God Stand Up
for Bastards

♣

David Leitch

GOD STAND UP
FOR BASTARDS

♣

HOUGHTON MIFFLIN COMPANY BOSTON

1973

First Printing   c

First American Edition

ISBN: 0-395-15469-3
Library of Congress Catalog Card Number: 72-6814
Printed in the United States of America

To Jill Neville, With Love

Preface

♣

THIS title may seem like a calculated insult to my mother Truda. In a way it is. But I have a sneaking hunch – and hope – that hard words may entice her out of the shadows where she has been lurking, crafty as a trout, for about thirty-four years. She may even bring a father and siblings with her. Mother, where are you?

Paradoxically, of all the characters who have collectively seduced me into writing, my mother is the one I know least well. Truda and I only really met in the womb (no stage for detailed observation or memory-jogging tape recordings) and thereafter our acquaintance was at best nodding.

With the other characters I am on firmer ground and the reader is entitled to ask how much is true. The answer is very nearly all. Only apparently plausible stories, in my experience, invariably prove to be lies, and if some episode appears particularly bizarre – Piers and his obsession with breasts, for instance – then it is certain to be unadorned *reportage*. The common link is 'I', a kind of special correspondent who happened to be on the spot, geographically or emotionally.

My obsession has been with people, some famous, some obscure, and nearly all funny in one way or another. They are people who have bobbed up in the course of a gypsy-like life; people I don't want to lose.

Truda I have no research files on (she covers her tracks as professionally as Howard Hughes, and has apparently even managed to evade the Registrar of Births and Deaths). My portraits of the others, particularly the famous ones, are underpinned with copious notes taken at the time, usually a dramatic moment of contemporary history. They are, for various reasons, portrayed more honestly than would have been possible even in the pages of a newspaper as open-minded as *The Sunday Times* of London (to whose successive editors, C. D. Hamilton and Harold Evans, I owe a great debt. They paid, as it were, for all those tickets in the front stalls, and sometimes enabled me to play a minor role in the action itself.)

Unconsciously I seem to have devoted a decade or more to preparing this book in meticulous detail. Almost the only things I haven't lost while roaming around in odd places are a collection of over five hundred notebooks, safe in a Paris filing cabinet. Latterly they have been reinforced by innumerable recording cassettes. Some notes are lucid, and even elegant; others are indecipherable hieroglyphs, or irrelevancies like 'phone numbers of burning young girls now uxoriously attending their fourth babies. The record I kept while flying into the infamous and beleaguered garrison of Khe Sanh includes my only will. These notes exude terror, and I still cannot look at them without emotion.

The characters – Starbuck, Piers, Jay – are composites, amalgams of two or more people, with the details of each again taken from notes made at the time. Readers who, like myself, treasure Harold Nicolson's *Some People*, will see their literary *provenance* at once.

As for the 'originals', when they recognize themselves or are recognized by others, I hope they will see I have portrayed them with affection. I have as far as possible avoided writing about people I dislike. When it has been unavoidable, as in the case of the Duke of Edinburgh, I have made the dislike explicit.

The book was written as it was experienced, mainly on the road to somewhere or another, so there are many good friends and generous hosts to remember. They include Mr Victor Herbert, who lent us one of his houses in the South of France and also his remarkable apartment in the *quartier latin*. Mr Robert Pickering let us have his home during a magnificent spring in Ardèche and also his polyglot library. Mrs Clive Neville welcomed me on the last – and most nervous – lap in her house 'Upalong' in the Blue Mountains of New South Wales, Australia. In London, editing, Dr James Spillius provided yet another temporary refuge and so did Miss Barley Alison, who has been guardian angel to so many writers, some of awe-inspiring eminence.

The original manuscript was read, to its considerable benefit, by Mr Christopher Booker, Mr Derek O'Driscoll, Mr Phillip Knightley, Mr Richard Neville, and Mr Nicholas Tomalin, a motley but expert and battle-hardened crew, to whom sincerest thanks. The errors are all mine.

Just as *God Stand Up For Bastards* is, in so many ways, my wife's. She stayed with the gypsy caravan when the going was good and – better yet – when it wasn't.

DAVID LEITCH

Contents

♣

God Stand Up
for Bastards

♣

CHAPTER I

Truda

♣

ON Guy Fawkes's Day 1937, eight days after I was born, my mother Truda published an advertisement in the Personal Column of the London *Daily Express* offering me, in effect, to the highest bidder. She specified a date, one week later, when prospective foster parents could attend a kind of private view of the infant. For this unusual ceremony she had selected the Russell Hotel which dominated the east end of Bloomsbury with its lunatic façade – all in all, a happy choice.

Still the hotel, despite its minor mock-Gothic contribution, played an unimportant part in the transaction compared to that of the newspaper. I have never been able to dredge up much affection for the *Express*, but its influence on my life has been positively zodiacal.

God knows where the infant would have finished up had Truda gone for *The Times*, *The Daily Mirror*, or *The News of the World*. Presumably the first would have prudently rejected such a *louche* advertisement or, in the Timespeak of the period, 'regretfully declined the insertion'. As for the last, Truda might easily have found herself the reluctant heroine of one of their inimitable 'I Took a Lorry Ride to Shame' serializations. In any case things would doubtless have been very different.

As it was the *Express imprimatur* guaranteed that much of what followed was predictable, if not virtually preordained. By definition the foster parents had to be *Express* readers, and as such were a pretty tightly defined group. Beaverbrook surrounded his paper with a highly individual aura of half-crazed megalomania but those who bought it (as well as the lost souls who actually worked on it) were invariably characterized by a sturdy, forward-defensive kind of middlingness. They were solid citizens; the contemporary version of the yeomen of England.

Such were my foster parents. They lived in the outer north-west suburbs of London (a commuting area then known, after the railway, as 'Metroland'). My foster father, like all neighbouring fathers, worked in central London. Each morning shortly after eight he travelled to his office in a brown train which passed through a series of brown stations plastered with advertisements for a brown tonic called *Virol* – even at this distance it is slightly frightening to calculate how many thousand times his eye must have caught the hoarding between Pinner and North Harrow: 'Nursing Mothers Need It, Growing Girls Need It.' Behind them this regiment of strained men in blue suits (which became more strained over the years), left their wives to shop, gossip and devise ways of killing time. It was, of course, pre-television; spiritual resources were spread thin, but the suburbs were unified by their pride in a certain marginal gentility. Again, over the years, the pride grew fiercer, the gentility increasingly tenuous. The female empire of the daylight hours remained, however, unchanged. Such excitement as there was came from female conflicts, petty yet passionate jealousies which often sprouted after much careful nurture into feuds of atavistic potency. Yet, strangely, blood was never spilled inside those solid walls adorned with Paul Scarlett roses. Suburban hate invariably worked itself out obliquely beneath a veil of euphemism.

Old enemies met with tight smiles and mean nods beneath the willows of Cuckoo Hill Drive. Instead of bellowing curses over their shopping bags, the bored ladies exchanged their poison darts so chastely that a stranger could easily have been misled into believing they actually liked each other. There were few affairs down in Metroland: too many keen eyes. No wonder local dentists confidentially compared the shocking obscenities these ladies let rip when the gas had got at their inhibitions.

Still, for my foster parents and millions like them, life was comfortable on the eve of the war. Mock-Tudor houses with half-acre gardens waiting for pansies and marigolds, apple trees and loganberries, were a drug on the market at one hundred pounds down, and the balance over twenty-five years. Everyone

had, at the least, a car; a daily woman to clean; and a maid to
open the door when other ladies came to tea. The maid cost
only fifty pounds a year, and it must have been obvious to everyone it could not last. While it did, Metroland provided a very
comfortable cocoon for people who liked their horizons tight.
The fifty pound maids doubtless looked back on the epoch with
little nostalgia, but to the unemployed, among whom my real
parents were probably numbered, the Metroland of my foster
parents must have seemed a paradise of security and ease.

It is hard to say for sure because my real parents were a
highly mysterious couple who surrounded themselves with the
maximum possible anonymity. But it seems that during the
Russell Hotel negotiations they concentrated mainly on the
financial standing of the potential foster parents, and they did
borrow the fare back to Nottingham from the ones they chose.
I have often wondered whether they put the touch on the un-
successful aspirants as well. Still, my impression is that they
were not simply on the make. Rather they were conscientiously
and quite sensibly concerned to select the most reliable and
financially secure of the couples who had replied to the *Express*
box number. Why they decided to dispose of their son to strangers in the first place remains entirely a matter of conjecture. It
looks as though they were in trouble.

It was not 'trouble' of the traditional kind; in 1937 Truda
was in her twenties, a pretty blonde according to my foster
parents, and a respectable married woman of some years standing according to the Somerset House records. I only discovered
this fact when I was an undergraduate, and felt slightly
aggrieved. Ever since I had been old enough to understand
what illegitimacy was, I had assumed that must be me. At
school there had been a few boys who were orphans, or whose
parents had been divorced, and I developed an instinct for spot-
ting them. It may have been a two way process because, to my
delight, I was selected for the stage-stealing role of Edmund in
King Lear, and had subsequently developed the habit of murmuring his bellow of defiance 'Now God stand up for bastards'
as a kind of war cry to myself in moments of stress. (Really it
should have been 'the gods' but I found it hard enough to take

one seriously, let alone a whole pantheon.) Paul, Truda's husband, may of course not have been the real father, but as birth certificates do not carry that kind of information there was no way of telling. Technically, at least, I am no bastard. Psychologically, the mould had long set like concrete.

The Russell Hotel meeting had been brief and to the point. Truda's scheme was that the foster parents should take the child for a few weeks, on approval as it were. This would give them time to make up their minds and if they decided to keep the child the legal details could then be settled. In the meantime she would come down periodically from the Midlands to check all was well with 'Paul' – as I was then called – and assuage her maternal instincts.

Truda's husband Paul Griffith, (whom, without any evidence, I have always suspected of not being my real father), preserved a grim silence throughout the meeting. From Somerset House I later learned that he was twenty-nine at the time, and his profession on my birth certificate was given as 'advertising agent', which could obviously embrace most things from freelance con man to bookie's runner. The adoption was very much Truda's show. Perhaps he asserted himself more on other issues but on this occasion anyway she had been boss.

And so the matter was left and the couples parted, Truda and Paul to Nottingham with their newly acquired fares, me to Metroland to be equipped with a pram, a cot, booties and other accoutrements necessary for suburban babyhood. Theoretically, it was still a temporary arrangement, and in the next month Truda wrote three letters which under the terms of my foster father's will I acquired at twenty-one.

Whatever Truda's other defects she wrote a pretty slick and convincing letter when necessary. How convinced my foster parents were I don't know, but to me they spoke loud and clear in their pale blue ink. A good deal of my education had been concerned with examining what people had written and extracting the ultimate *nuance*. Truda's few hundred words evoked a sense of total comprehension and sympathy I had never previously experienced. For people who actually know their blood relations I imagine instant recognition of precisely what a brother's frown, or a father's cough signifies is pretty common-place. I have heard twins describing their irritation at being constantly confronted with themselves via their sibling. Before reading Truda's letters I had never known with absolute certainty, precisely how someone else was feeling at a given moment, and I have never had the same experience since.

'I miss the little lamb dreadfully', she wrote, 'and long to see him in his new booties, but unfortunately we must go to Leicester by train tomorrow and won't be able to fit in the trip to London as promised . . .'

And so on. The letters revealed a neat combination of weakness and resolve, prevarication and self deceit. Not only was Truda concerned to put up a show of behaving well in front of the foster parents, she was also busily trying to persuade herself that what she was doing was for the best. I don't know how well she succeeded on either front.

The letters told the story of a woman doing her inadequate best to behave decently, but failing to pull it off. I have often thought that good behaviour is a kind of very desirable trick that only some people are fortunate enough to learn. Truda lacked the courage, or stamina, or perhaps quite simply the good luck to qualify even for entry into those leagues where people are given merit marks for good conduct. A small private income or a different husband might have made a lot of difference.

As it was she was trying to make moral bricks without straw. The women's magazine gush about booties was Truda flashing a dog-eared identity card testifying to her human status as a mother. Doubtless, she *did* miss the child but her undertone of bothered petulance – why do we have to go through all this *performance*, I can hear her mutter irritably – gave the show away as far as I was concerned.

I have felt much the same way myself, though marriage rather than unwanted babies has usually set the syndrome in motion. Through the morass of guilt and biological disturbance Truda was very well aware that one voice spoke louder than any of the others.

It was clearly only a matter of time before she packed her grip and headed for the hills.

In fact, it turned out to be just under four weeks before my foster parents' letters started coming back with the information that the addressee had departed without informing the Post Office of her next destination. Truda, with or without Paul, had gone very effectively to ground, and there has been no word of her since. My relationship with my parents had been on the brief side – just under nine days.

When I was told this story, or most of it, at the age of eight, my overriding reaction was one of scepticism. There were others too: it occurred to me, for instance, that I was actually nine days older than had been previously believed, and therefore might qualify for two rounds of birthday presents instead of one. There was also an inchoate sense of confusion and dispossession. But, above all, I just flatly didn't believe what my foster mother was making such a hash of trying to explain to me.

People did, this much I knew, sometimes leave babies in swaddling clothes – whatever *they* were – around bullrushes, or from time to time on doorsteps. But there seemed no precedent for hotel suites. To a child precociously ploughing through the works of Walter Scott, our main literary authority on doorstep babies, the inherent improbability of the tale was blindingly obvious. I was not sufficiently seduced by Scott to believe that one day it would be established beyond doubt that I was Bonnie Prince Charlie's son and heir – apart from anything else I possessed no eccentric birthmarks, which I knew were obligatory in these cases. But, to a child, the story was somehow wrong. And for that matter it still is. Somewhere around there is an unknown, and probably unimagined factor, which only Truda could elucidate. And, as we know, Truda is not talking.

As it stands the story is resonant but basically unsatisfactory. It lacks neatness and, above all, a last chapter *dénouement*. I caught on to this too at an early age but for a long time lacked confidence on the subject because I obeyed my foster mother's passionate injunctions to keep the whole thing a deep secret. Somehow, she had inadvertently suggested, the whole lopsided narrative was something to be ashamed of, and should be brushed under the carpet.

And so, for many years, I kept very quiet indeed about my

ambiguous origins. Other children with odd backgrounds I
recognized through intuition or because their status had been
made public. They were, I noticed, usually unhappy – the boys
who ran away, or wet their beds, or failed Common Entrance.

I did not wish to join the camp of these natural losers, and in
any case the schools I attended did not create the kind of environment where children confided in each other. Home was
something apart, something only a sissy talked about. I accordingly concentrated on learning to bowl an off-break out of the
back of my hand and on Caesar's relationship with the Gauls
and Helvetii. My secrecy was entirely negative, and I don't
suppose I even thought about Truda more than once a year.

My new parents, on the other hand, found themselves in a
difficult position. For them secrecy and evasion were something
they had to work at.

Truda's disappearance into God knows what Midlands gloom
must have come as a very nasty shock. There they were in
Metroland holding the baby as in the oldest music hall joke. The
weeks passed and still there was no trace of Truda. Eventually
they consulted their lawyer and discovered that adopting babies
was not a simple process like buying a secondhand car: there
were officials to be consulted, forms to be signed and, above all,
the real parents had formally to acknowledge their agreement.
Evidently Truda and Paul were highly unlikely to contribute
anything to these legalistic processes – it was not their style at
all, and in any case no one knew where they were.

The lawyer's advice was admirably correct. There was, he
said, only one legal course to follow.

In the first instance the infant should be transferred to a
properly constituted institution, in this case one run by the
Hertfordshire County Council. After a specified period had
elapsed, assuming the real parents had not appeared, it would
then be possible to begin the procedure which leads to legal
adoption. Nothing, however, could be guaranteed. It was up to
the County Council to decide whether or not they would be
allowed to have the child.

At this juncture my new parents (or simply parents as I will
call them from now on), did something which by their standards

was wildly eccentric. They simply moved fifteen miles away and introduced me to the neighbours as their new-born son. They were not quite such an ordinary couple as they must have appeared on that bizarre November afternoon beneath the crenellated Gothic of the Russell Hotel. True, they were suburbanites, and *Express* readers. But for various reasons neither of them fitted very well into the environment in which they found themselves. In the first place they had both, at an earlier stage in their lives, been very rich. They were gradually being reconciled to a genteel sufficiency, and that was all it was, particularly after Labour's victory in 1945, but my mother in particular regretted the past and resented the present. Their interests, almost entirely domestic ones, were shared, but they did not talk much – my father's habitual taciturnity was a constant cause of strife. Even at times of apparent marital harmony they often conveyed an impression of wishing they were somewhere else, though being too resigned or indolent to actually get up and go there. Their prime reason for adopting me was, I suppose, a hope that their distinctly low-key marriage might be improved as a result. At least, I do not suppose it got any worse.

I have cynically learnt that even a perfunctory account of this story, particularly when told at the end of a long dinner, provokes the most violent maternal instincts in all women. Tender, thoroughly unlikely passions have risen to the surface even in hard-minded women reporters who heard everything that Fleet Street can offer in their own cradles.

A very common reaction has been to insist that a full-scale hunt for Truda and Father Paul should be initiated immediately. The underlying implication has usually been unflattering – that the discovery of my real parents was the only way to clear up at least some of my more manifest and crippling neuroses. Occasionally, influenced by alcohol or sex or eloquence, or simply taking the course of least resistance, I have promised to do something – hire detectives, launch an appeal via the *Express*, devote a year of my life to snuffling around for traces. But the next morning reason, or sheer indolence has always prevailed, and apart from the odd trip to Somerset House, I have made no efforts to confront my roots.

Private detectives come expensive and in any case they are an unreliable and incompetent race. It would be no light task to trace Truda, whose spoor was effectively obliterated in 1937. The name David Leitch has never been blazed in sixty-four point neon exactly, but it has at least achieved sufficient prominence to attract the attention of his mother. Still Truda and Paul have given no sign. Perhaps they are dead; in any case it is unlikely that they would be overjoyed to find a stranger on their doorstep bearing filial tidings.

All the same – and if Truda reads these pages by any chance she might bear it in mind – it would be interesting to know if there are any brothers and sisters knocking around.

* * * *

Around twenty years later I met the famous Beaver, proprietor of my birth paper, in circumstances of appropriate farce. It was on a summer day of great beauty in London and the old man, then in his seventies, was holding a vulgar party. This was to celebrate the rebuilding of Stornoway House, his residence off St James's, which during the war had been gutted by a clutch of incendiary bombs.

After admiring the skill with which the architect had re-created the eighteenth-century excellence of the house – so unlike its owner – I fell into drinking a lot of Dom Perignon and talking to an *Express* senior executive, now as dead as his master. He was compounding the many years maltreatment his sad capillaries had undergone with neat malt whisky out of a tumbler; champagne, he told me, was a girl's drink. (What he really meant was that champagne was the drink you gave to girls you were firing three months after hiring them as feature writers in order to get them into bed. The form was you gave them 'bubbly' and sent them to the Manchester or Glasgow office 'to broaden their experience'. There were invariably tears, sometimes, when the more cynical executives were involved, on both sides.)

This agreeable drunk had a theory about Stornoway House which indicated, in a minor kind of way, the gifts which had led to his success within the frenzied corridors of *The Daily Express*.

Reichsmarschall Goering, he insisted, had made the destruction of Stornoway House a top priority, and had assigned a crack wing of Heinkels and Junkers 88's to carry out the task.

'Top priority,' insisted my friend. 'Getting "the Lord" was the top priority of all those bloody Nazis, after Churchill of course.'

It was a pious qualification which indicated an instinctive comprehension of hierarchy, without in any way diminishing his master. In such tones a disciple of John the Baptist might have accorded primacy to the Archangel Gabriel.

I was aware, of course, of the Beaver's stint as Minister of Air-craft Production. His efforts had been widely publicised, and not least by his own newspapers, both at the time and subse-quently. A million suburban gardens had been stripped of their prized wrought iron gates at his command. No one had ever discovered how many hundred thousands of housewives had sacrificed their aluminium pots and pans because of the Minister's (mistaken) impression that they could be used in the manufacture of Spitfires. It was widely believed that these domestic utensils had been subsequently buried in an enormous trench deliberately excavated for the purpose somewhere in Somerset with the help of high explosives that might otherwise have furthered the war effort by being dropped on other house-wives in Hamburg or Dresden.

Had the *Luftwaffe* really been aiming deliberately at Storno-way House, I wondered mildly. After all, there were many other targets in the near proximity that the Reichsmarschall might have noted as significant to the war effort. Buckingham Palace, for example. The *Express* executive was unimpressed. Well then, what about St James's Palace, or – getting a bit more fanciful – Prunier's say, or Boodle's bow window or even Laurie's down-stairs Bar at the Ritz? This last weighed a bit more heavily, but my argument was still far from being accepted.

At that moment the great man appeared, walking very slowly in the exact middle of the little street that runs up from St James's past the sentry boxes. A venerable newsboy, encrusted with war medals, popped up simultaneously, carrying lunch-time editions of *The Evening Standard*, the *Express*'s stablemate.

The Beaver bought a paper, and cameras clicked. They didn't all click quite quickly enough because the Beaver was forced to buy several more copies to cater for the tardier practitioners who jostled each other, cursing and letting off flashbulbs. Finally, the senile newsboy saluted – perhaps the medals were from the Boer War.

'Ask him yourself,' suggested the executive. 'But don't mention my name.'

Later on, inspired by the champagne, I did. It was, after all, in the line of duty. The affair, which had some very marginal news value – maybe three paragraphs – would be recorded in *The Times*. That was why I was there. It was the kind of occasion attended by young reporters climbing up, and middle-aged ones sliding down.

His face was like an old apple, infinitely brown, wrinkled, and knowing. Despite what I had heard he emitted no swirling mists of evil. Rather he struck me as mischievous; the kind of man who might offer one an explosive cigar, or place cushions with built-in farts under portly dinner guests. We disposed of the Goering myth, for such it was, and he solicited my opinion of *The Daily Express*. I was a foolish young man, but not foolish enough to tell him.

Instead I expressed regrets that the personal column was extinct, and when pressed explained my own affection for it. The bright eyes grew brighter at this human interest story which, had it not actually been true, might have been picked straight out of his Sunday paper.

'We have to check this out,' he said enthusiastically. And he grasped my wrist sincerely with his little monkey hand.

He gave me the name of someone to ring for an appointment, and moved on. The senior executive, who had sidled sideways into the exchange, was deeply impressed.

'You mustn't forget to ring, whatever happens,' he said, much moved. 'You will be sure to ring, won't you?'

I said I would be sure, placatingly. Thank God I never did.

CHAPTER 2

Max and Wilma

♣

WILMA was a crumpled, anxious woman of forty with a passion for Mozart, which my parents, who were devotees of Albert Sandler and his Palm Court Orchestra, would discuss years later with the benign confusion they reserved for everything foreign. She taught me 'Oh Tannenbaum' and 'Stille Nacht, Heilige Nacht'. When she sang herself it was possible to see she was beautiful, or had been. Of her husband Max, who arrived shortly, I remember little. He spoke no English and in any case speech in any language was difficult for him at that time. A Nazi functionary had kicked all his teeth out, and Max was saving up to replace them. In the meantime he worked in our garden and cleaned the car, pursing his lips like a whistler, though no sound emerged from his ill-treated gums. He had owned the largest handbag factory in Vienna and my parents were surprised at how contentedly he accepted his lowly new role. Unlike him, of course, they did not really understand what the Germans had been doing to the Viennese Jews.

Afterwards I learnt a lot about the concentration camps, and even visited the sites of a couple. Even so, no recital of horrors from my Israeli friends wearing their blue Auschwitz tattoos much as Frenchmen display the Legion of Honour, no photographs or war crimes statistics, have ever affected me as deeply as the thought of Max and his teeth. He was a man of such gentleness, such consummate harmlessness. Whoever did that to him must have been capable of beating a mouse with a hammer. I hope he was subsequently kicked in turn, and with accrued interest.

Max and Wilma did not last long after the official beginning of the war. They were interned under Regulation 18B as 'enemy aliens' in the Isle of Man, which also housed Tom Mosley and other well-known British fascists. Mosley and Max must have made odd bedfellows.

When the day came for them to leave we all wept, Max sobbing copiously into an old mackintosh my father had given him for the journey north. They drove off, my father in the chauffeur's seat because Max was thought to be too *distrait* to drive himself. It was an ironic prefigurement of future roles and reversals. The dispossessed, toothless ex-handbag manufacture and his musical wife were the last servants my parents ever had.

My father's occupation kept him in central London 'for the duration'. For my mother and myself it was a vagabond period, a foretaste of so much vagabondage that was to follow. To my bitter chagrin we left within a few days of the start of the blitz. I had adored sleeping in an indoor Morrison shelter, particularly at a time when the *Luftwaffe* was laying on the most lavish fireworks display in the history of man. It was more than twenty-five years before I saw anything remotely in the same pyrotechnic league. Then, watching Tân Son Nhut airbase in Saigon under attack during the Têt offensive from the grandstand of the Caravelle Hotel roof, it all came back. Arnaud de Borchgrave, as always a mine of unlikely information, informed me that each of the huge sodium flares which illuminated the ten mile perimeter to discourage marauding vc with their bilious yellow glare cost the us taxpayer eighty dollars. 'And they drop four thousand a night,' said Arnaud. 'You know what that adds up to in a week?' The arithmetic was beyond me but even if you threw in the red and white tracer trails spurting out of the armoured helicopters the Air Force had christened 'Puff Puff the Magic Dragon' I reckon our domestic little cut-price untechnological blitz made a better display. Not wishing to spoil my American friend's patriotic pride I forbore to say so.

There was no blitz in Llanfairfechan, North Wales, the first of our wartime homes, indeed little light of any kind. We stayed in a vast Gothic mansion owned by a retired bishop and because of some wartime snag my mother was having trouble getting money from London. She was therefore about five pounds short of the three months' rent deposit money. The saintly

bishop let us in, but had the electricity cut off in case we ran up
a big bill. For three weeks we lived by candlelight. It was typical
of the welcome refugees from London and the Midlands cities
received. People stopped us in the street and accused us of steal-
ing their rations. Several small local boys broke into our enormous garden to sneer at me in accents so thick it was hard to
tell what they were saying, though the tone was recognizable
enough. Filled with fear and hate I struck the largest over the
head with a toy rifle, wielded like a baseball bat. His father came
round several times to threaten court proceedings and we moved
on, first to Lytham St Anne's with its rolling whiskery sand
dunes, and later to Bovingdon in Hertfordshire. Cards and
letters from Max and Wilma followed us round our various
addresses. In Bovingdon I spent weeks with my eyes glued to
the sky. From this aerodrome the giant Flying Fortresses, flown
by those elegant giants who were so generous with their chewing-
gum, were flying suicidal low-level bombing raids. The first
time they gave me gum it was such a novelty that I thought they
were offering razor blades. The first, vaguely medicinal yet
infinitely delicious chew taught me better, and at that moment
I became an Americanophile for life. I loved those battered,
disintegrating 'planes as they limped home. There was a contemporary song about coming in on a wing and a prayer. No
one could assess the piety of the aircrews, but that spring we saw
plenty of planes coming in without much more than one wing.

About that time I learnt Max and Wilma were trying to go
to America. America!

For a generation growing up during the war it was the
Newfoundland. There were the GI's in their *chic* barathea, their
pockets stuffed with candy, everyone of them – for children
anyway – a kind of walking public relations officer for their
country. We loved them, and they seemed to love us. Probably
many of them were lonely. We also loved their comics, which I
noticed many of the soldiers used to read, as if they themselves
were children. They were so thick, so lush, the colours were
deep and satisfying, and the paper had a kind of gloss on it. The
going rate in the barter market was one *Superman* against six
mean little *Hotspurs* or *Champions* with their sad format of pinch-

penny wartime newsprint. A lot of the children read them, I think, for the advertisements, which often carried a tragic note saying the items could be obtained only within the USA. Sweets that crunched, breakfast food that crackled, electric trains and remote control aircraft and Superman suits . . . the richness of it all was beyond belief. One got further indications of the same cornucopian amplitude at the cinema – those cars, their size, their streamlined pointed noses . . . Besides them the Ford Eights and Standard Tens that sometimes crept along, powered doubtless by illegal petrol purchased from lorry drivers who chained two trucks together on country roads so they could sell a gallon or two, why English cars were like mobile dog-kennels. An Air Force officer with whom I was on good waving terms possessed a dove-grey Packard Clipper Convertible and I dreamt about it for several years.

Just as the children loved the Americans so the parents hated them. They showed off, they monopolized the taxis and girls, they had changed Piccadilly Circus – 'Rainbow Corner' – into an *al fresco* brothel, wherever you went they seemed to be copulating in public like so many jack-rabbits. I overheard enough adult conversations to know some of these things. What I did not understand was that these criticisms stemmed from a growing awareness that a few million Errol Flynns really were winning the war, and an uneasy feeling that they were going to win the peace as well.

It was hard to understand why my father got so angry when I suggested he commission Max and Wilma to send him a batch of rainbow ties from America. Then he could throw away all his black ones with tiny white dots. Only spivs wore ties like that, he said. But *Americans* wore them. I had seen a sergeant from the base who had a brown silk tie six inches wide with a palm tree on it. It was a beautiful tie, probably the most beautiful in the *world*.

Americans and spivs had much in common, he countered. They never did any proper work, they were common and had no manners, they thought about nothing but money. This was puzzling because my parents seldom discussed anything else. There was, for example, the long-debated question of a maid but she never arrived because, it seemed, the girls who in 1939

had been delighted with a pound a week and their board now
had the impudence to ask four times that. They had been spoiled
by war work, the factories, the way they carried on with the
Yanks . . . and here, frustratingly, always at the same point in
my parents evening litany, the voices would drop to a hissing
whisper of disapproval and resentment, or else I would be sent
off to play. My mother was forced to settle for a slatternly char-
woman, Mrs Archard, who often arrived late, and always called
her 'Ducks'.

The end of the war was an anti-climax. We were given the
afternoon off from my prep school and I raced home. Bananas,
oranges and pineapples, I sang to myself. These were the fruit I
had never seen, except in pictures. But, I had been assured,
when the war was over they would be available by the basket, by
the ton even. Yet there was no sign of them, not so much as a
rotten old Victoria plum, the kind we rather amateurishly grew
ourselves. I lay on the drawing-room carpet wailing my protests
about this fraudulent VE Day, and was rightly rebuked. But my
feelings were shared, I imagine, by my parents and millions of
others who knew that the war had written 'finis' to their way of
life. Technically, it might be over, but nothing seemed to have
changed. There was no petrol, no car, no servant, no whisky –
only snoek, which even our notoriously undiscriminating dog
turned his muzzle up at – whale steak and recipes for making
cakes with castor oil. Two years later 'They' – to be precise the
evil John Strachey who had been, and probably still was, a
communist – even put bread back on ration, or 'on coupons' as
we said.

England can seldom have lived through a period of such
mean-spirited bitterness, such pervading sourness. My parents
found their spokesman in Angela Thirkell with her nostalgia for
the older order; their intellectual nutriment came from the four
austerity pages of my old friend, *The Daily Express*. They wore a
little beetle badge in their buttonholes, because Nye Bevan was
said to have referred to the middle classes as 'vermin'. It was all
just like the war, except now the enemy was the Labour
Government.

* * * *

The bananas, the oranges, the pineapples were suddenly all there. There were even hothouse grapes, blue-black, and huge – they made a little pop when they burst in your mouth. The long-awaited cornucopia sat on a table in Max and Wilma's drawing room, a vast wicker basket covered in cellophane. I had seen such things in Hollywood films, usually dispatched by infatuated suitors to Mae West.

Wilma had been released in 1943, and Max rather later. They had opened a dress shop with someone they had met in the camp, and then a second. They had bought a very big and ugly house in Hendon; the first of the post-war Jaguars gleamed in the drive.

Max looked different with teeth, he was fat in face, fat all over beneath his lushly cut double-breasted suit, the lapels wide, the shoulders hand-stitched and solidly padded. His English was now fluent, if strongly Viennese; he had a lilting, persuasive voice, and soft hands, designed apparently for grape peeling or holding up peaches for approval.

'Lovely, aren't they? Chap I know grows them in his hot-house and sells a few – on the QT of course.'

He winked. 'Paid twenty pounds for that basket. How we should live with these prices . . .' Wilma clucked in connubial support, my father said something stern about Stafford Cripps.

For me the fruit overshadowed everything, except perhaps for the heavy cream cakes which Wilma proudly produced on a silver tray. Years later I was to see their twins in Demmel's in Vienna – *Malakofftorte, Bischofsbrot, Mohnschnitte*. Through the gastronomic haze I gathered that Max seemed to know an awful lot of people. There was the man who had introduced him to the sales manager at the Jaguar showroom; the man who had helped him with the building permit for the second garage; the man with the villa in Biarritz where they had just been staying. One man, in particular, I remembered long after – Rudi Stitcher, who like a Happy Families card, turned out to be Max's tailor.

Max, the new Max, gave my father Stitcher's card. 'Just say you're a friend of mine.' The wink. 'No coupons, of course.'

And Max made a gesture of producing something from under a counter.

The reason for the visit was, in fact, to say goodbye. They had swung their American visas – Max knew a man – and someone else they had met in the camp had a nice little business in Chicago. Handbags: Max and Wilma were going back to their first love, leaving behind the ration books, the castor oil cakes, the little beetle badges. They presented us with some furniture they would not be needing, including a vast utility wardrobe in which Max had his Rudi Stitchers hanging – there must have been thirty of them. Wilma asked me what I wanted from America and I was compiling a long list of items memorized from the *Superman* small ads when my mother stopped me, because it was bad manners.

All the same the food parcels arrived once a month for years afterwards. I was the only boy in prep school with bubble gum, *Caran d'Ache* crayons, a two-colour ball-pen – the first domestic 'Biros' cost three pounds each – real Indian mocassins.

On the way home in our Standard Ten my father flipped Rudi Stitcher's card out of the window, a gesture so untypical it must have sprung from deep emotion. 'Fifty guineas for a suit,' he said. 'Fifty guineas. What a hope.'

'Those Jews know how to look after number one,' contributed my mother. The confrontation with her former maid and gardener had obviously shaken her. It was the end of something, that much was clear.

We kept the wardrobe for years, but it was always a nuisance. It was far too big to fit into any of our little rooms. And never again would there be enough suits to come near filling it.

CHAPTER 3

Becky

♣

BECKY's gaze was jade green, mildly diluted with flecks the colour of Oxford marmalade. She had a cool, assessing look that I found hard to meet without blushing or fumbling.

'I bet,' said Becky, 'you can't French kiss.' They were the first words she had ever addressed to me, and I was taken aback. But if a year's public school education had taught me anything it was to lash out, blindly if necessary, as soon as you found yourself pinned against the ropes.

'Of course I bloody do. *Everyone* knows that.' Becky appraised me, unimpressed.

'I bet you don't even know what French kissing *is*,' she announced.

I performed a few virtuoso arabesques around her, casually demonstrating the skill with which I controlled my pea-green Raleigh Lenton with drop handle-bars, 531 lightweight tubing, and silver pump. It provided an excuse for not meeting those jade eyes.

She stirred, irritated. Becky liked to come to the point.

'Come here and I'll show you.'

Becky had been born knowing; she was undeceived by my bluff confidence, my elegant bike style. No man or boy had put anything over on her in the course of her fourteen years and two months. I would lay odds none have in the two decades that have elapsed since our meeting in that happily dense wood cradling the Metropolitan Railway Line at a point some two hundred yards due south of the rustic station of Moor Park, in Hertfordshire. Moor Park possessed several avenues of ample residences in stockbroker Tudor, three championship golf courses, a palace originally constructed for Cardinal Wolsey and also, some way down the architectural scale, my school. At the time I was just thirteen and a half, which was by no means old enough to cope with Becky on anything like equal terms.

'Follow me.' She snapped a padlock on her bike with the deftness that characterized all her physical activities. No element of choice was offered: I followed, rapt, obedient and burning, past some oaks, across a tangle of blackberry bushes, and finally through a patch of nettles. My legs were protected by my first pair of long trousers. Becky's, in trim white ankle socks, emerged as golden and unscathed as the sands of Bude. Probably the nettles were too intimidated to sting her.

She nipped goat-like across a tree-trunk bridge over a small stream and we were in a totally enclosed glade. She sank down in the middle, primly adjusting her green-pleated school skirt over her knees, and removing her broad-brimmed straw boater to reveal blonde, bobbed hair.

'Here.'

With a gesture of total self-sufficiency she patted the grass next to her. Her hands were freckled, and lightly smudged with ink; the finger nails had been bitten. Becky was responsible for convincing me that girls who neglect their hands while lavishing care on the rest of their bodies are invariably highly erotic. This has sometimes led me into error but more often than not the Becky principle has proved sound. When grubby hands are combined with a good deal of self-touching I remain convinced the sexual signal is as reliable as a red light in Bangkok. As I hesitated, Becky stroked her left arm, which was crowned with a wispy line of hairs the colour of platinum.

She clucked at me between her teeth, impatient yet encouraging. It was a noise she used when dealing with recalcitrant horses – Becky was a talented rider, her stables were decorated with innumerable rosettes commemorating victorious gymkhanas.

'Better not talk,' she said. 'It spoils the quiet. You do it like this.'

The preliminary lesson was carried out on a nettle sting below my wrist; she had spotted a good erogenous zone.

'You kind of wiggle your tongue,' she said unnecessarily.

'It's like a butterfly's wings. Breathe through your nose. See, it's easy.'

Becky *made* everything easy. There was, for instance, the problem of undoing her coral-blue brassière, a colour she had selected because its outline showed clearly through her starched school blouse. The authorities evidently believed that these shapeless garments kept the girls looking reassuringly pre-adolescent, but they were no match for Becky. She always bought them two sizes too small; both her mother and the Matron complained vaguely, but were too embarrassed to specify why. Becky said they had shrunk in the laundry, and looked demure.

'You kind of pull to the left *there*, it's easier when I turn over a bit. There's no need to crush me.' The brassière sprung apart, like all her bras, as if she had built some patented quick release mechanism into it. She sighed, turned on her back, and revealed her taut breasts with their babyish pink aureoles and precocious erect nipples. One inkstained hand closed on the base of my skull, and guided my mouth towards the middle of her chest.

'Tongue like a butterfly's wings,' she breathed in my ear. She bit the lobe to make sure I was concentrating, and then pushed her tongue inside to give a further demonstration. I worried briefly that it might be waxy, but not for long. With Becky such anxieties never lasted, and even the rankest beginner, like myself, found it hard to be physically clumsy. She guided, instructed, nudged, cajoled and how often I remembered her skills in later adolescence, when tugging frantically at the maze-like infrastructure of a Newnham virgin's underwear, and wondering whether the straps and buckles had been deliberately constructed to embarrass us both, psychological chastity belts encasing breast and buttocks. But these later exchanges took place either in pitch dark, or by the unreliable light of a winter gas fire. Becky liked to make love in the daytime, preferably in the sun, and at the moment of orgasm her eyes examined one minutely in a spirit of friendly co-operation and interest.

'If you lift me up there with your hands, and then you sort of push a bit . . .' The final part of the operation was accomplished

with the same deftness as the preliminaries. By then even the
most dim-witted schoolboy would have started to grasp certain
principles for himself.

Stephen Wiczinsky, whose central European origins have left
him something of a traditionalist, once lectured me in the
Boboli Gardens on the importance of young men having older
mistresses. He sounded oddly like Maupassant, and I tepidly
advanced the thesis that the Beckys of this world, rarities in
Hertfordshire twenty years ago but doubtless commoner now,
were even better partners. Their youth, it seemed to me, made
for a level of sexual mutuality impossible between an awkward
young man and a poised married woman.

'There was this girl Becky,' I told him. 'If only I knew what
happened to her afterwards. She could be the heroine of a book
In Praise of Younger Women.'

Stephen, unimpressed, interrupted this rich vein to make me
pose next to the repellent and gross marble satyr behind the
Pitti Palace. Some American college girls giggled at it and us.
Becky would never have giggled.

Becky had dismissed me economically with instructions to
be there again at the same time the following day. I wandered
schoolwards in a haze, but not so much of a haze that I failed
to dive briskly behind a hedge when I heard the bumping of
an approaching bike. After the unknown rider had passed along
this short-cut to the school I sneaked out to identify him. The
exercise presented no difficulties.

The disappearing profile on its heavy black Hercules – no
flashy dropped handle-bars, no silver Italian pump for *him* –
was unmistakeably that of Macintyre. No other boy, even those
of eighteen, was six feet four and about three feet broad across
the shoulder blades. No one else rode a bike as if at attention,
Macintyre, Frank John Macintyre, was returning punctually,
after some doubtless authorized visit to the village, to preside
over prep.

Even seen from behind, and at a safe distance, his physical
presence was chilling. It was at least certain that he had failed
to spot my bike with its telltale school number and worse, with

my cap (which I regarded as unglamorous) stuffed illegally under the saddle. The faintest trace of my spoor and he would have been on the trail without hesitation; that soft stern voice would soon have established that, as usual, I was involved in something illegal. This was normal enough. There were few human activities that were not proscribed either by the school rules or the house rules, or both. Inevitably one lived, if one lived at all, outside the law. But Becky . . . if he had discovered her, would surely have reeled Macintyre's world on its normally solid axis.

'Coo,' I thought, and pedalled frenziedly back across the golf course.

Becky and Macintyre became the twin poles of that summer term; Becky the Id, Macintyre the Super-Ego. The situation, with minor variations, is one I have grown accustomed to over the years. The two of them have reappeared in many disguises. Becky's cool shadow has lurked behind a whole string of irresponsible but irresistible women. Sometimes she has been subtly transmogrified and manifested herself in the form of a bottle of Scotch or even a whole country, almost always a Mediterranean one. Her message has been invariably the same: 'Come on, it's easy. Just enjoy yourself.' And her cool voice has encouraged me to unzip a dress, pull a corkscrew, set up a sun umbrella, and to hell with Macintyre. Macintyre has reappeared as the Dean of St John's College, Cambridge; the Night Editor of *The Manchester Guardian*; a man I briefly shared a flat with who kept his shoes in lasts; finally, and most horribly of all, as a newspaper executive who subtly combined the archetypal shrivelled Macintyre soul with a surface gloss of snobbery and *insouciance*, a disguise which deceived me. Macintyre has always wielded the lash, and no Macintyre strikes until he knows, Montgomery-like, that his tanks so outnumber the enemy that the result is a foregone conclusion. Even so Becky's voice has always been the stronger in the end.

The voice of Macintyre, the real original Macintyre that is, echoed through the school day, gravelly and commanding. It was an expressive voice. When he read Grace – a terse 'Benedicat, Benedicatur' – it was with a heavy overtone of distaste:

no doubt his broad Calvinist streak disapproved of the Popish-
ness inherent in the Latin. Macintyre disapproved of so much;
there were few things, certainly very few things to do with me,
which he did not find morally reprehensible for some reason
or another: my not knowing, for instance, that the House was
named after Lancelot Andrewes, the Elizabethan prelate and
sermonizer beloved by T. S. Eliot. I, of course, had never heard
of T. S. Eliot and neither I suspect had Macintyre. But he was
perfectly confident on the subject of Andrewes, even though he
must have privately disapproved of him as 'High Church'. This
was only one issue of many. In the winter there had been my
inability to swim three lengths of icy water, and my preference
for effeminate squash at the expense of honest, hand-bruising
fives. The tone of all our future *rapports* had been set at our first
meeting on my first, miserable day in the school. Those frank
brown eyes had examined me sternly, and found me wanting.

'Why,' his first words had been, 'is your hair so filthy long?
And why have you got that dirty big knot in your tie? And
your shoes are muddy, and I'm not quite sure that pullover is
regulation.'

He peered at it earnestly and suspiciously, as if trying to
assess whether it was poisonous. His look was that of one of
nature's lay preachers.

'Most boys in this house wear waistcoats' – he nodded his
beaky nose at his own, tightly buttoned over an exotic tie which
I later learnt was the School fives colours, olive green striped
with black and silver.

'I personally *prefer* waistcoats, they look smarter. But if
you've *got* to wear a pullover it must be dark grey with a v-neck.
Bring me two hundred lines this time tomorrow and if your
collar's dirty or your hair hasn't been cut you'll be beaten.
You can go now.'

'Lines' could be anything you liked, as long as the chosen
sentence contained forty letters. 'To be or not to be that is
the question said Hamlet', was the most popular. The experts,
whom one paid sixpence a hundred to turn them out, wrote
all the 'To's' vertically, then all the 'be's', and so on, claiming
it saved time. Macintyre cost me a fortune that year.

'Andrewes is a *keen* House,' he would say, after counting them solemnly. And so, God help me, it was. The very word, always used with its antonym 'slack', haunted me. My persecution seemed unjust. Who had been top in French, and English and History, only to be rebuked by Macintyre for 'slackness' in Maths? Even my small sporting triumphs failed to mollify him.

I had hoped that the try for the under-fourteens against Harrow might have placated him, but the next day he beat me for whistling. More recently, there had been the five wickets against Highgate, and the nineteen not out against St Paul's, the day they had brought a fast bowler who looked seventeen, wore an incipient moustache, and was so ferocious he hit his own wicket-keeper in the teeth. And that was for the Colts, under-fifteens, and I wasn't yet even fourteen! Macintyre must have known about it, he made it his business to be informed on all the *minutiae* of school life. Yet no praise came from Macintyre, not even when I won a copy of *Tess of the D'Urbevilles* with a map of Wessex inside and the school crest in gold on the cover, for writing the best Upper Fourth essay on the journeys of St Paul. He continued to load me with punishments and lectures and whenever his eyes fell on me an expression of melancholy *gravitas* settled on his vast, boney face.

Macintyre, of course, was simply doing what he regarded as his duty as Head of House. If anyone had told him he had made my first terms at the school a misery, which he had, Macintyre would have thought them deranged. In some ways I was an odd choice; of all the new boys in his house I had been by far the most successful at games, which counted most; my academic work had also been good. There were many dirtier, idler boys than me around whom he might have tormented. By choosing me he had revealed an unexpected intuitive gift; a keen nose for the whiff of brimstone. Macintyre was operating his own instinctive character classification, not unlike that of Graham Greene's Major Jones who reckoned the world consisted of Toffs and Tarts. I had plenty of Toff accomplishments, especially cricketing ones, and a less acute observer would probably have been deceived; I had even gone a fair way towards deceiving myself. But Macintyre, the implacable moralist and enemy of pleasure, had sniffed out the Truda side of my character, the atavistic core of Tartiness. My successes, he saw, had not been painfully achieved by masochistic grind, or what he would have called 'keenness'. To be top in History because one found the subject came easily was, by Macintyre's standards, worthless – it was virtually sinful. Almost as reprehensible indeed as being bottom in Maths because one found trigonometry incomprehensible and pointless. Macintyre saw Andrewes as a house composed of earnest Toffs; he wanted no high-flying Tarts.

My tormentor himself personified this joyless philosophy. He was, apart from House Captain, Head Monitor of the School, and captain of the First XV. Typically, he played full-back, and with his great shoulders hunched into a gorilla-like attitude of menace, I can still see him galloping through the blind side. His preternaturally huge boot, size eleven-and-a-half, would blast penalty goals from distances where puny six-footers representing other schools were content to punt into touch. Macintyre's knobbly, Free Church knees, plastered with mud beneath his chastely long shorts, pounded along like animated hams. When I read *Coriolanus* I recognized the character at once. An inhuman engine of war compounded of fire and death: Coriolanus was Macintyre playing against Haileybury.

As he was no cricketer – he probably despised the game as insufficiently violent – Macintyre had ample time for snooping and trouble-making that summer term. I cowered from him on the Parade Ground where as senior Under Officer in the Combined Cadet Force (democratically downgraded, to everyone's wrath, from its former title of Officer Training Corps) his polished boots rang like hammers. I watched him with loathing when, in the grip of late-adolescent religious mania, he lectured the House on the Saving Blood of the Lamb, and issued blood-curdling warnings against 'Smut'. There was no sex in Macintyre; even the most depraved and promiscuous of his fellows would have drawn the line at manipulating that horse sized phallus in the communal rugger bath, or behind the bike sheds. I regarded him with fear, but I knew my life was better than his, better probably than anyone's, anywhere.

For each afternoon at four I sneaked off, by now skilled as an Indian tracker, to the secret clearing where I knew Becky would be placidly smoking a Player's Weight.

Becky's interest was almost entirely sexual. I think she quite enjoyed the deceit and the element of danger but these refinements were strictly secondary. For nearly two months I never saw her anywhere except in the wood. Even if had it been possible to go on excursions together I doubt she would have been very interested. The peripheries of courtship were not her style at all. Miraculously we were undetected, and I lived in a haze of content. The only problem was to get through the day – I sometimes looked at my watch five times in as many minutes – and to prevent Macintyre or his henchmen from putting an end to by far the best thing that had ever happened to me. I took enormous risks and grew increasingly confident; perfect lust had cast out most of my fear, if not all.

The half-term holiday brought a change. For the first time I visited Becky's house, or rather her section of it – a fairly extensive stables at the end of a field where her three horses were kept. A large part of every day was devoted to these animals, feeding them, grooming them, and practising jumps. For the rest we continued as usual with one exception. For the first time there were other people around and in particular one – a dull girl called Peg, supposedly Becky's best friend. Becky, however, held her in contempt.

'She's a year older than me, and she's still a virgin. She asked me once if I thought she should let Jonathan kiss her.' Becky snorted scornfully. '*He* must be pretty slow.'

I turned the conversation because I had seen Becky eyeing Jonathan, Peg's fumbling swain, in a speculative way which I suspected boded no good. I disliked him. He was at St Paul's, and was Peg's devoted squire and shadow. They had picnics together, went to the cinema, had long excursions on bicycles and generally did all the things for which Becky had so little time.

'Peg's wet as water, she's awful,' Becky said. 'My parents say she's a good influence, good, ugh.'

Had my antennae been more delicately attuned I might have picked up the warning. On the last day of the holiday all four of us were in the stables when another girl from their school turned up with a camera. She took some photographs, me with my arm round Becky, Jonathan standing awkwardly some distance from Peg. The girls giggled and I forgot about it. It was a small incident, but enough.

The Headmaster, Dr George Arbuthnot (M.A. Edinburgh; B.Litt.Oxon) was a formidable figure for a fourteen-year-old to take on. He kept me standing on the good Persian rug in front of his desk for several minutes while he signed letters, and then removing his rimless glasses looked at me with unconcealed revulsion. I knew what to expect.

The Michaelmas term had come swiftly and savagely and daily as I rode my bike up the drive to the school a driving east wind blew a thousand yellowing chestnut leaves in my face. I used to imagine I was on the retreat from Moscow – 'only another thousand miles, Murat' – and already there was rime on the rugger pitches in the morning. On the first afternoon I arrived punctual and excited at the glade, full of plans for a winter headquarters in a disued golf hut I had discovered. Becky strongly disapproved of any love-making which did not involve the rapid removal of all clothes as a preliminary.

To my despair she was not there; not did she turn up on the three subsequent days. Becky had always been even more concerned than me to preserve the utmost secrecy, and it did not as much as occur to me to risk her wrath by sending a letter to her at school. Instead I sweated it out until I received a frantic note from Jonathan written on graph paper in a spirit of abject terror. He had been summonsed by the St Paul's High Master, and been beaten – though whether this was for anything specific, or simply on principle was far from clear. There was something incomprehensible about photographs, and a warning 'to stay mum WHATEVER HAPPENS'. A long twelve hours later I was commanded to present myself before Arbuthnot – a message that was delivered to my form master by Macintyre and passed on to me in the middle of German grammar.

I slouched off to discover my fate, leaving the form in a state of wild excitement. None of my form-mates had ever spoken to the headmaster and I did not suppose that our master, a foxy hysterical figure who brooded because he was obliged to oversee the scouts and was thus forced to travel twice a week on his suburban train in humiliating shorts was on very intimate terms with Dr Arbuthnot either. Our society was probably less democratic than Thomas Arnold's Rugby.

Arbuthnot's study was piquant with carbolic, and shone with sporting trophies. Otherwise the doctor's taste ran to photographs of himself in various rugger teams at the universities of Edinburgh and Oxford, both of which he had represented as a lock forward. He had probably chosen this position as the least comfortable on the field – Arbuthnot viewed the world with the kind of masochistic relish a fakir feels for a bed of nails.

This showed on his face which settled naturally in repose into an expression simultaneously combining disgust and anguish. These reactions, his dominant ones presumably over the years, were not normally provoked by some specifically distasteful occurrence, but were rather the Head's portmanteau response to the world in general. Between the crests of Edinburgh and Oxford, Christ writhed on an eighteenth-century Spanish Cross, which despite its Popish associations had evidently slipped through the nonconformist defences on the grounds of its extreme sadism.

When Arbuthnot spoke, which was often, his voice boomed and bellowed in the clipped accents of John Buchan or Lord Reith, a surprising effect. He may have seen himself as a Covenanting minister admonishing his flock on some misty crag, or the volume may simply have been the product of a life time spent rebuking large and captive audiences. In the confines of his study a sentence from Arbuthnot hit one like a box on the ears.

'I know you've been messing about with *girls*,' he bellowed, crashing a fist on his blotting pad, as if any additional emphasis were required.

There was something about the stress he put on 'girls' which made it clear beyond any doubt that he hated and despised women. At a more mature age I would have wondered whether he would have felt the same moral outrage, or indeed any outrage at all, had the 'messing' been with boys – a much commoner misdemeanour in our male ghetto, and one that in my experience anyway had never been punished, and seldom even mentioned. But I was too young – and too frightened – to ask either the Doctor or myself why this obvious madman was yelling at me while my form-mates Finch and Fletcher, who had slept in the same bed together for the last three terms, were now peacefully holding hands or feeling each other up in the back row of the scoutmaster's German class.

But though I was too innocent to think of this, the combination of firstly, the 'I know', and secondly, the 'messing about with girls', somehow raised my cowed spirits. It had been girl singular, not 'girls' for a start, and it was hard to think of what Becky and I had done in the hay-loft as 'messing about': he had got it wrong, he was trying to bluff. When Arbuthnot said 'I know' he did not, not at all, and therefore it followed that the great man must be lying. Dimly I began to feel the faintest stirring of hope.

And as Arbutnnot continued, as he did for some time, I found the heterodox idea that I might be right and he wrong growing in me, even though I did not fully understand how so unlikely a state of affairs had come about. It was a total reversal of one's normal response because the school and the house were so hedged around with regulations, both written and unwritten that I was long accustomed to living in a state of more or less permanent delinquency. Only when asleep, and then between regulation hours in a regulated cubicle, could one possibly imagine being in a state of grace. Yet the Doctor had lied, and as far as I could see, was still lying.

It was easy to see his sources of information were pretty lean, despite the unfortunate coincidence of his being a governor of St Marina's, the snobbish school Becky attended. I knew enough about her to be sure she had given nothing away; Jonathan, who anyway knew little, did not sound as if he had blabbed either. I decided that if the Doctor could lie so could

I and at the end of half an hour I think he was reassured that the worst had not happened. Indeed by then the charge had been subtly diminished, and I was really being accused of no more than seeing a *girl* who was demonstrably not my sister, and having appeared next to her on a series of amateurish and entirely wholesome snapshots. There were in due course a couple more sessions with Arbuthnot in the same Covenanting vein which included a bizarre sexual lecture. The Doctor, puffing and panting, roared that those foolish enough not to practise total abstinence before marriage were like boys eating the icing off a Christmas cake. 'If you do that when you come to, er, scoff the cake it doesn't *taste* so nice, understand? It makes you feel sick.' Though I nodded solemnly this pastry shop view of matrimony left me cold. Becky was not remotely like a cake, or even a box of chocolates – another Arbuthnot metaphor – which goes stale if prematurely unwrapped. In fact the oftener she was unwrapped, the fresher Becky became.

What really bothered me was the fact that she had disappeared without trace. By the time I discovered what had really happened she had been taken out of my life for ever. I was punished, but St Marina's had no doubts about Becky's total culpability; she was expelled overnight. Becky had, it turned out, what criminal lawyers call 'form', and St Marina's was only the most recent in a long line of pretentious boarding-schools from which Becky had suddenly disappeared, her trunk packed, her Sunday 'walking out uniform' (for which I felt particular affection and longing) deposited with Matron to be sold secondhand to some other girl. Becky had left a lot of uniforms in virtually mint condition with a series of matrons throughout the English countryside. The reasons for her abrupt departures were always spoken of, one imagines, in shocked behind-hand whispers.

She had, of course, brought it on herself. Becky disliked Jonathan, whom she thought wet, but this had not prevented her from seducing him with her usual despatch. For her, male sexual innocence was virtually tantamount to a personal affront. Jonathan in turn had tried his Becky acquired lore on the chaste Peg, who had soon discovered the explanation of this new confidence and denounced Becky through, one supposes, jealousy rather than prudery. With Becky's reputation even those innocent photographs had acquired all the evil lineaments of dirty postcards from Port Said as far as the St Marina's headmistress was concerned.

But the history of the disaster left me unmoved. All that mattered to me was that Becky had been whisked away, for ever as it turned out. For over three years I visited 'our place' regularly, and would sometimes spend hours waiting on the grass. But needless to say the glade was always deserted, and I smoked my Player's Weights in bitter solitude.

* * * *

Becky, even in memory, had a profound influence on me. She ensured, for example, that it was at least ten years before I was even prepared to consider whether life had anything to offer which was remotely comparable to making love with an attractive and gifted woman. She also resolved my future status. On the day of her first appearance in that wood I was, I suppose, suspended somewhere between the Toff and Tart encampments; I might have joined either side. She made me a Tart for life, and implacable enemy of the Macintyres and the Arbuthnots, a poseur, sceptic and callow cynic. I shortly afterwards discovered my heroes in the novels of Aldous Huxley, like many bookish adolescents, and I suppose Becky would have approved, though she viewed reading as a waste of time that might have been spent more profitably coaxing horses over dangerous jumps, or shy boys into bed. When later on, a time came to choose between the Toff world of the Foreign Service, and the Tart society of newspapers, Becky had effectively made the decision for me in advance, and I was in Fleet Street before I was twenty-one.

It was through the agency of a newspaper that I had my last news of her. Returning to London Airport after some nerve-jangling assignment I bought an *Evening Standard* to read in the cab and found Becky, though her name had changed, all over the front page. The story was Becky's divorce (her third) and I still remember how reading the evidence soothed my nerves and induced a warm glow of affection, amusement and distinct randiness – thousands of commuters between Baker Street and Pinner, Victoria and Croydon, would have been similarly affected, and the evening papers must have beaten all circulation records. Even at a distance she had a gift for making people happy.

The case had a particular piquancy because her husband, a polo player of some celebrity, had employed a *louche* firm of private detectives to bug her bedroom – God almighty, I remember exclaiming aloud – and there had been a considerable legal debate about whether the tapes could be admitted as evidence. They were not, unfortunately for me and the commuters, quoted verbatim, but the lawyers acting for the traduced husband cited her adultery with, among others, her fifteen-year-old godson; a sixteen-year-old stable-boy; the MFH of her local Hunt, and her husband's best friend. It was also suggested that she had enjoyed an unnatural relationship with the Italian *au pair* girl which, unlike the equestrian element in the other seductions (which was strictly traditional), implied that Becky, like some intrepid geographer, was pushing the sexual boundaries ever further into the hinterland.

It was a shame about the tapes. But I knew perfectly well what was on them. 'Much better if we take all our clothes off straight away,' I could hear her saying in that lucid voice. 'Now, you shove a bit to the left like that . . . easy now, there's no need to suffocate me you know.'

CHAPTER 4

Arthur

♣

THERE was no difficulty in getting a job at W. Bean and Co – they would have welcomed Count Dracula, and offered him twenty per cent below union rates. I was virtually the only Bean's employee not suffering from some obvious physical or mental deformity. There were workers with hooks instead of hands; pegs instead of legs; eye-patches, cleft palates, and spastic shudders under the shapeless blue overalls we at the bottom wore to distinguish us from the white-smocked 'Staff' – employees who had been there long enough to qualify for the wretched pension scheme and the annual daytrip to Clacton. We of the Stock Room, shuffling, limping and in one case virtually crawling through the gate to clock in on the morning shift, wore the unreassuring air of the Marat-Sade cast getting into full stride.

Arthur was a notable exception. Aged perhaps thirty-five, he cut a dapper figure in gaberdine mackintosh and white shirt. He walked with a springy, cocky step, but there was something indefinably furtive about him. We eyed each other warily.

Whenever the foreman headed my way I had fallen into the habit of sneaking round the stacks on his blind side and walking briskly, as if busily occupied, in a random direction. One morning I found Arthur marching smartly in step.

'You picked it up very fast,' he whispered approvingly, looking straight ahead. 'But always carry something.'

I glanced down. Arthur was holding an empty cardboard box marked 'Periwinkle Blue' in front of him, like a shield against authority.

Bean's Dante-esque stockroom, lined with millions of lead tubes containing Burnt Sienna, Brown Ochre, Prussian Blue and Periwinkle Blue, was my temporary home until there was enough cash in hand to take off for Italy. It was a distinctly Victorian throwback, a murky peeling building dedicated to 'Very Finest Quality Artists' Paints'.

A non-union shop it had been allowed to stay that way because the arrangement suited everyone. The outer London industrial estate where Bean's made their paint boasted dozens of modern factories where semi-skilled, or at any rate not totally incapable workers, picked up respectable union-agreed wages.

Unfortunately, none of these places had wanted my services, because they reckoned I was too educated, so I was relegated to the stockroom. (Over-qualification is a curse. I still bitterly remember the day a talented girl-friend in Rome lost her clerk's job with FAO because some busy-body had discovered she held a good Cambridge law degree. From then on we had to switch from Commissary Vat 69 at a dollar a quart to undrinkable Italian brandy at twice the price.)

One day at Bean's Arthur bought me a Lyons individual fruit pie from the rusty trolley, which was wheeled round periodically by Dottie, who had a club foot. While we munched he nodded towards the white-coated foreman.

'Six months ago I had a white smock like that,' he said. 'Very nifty. Progress Chaser I was. Thirty quid a week, plus bonus.'

'What happened?'

'Got the chop.'

'Bad luck.'

'Too bloody right. I should never've touched the rum at the Christmas Party. Some cow said I tried to rape her.'

After this confidence our relationship prospered. There was literally no one else to talk to among the cripples, geriatrics and housewives in curlers who worked the morning shift for pin money, and kept up a continuous flow of hissing gynaecological gossip among themselves. Time, among the paint stacks, moved almost in reverse, and the boredom was as palpable as toothache. Arthur and I were as companionable as fellow convicts.

Before Bean's and the Christmas Party *débâcle* he had been employed, as he put it, 'in retail distribution'. The distribution was strictly one way: from the owners' till into Arthur's pocket, and thence to bookmakers at Wembley, the White City and Harringay, dog tracks he visited each week. He had once been over four thousand pounds ahead, and bought a house 'cash on the nail'. While I knew him he brought off a flashy double at Newmarket, and cleared over a hundred pounds. Mostly he lost.

But if his gambling career had been chequered, when it came to cash registers he was a virtuoso. He talked about them in tones of intermingled contempt and lust, as if they were women whose deceitfulness did not entirely cancel out their ability to inflame.

'Crazy bloody devices they are,' he remarked one bleak morning, moodily shuffling a pile of Brown Ochre to create the illusion of useful activity.

'Women or tills?'

'Don't be so bloody smart. One day what I'm telling you might come in useful.'

His thesis had the appeal of simplicity. Arthur believed that cash registers were entirely decorative, a gigantic con trick on the part of their manufacturers. This was partly because no machine had ever been devised to record an assistant putting the cash for the sale straight into his pocket; and partly because they were too mechanically sophisticated for simple folks – like shop managers – to make them function properly.

'I've never, repeat never known a shop manager who could make his register work,' insisted Arthur dogmatically. 'Nobody understands them, except me that is. It's an axiom like, like the Second Law of Thermodynamics.'

'Of what?'

'*You* know, the equation of heat and mechanical energy. Thought you were supposed to be going to college.'

'Not so I can be a thermodynamicist.'

Arthur looked disgusted. He had never fully adapted to the fact that he knew so much more about everything than anyone he met in the course of his circumscribed social round between Bean's and the dog tracks. It must have been like that for many years, for Arthur's conversation had acquired an elliptical quality. Even when he was ostensibly chatting to someone else one had the impression he was more than half talking to himself. He was a rare modern phenomenon; a man of brilliant intelligence with virtually no formal education.

His parents had been itinerants, and he had attended over fifty different schools before being discharged on the world at fourteen, totally illiterate. In the nineteenth century he would have taken his place among a multitude of Jude the Obscures learning Latin by candlelight and queuing outside the Mechanics' Institute. A few decades later there would have been kindred spirits in the trades union and labour movements. Now, in the post 1944 world, he was almost on his own. The Butler Act had made it highly unusual for children as gifted as this to slide through the educational net.

'Tell me more about cash registers,' I encouraged.

'Nothing to them *if you understand*. One job I had in the wine trade, Mayfair it was, very flash. Very first morning I saw the manager cursing and swearing with his till, dreadful mess he was in with the ribbon. "Arthur," he says. "Know anything about these bastards?" "I'll have a bash," I said. And that was it. In a week I was in charge of all the stock books as well, and the gaffer was as happy as a lark. We turned over eight hundred pounds a week in that shop. I reckon I did nearly three thou in eight months.'

'*Three thousand pounds?*'

'Near enough.'

'Did they get you?'

'Not likely. The way I used that register – it was a National, very pretty – I don't suppose they ever even knew. Heartbroken the company was when I said I was moving along. Offered me a shop of my own, they did. But you've got to know when the time has come to scarper.'

'When's that?'

Arthur winked.

'I reckon the first week of December's the ideal. Always leave a clear four weeks before stocktaking.'

Soon after I began visiting Arthur's extremely comfortable suburban house, a relic doubtless of the lush days in 'retail distribution'. His passion, it turned out, was classical music, and he had a truly astonishing record collection, which must have cost several times his annual earnings from Bean's. There were thousands of records, all elaborately catalogued, and he subscribed to several specialist magazines. I noticed the back numbers extending over several years were neatly stacked on several yards of shelves identical to those Bean's Stock Room employed for the paint tubes. He decided to further my musical education, and I cooperated enthusiastically. Apart from a repertoire of the better known Anglican hymns, and a few hundred verses of the Ball of Kerriemuir, my venerable school had contributed little in this direction.

Arthur's teaching methods were eccentric but strikingly similar to those my director of studies in Cambridge was to employ some time later on. Both he and Arthur specialized in a flow of allusive, and almost surrealist comment. Only the subject matter differed.

'Take pox now,' my Cambridge mentor would begin on a typical day. 'It's a kind of touchstone of chauvinism. To the Elizabethans it was the French evil while Catherine de' Medicis would undoubtedly have thought of it as *"la maladie anglaise"*. The Dutch usually attributed pox to the Spaniards, and the Tahitians always did (doubtless with good reason too, haw, haw). Is your glass full? Good. Did you know by the way there is a charming town called Condom in the Bas-Pyrénées?' And so on.

Arthur too liked his seminars to be accompanied by drink, but instead of Tio Pepe, offered sweet tea out of a Coronation Mug trellised with tannin impregnated fissures.

'Nice that, in'it?' he would begin, waving vaguely towards the Hi-Fi. 'Gregorian, you reckon, or Ambrosian? Naw, that's too easy. Two different pitches at once, get it? They call it diaphony, now you're the kind of bloke who'd know whether that's Latin or Greek. Funny thing the Bantus – that's a nigger tribe in South Africa – play a stringed instrument the same way. All fourths and fifths: makes you think, eh?'

Occasionally he would divert conversational channels to take in one of his other hobbies.

'Jolly Roger's never going to give Royal Jubilee five pounds,

especially if the going's wet, as it often is in Carlisle at this time
of the year. Jubilee's out of Minnehaha of course, wonderful
stayer . . .'

When racing was exhausted he liked to work through the
Daily Telegraph, and comment on items he found stimulating.

'See a bloke's drawn five years at London Quarter Sessions
for nicking lead. Silly bugger. Bottom's fallen right out of the
Church roof caper. Three years ago now, that was a *very* different kettle of fish. Bloke I know in South Harrow, calls himself
a "general dealer", that's a laugh he's a right villain, anyway
he used to say . . .'

Invariably the flow would be interrupted by Arthur's elder
sister Tilly, an immense good-natured woman who worked as
a cook in a transport café. She nagged him incessantly about
'bettering himself', and would sometimes provoke his stylized
fury by sneaking to the gramophone and putting on a Mario
Lanza record while he was in the lavatory. His counter-attack
was Debussy orchestral music, which she claimed always made
her flesh come up in goose-pimples.

Eventually, a better job did come up; Arthur was 'tipped
the word' by a contact 'in the wines and spirits'. I was given a
smart yellow van and became a comparatively free man overnight. The day before I began work Arthur explained how to
exploit the system of deposits on bottles and delivered a lecture
on 'ullage' – the arrangement by which wholesalers' replace
bottles of spirits that have broken, *as long as the break is below
the neck and the seal has not been tampered with.* Arthur recommended
a method involving the use of brown sticky paper, a plastic
funnel, and a hack-saw.

'With bottles and ullage and tips you'll clear twenty a week
easy,' Arthur said. 'And then there's your wages on top.'

It was typical he should have put wages last. In his mind
official payment was a kind of ancillary tip, a bonus you
pocketed after acquiring the real money by stealth.

I noticed he had taken up oil painting, and equipped a
'studio' with Bean's paints and brushes, even a Bean's easel.

'If this job's so wonderful why didn't you take it yourself?'
I asked him.

Arthur looked cunning.

'Don't want to fall into temptation,' he said. 'Anyway you get time to think at Bean's. I'll go on keeping my head down.'

So I graduated to bourgeois Golders Green, and began delivering kosher wines to houses full of white carpet. Arthur's head stayed so well down I never saw him again.

*   *   *   *

Some of Arthur's lore turned out to be useful, though not all. At least, thanks to him, I have always had a horror of ante-post betting; avoided backing second favourites over the sticks; remembered to carry something when engaged in simulating innocent activity; and made good resolutions about staying sober at office parties.

Because of Arthur I also retain prejudices against Tchaikovsky and in favour of the Budapest rather than the Prague interpretation of the late Beethoven Quartets. When in gainful employment I have noticed a distinct restlessness and impulse to scarper early in December, as if to pre-empt some spiritual January stocktaking. I regard cash registers with disdain.

It would be nice to think he took some of my advice and has eschewed office work, particularly any office which habitually carried a 'cash float'. If he forgot about this Arthur will probably read these words in prison, if at all. There could be few people more comprehensively equipped with spiritual resources for dealing with a long stretch.

CHAPTER 5

Starbuck

♣

LIKE several hundred other undergraduates I was made aware of Starbuck's presence on his first day in Cambridge. He arranged things so that it was virtually impossible not to notice him as he drove with royal deliberation past St John's, along Trinity Street, and in front of King's Chapel. His car was a long, black Jaguar which would have caused no great stir in the world of, say, Harley Street abortionists. But in Cambridge, particularly when driven by an eighteen-year-old, it had rarity value, and so had Starbuck's passenger, a girl with chemical silver hair and a bosom of such improbable dimensions that it later brought her a kind of fame. In those days Ruby was only sixteen, and had yet to make her first appearance on television, but she was an impressive vision for Cambridge in October. At the time Ruby was humbly employed as a chorus girl at the Tower Ballroom in Blackpool, which happened to be Starbuck's home town.

Ruby's totally knowing blonde stare through that shining windscreen must have caused not a few Newnham girls in blue jeans and dirty duffle coats to shift uneasily on their bicycle saddles as they headed back to their Victorian rooms; crumpets by the gas-fire; the prints of Van Gogh or Picasso; the obligatory copies of Donne's poems and *Dusty Answer* with their owners' names – Antonia, Caroline, Joanna – inscribed in sensitive black italic on the flyleaf. The university girls, with rare delightful exceptions, tended to conduct their *affaires* on an anguished epistolary level of great complexity and frustrating abstraction. One girl, who caused me an inordinate amount of trouble, spent three dramatic years enveloped in a Boulevard St Germain black cloak writing poems about the beauty of her Girtonian buddies, and talking gnomically of Sappho. Most people assumed this was no more than a not very original Lesbian pose: and so amazingly did she. It took her ten years to acquire the courage of her adolescent affectations, and when at thirty she finally discovered she really had been homosexual all the time, she was as surprised as she was delighted.

Neither Starbuck nor the sexy Ruby looked as if they were much worried by problems of this order. Perhaps, in Blackpool, puberty ended at ten, or maybe Starbuck had simply been born older than his contemporaries in the great middle class.

She soon disappeared, to universal male regret, and so did the Jaguar (undergraduates were not allowed cars). Starbuck however, remained, and it occurred to me even at the time that he constituted a living challenge to everything that venerable university held most dear. As always, of course, there were lots of young men around, including myself, who reckoned they were rebelling against something or another; at that time the most popular targets were the class system and the so-called Establishment (which, in various disguises, most of the young radicals were soon to join). But we were generally self-conscious, unimaginative, and noticeably lacking in spontaneity, a quality which Cambridge has always suspected because it can so easily get out of hand.

In contrast, Starbuck's revolutionary qualities were so entirely a function of his own personality that he would have no more considered discussing them as a thing apart than he would have thought to analyse his need to breathe, eat or fuck. His very appearance was revolutionary, as I realized one Sunday when I ran into him conducting a large party of very flash looking Blackpool relations across the Bridge of Sighs in St John's. Most undergraduates would have entertained ambiguous feelings about such an occasion, but not Starbuck. He found the whole thing side-splittingly funny.

'Meet me mum,' he said, doing his maniac grin. 'And that's Aunt Florrie wearin' the 'at with the feathers. They're enjoying it as much as the zoo at Bellevue, all 'aving a grand time.'

I passed on with an aesthetic young man, now a fellow of that splendid college. He was shocked, not to say horrified. As

Starbuck was wearing a ragged looking gown which he had no doubt stolen in order to amuse or impress his relatives, my friend was also genuinely alarmed. '*That's* not one of ours, is it?' he said, once we were safely established against the well-mannered Elizabethan façade of Second Court.

'No,' I told him, 'unfortunately not. Don't you think he'd cheer the place up?'

'You're being flippant, of course,' he replied briskly, much relieved to learn that Starbuck's presence on the Bridge was a mere geographical accident.

'My God, did you see his *hair*?'

Starbuck's appearance was, it must be admitted, rather special. His face was ugly and ageless with eyes the colour of black pudding – one of his favourite dishes – and a bothersome complexion that never remotely bothered him. His hair was particularly remarkable as it had been 'styled' in a cut then known as the 'Cherokee', a fashion which enjoyed a brief and limited vogue among Teddy-Boy pacesetters in places like Sunderland, Jarrow and the Gorbals. It involved the scalp being totally shaved except for a strip of greased hair about three inches broad running from a point above the centre of the forehead, if any, to the nape of the neck. Starbuck had it done that way because he thought it was 'a giggle'.

His clothes were similarly designed to amuse, primarily to amuse him. He had a weakness for blue suede shoes; ruffled shirts with boot-string ties; eccentric Italian inspired trousers with fly-buttons on the outside; and midnight blue blazers with narrow, notched lapels and big plastic buttons. Starbuck's outfits were to me totally original – I had never seen clothes remotely like them – but I suspect his sartorial inspiration stemmed from some specific sharp dresser he admired – probably a comedian he had seen at home in the Tower Ballroom, or perhaps on Blackpool Pier.

The run-of-the-mill Cambridge nonconformists of the Left tended to dress in a manner which was just as formalized as the uniform – pinched-in felt hat, club tie, narrow cavalry twills, chukka boots – of their social and political opponents. The 'angries', *pace* Osborne, cultivated an Orwellian austerity: the jeans and shapeless jerseys, the duffle coats and beards, were intended to indicate working-class solidarity, though in fact their clothes were at least as dissimilar to those of the proletariat as the kind of outfit our college's resident South American millionaire wore for an afternoon's polo. The bourgeois intellectuals were accordingly as recognizable as the bourgeois *tout court*. God knows what Starbuck was recognizable as, but that 'Cherokee' had nothing middle class about it, while disordered Einsteinian locks were in a well-established and eminently respectable tradition of acceptable dissent.

The bizarre gear set Starbuck apart, but nothing like so far apart as his total confidence and lack of neurosis. Years later a distinguished zoologist lectured me at length about chimpanzees, and introduced me to one of his flock, a playful and interesting companion who ruffled my hair and held my hand. Immediately I had a vision of Starbuck, whom I had neither seen nor thought of for a decade. It was not simply that the animal bore a striking physical resemblance to him, which it did. It was the over-powering impression I had of its pure, unfallen instinct. Through that tender paw flowed animal ease, like poured oil. When my chimp saw, or touched or smelt something in the outside world, its reaction was simultaneous and entirely reflexive. No ratiocination, no neurotic cerebral process, came between it and the thing. I had seen Starbuck react similarly when confronted with girls, the prospect of money, and on one occasion a police sergeant who rightly suspected that something illegal (in this case enough pot to keep the university high for the whole of the Michaelmas term) was going on round Starbuck, but without knowing exactly what.

This highly developed instinct did not preclude foresight. Compulsory National Service meant that Oxford and Cambridge selected most of their entrants three years in advance, reserving their places for when they had finished with the services. Starbuck accordingly took entrance exams at both universities, and narrowly passed. He had previously arranged to fail his National Service Medical, and also established that the two ancient universities differed diametrically in their attitude

towards borderline students. Cambridge, liberal as always, held
the view that once an undergraduate had been admitted he
should be given every possible chance. Except for gross mis-
demeanours, no student was sent down for academic failure
before the end of his second year. Oxford, more brutally, simply
got rid of everyone who had not managed to pass a preliminary
examination by the end of his third term. Starbuck's vision of
the universities was too realistic for the idea of passing any
examinations to be part of it. That was not on his programme.
He therefore assured Oxford that they could expect him in two-
and-a-half years, once he had finished serving his country,
while telling Cambridge to expect him immediately, as he was
medically exempt from the army. This strategem, remarkably
far-sighted for a boy of eighteen, worked perfectly. Cambridge,
with few regrets, gave him marching orders at the end of his
second year, and with the minimum of disruption he shifted
his Presley records westwards to Oxford, where he presented
himself as fresh from the British Army of the Rhine. Oxford,
in turn, threw him out at the end of three terms, which meant
he had completed, as he had intended, three comfortable university years, even if in tandem. He was then able to concentrate
uninterruptedly on selling 'authentic display fruit' – plastic
imitation bananas, peaches and so forth, designed to sit in
bowls on the window-sills of houses in council estates, thus
creating an illusion of luxury and wealth for the benefit of
neighbours and passers-by. But this was some way ahead.

The invasion of Suez in November 1956 drove the university
collectively mad, though when the Russians moved into Budapest it was to go even madder. Some time between the two
events I called on Starbuck in his rooms, rightly suspecting
that I would find a change of atmosphere. For the time being
I felt I had signed enough petitions and carried several banners
too many. My director of studies, a remarkable man who was
among other things a veteran of the Spanish Civil War and a
life-long friend of Guy Burgess, had that morning interrupted
a discussion of Thomas Nashe's prose to remark that he had
known the university reach such a pitch of political excitement
on two previous occasions only. The first had been the visit of

the Jarrow Hunger Marchers in November 1933; the second was Munich. All in all I think by that time I would rather have stayed with Thomas Nashe.

Though ostensibly resident in his obscure and uncomfortable college Starbuck had acquired a large and scrupulously neat flat above a coffee bar which had a reputation for being *louche* and was often visited by the begowned proctors. He was occupied in watching the demonstrators in the Market Place, playing an Elvis Presley LP, and smoking a marihuana cigarette. Smoking pot was at this time an exotic vice almost entirely restricted to jazz musicians and West Indian immigrants. As usual Starbuck was ahead of his time. In the adjoining room the exquisitely pretty daughter of a bus-conductor on the Huntingdon route was demurely changing the sheets of the bed she had just vacated, and which would later be occupied by a 'chick' Starbuck had picked up in the only pub for twenty miles which possessed a juke box. It was hence patronized exclusively by American airmen, plough boys, and apprentice fifteen-year-old whores from sinister villages deep in the Fens.

Undergraduates, who would have found nothing in *The Blue Cock* to interest them anyway, were naturally barred. Starbuck was of course accepted because it never crossed anyone's mind that he might have any connexion with the university, except possibly in some domestic capacity.

In due course, he substituted Bill Haley for Elvis, and then put on Buddy Holly, of whom I had never heard. His 'chick' tottered off on her high heels in the direction of Huntingdon, and Starbuck remarked he would be spending Christmas in Blackpool, running a mock auction on the front and selling 'lucky dip' parcels of cheap toys from the back of a lorry at ten shillings a time. 'I pay two bob for the toys and stick silver stars, you know to make it Christmassey like, on the outside,' he informed me. With the profits he intended to spend a fortnight in New York because Ray Charles and Nat Adderley (again both names that meant nothing to me) would be performing in Harlem.

I replied, with I suppose unconcealed envy, that I too would have to work at Christmas – probably sorting the post at

Euston Station. Starbuck waved aside the idea languidly, and suggested instead I join the committee of the University Jazz Club, which by some unknown chicanery he had succeeded in taking over. It was a very good band indeed, and Starbuck devoted a couple of hours daily to arranging 'gigs' all over the country. He drove the band, and their followers who at a later stage would have been called 'groupies', to their engagements in a Rolls-Royce hearse he had recently acquired (out of club funds) to replace the defunct Jaguar.

'Easy enough to swing it,' he said encouragingly. 'You should clear a tenner a week, what with the admissions and all.'

I indicated that spending five nights a week clipping tickets on the door of places like the Masonic Hall, Bletchley, was not my idea of a good time. Starbuck never argued, and he saw the point at once.

'You'll have to flog books then,' he said.

'How do you mean?'

Starbuck sighed, and removed his dark glasses to fix me with his button eyes.

'How many people do you know in this place? Two hundred? Five hundred?'

I said I didn't know exactly, but certainly a lot. He did his monkey grin, pleased at having made a point.

'How many of 'em lock their doors when they go out? One in ten would you say? Right. How many of 'em read books? Most of 'em, right? So what you do is get a bag, one of those you put sports stuff in, and go round and call on your mates. When you find someone's out put all his new books in the bag and go straight round to Heffer's, they'll give a better price than Bowes & Bowes. If he's written his name in don't ink it over. Keep a pair of scissors with you, and just cut the page out altogether. Money for jam.'

It was a shocking concept for a boy who had been brought up to leave his penny bus fare with another passenger if the stop arrived before the conductor had been round.

I fell back on a traditional argument from prep school, sure that he would climb down.

'How would you feel if a friend did that to you?'

Starbuck leered contemptuously.

'Nobody could. Firstly I don't buy books, and secondly you'd need a bloody acetylene torch to get through the padlock on *that* door.'

Starbuck indicated his security arrangements with a nod of his 'Cherokee'.

'You don't think I'm daft, do you?'

When Starbuck originally arrived in Cambridge with his Jaguar and show-girl I suspect he entertained certain Gatsby-like aspirations about the university. Even an adolescent as unimpressionable as he was must have felt some tingle of excitement at the sheer plenitude of the city, a place so beautiful that one is left wondering perpetually how it has out-smarted all the planners and politicians and architects who in the best native traditions have been concerned to turn it into Hemel Hempstead or Harlow New Town or the University of Sussex. But the enchantment, if indeed it ever existed, did not last.

During his second year Starbuck's connexion with the university became increasingly peripheral, and I had the impression he was often away. Mentally, he was probably preparing himself for the inevitable transfer to Oxford. Once he arrived there – and had taken over the Oxford Jazz Club using techniques already tried out and perfected – he seemed to lose interest in that university too.

It was some time during my third year in Cambridge and Starbuck's first at Oxford that he acquired the franchise to import simulated oranges, bananas, pineapples and such fruit from Italy. These plastic 'simulated display items' enjoyed an enormous vogue at this time among the pace-setters on northern housing estates, and Starbuck was so busy selling them door to door out of the back of a Citroën estate wagon (the hearse's successor) that he had no time to waste in Oxford, where he was ostensibly a student. He had delegated the Jazz Club to a crazed young man who wrote poetry in lower case, and trembled when addressed. For a break he would come each weekend to stay in my rather grand flat opposite Parker's Piece. I should not have lived there at all as an undergraduate, but had made some kind of a case to the college authorities, claiming that the place really belonged to a drunken MA of my acquaintance, and that he would therefore be responsible for my conduct. It seems highly unlikely that they were deceived by this device but they were, as usual, far too urbane to shoot me down. Towards the end of my second year St John's seemed to have been trying to make up its mind whether to send me down or not, and having finally settled for a couple of weeks' rustication – a minor punishment which involves simply staying outside the city limits – they apparently decided, according to the traditions of the university, to look after their own, and put up with me for three more terms. My tutor, the classicist John Crook, is I think the best-mannered man I have ever met, and I imagine he did not wish to embarrass me by demolishing my doubtful qualifications for living in a flat without the supervision of some ex-College servant turned landlady. The College Dean, who was responsible for disciplinary matters, chose nine o'clock in the morning as a suitable hour for delivering a heavily Pauline lecture about the evils of alcohol, and arranged for me to be escorted to his mock-Gothic rooms in New Court by a brace of college porters, both of whom were close friends. They stood on either side of me during the reprimand like military policemen, having previously each drawn a frothy pint of bitter from a barrel the admirable Dean kept in his gyp room. He himself drank brandy out of an early nineteenth century balloon glass during his eloquent lecture, which he concluded by giving me an inscribed copy of his collected sermons with an epigraph from II Corinthians, the well-known section about children speaking as children and men like men. The moral was to go to hell in your own way but don't inconvenience us, or your fellow undergraduates, and thereafter I kept my head down.

Starbuck was earning something in the region of two hundred pounds a week from his plastic fruit sales, and for some reason I never worked out had the money sent to my flat in five pound notes every Friday for collection the following day. I only discovered the contents of these registered parcels when I signed for one in an early morning haze and threw it on a table where it was lost beneath a pile of books. When Starbuck demanded his parcel I denied ever having received it, and after a fraught Saturday we finally found it by mistake. Around this time Starbuck's sexual activities, always impressive, reached some kind of a peak.

He had acquired the habit of sending a postcard in the middle of the week, usually from somewhere like Wolverhampton, warning me of what I could expect over the weekend. His taste was eclectic, and encompassed the manageress of the perfume department in the Birmingham branch of the Cooperative Wholesale Society – to whom he was at one stage engaged – and a cousin of the Queen, a grim and spotty lady whose love letters he ungallantly sold to a Sunday newspaper for eighteen hundred pounds in cash.

One day he sent a long and slightly nervous telegram warning me that every time the telephone rang I was to answer: 'University Arms Hotel, Good Day.' I went along with this request, thus convincing various friends I had finally gone mad, but the precaution was justified. My flat was directly opposite this Victorian pile of the utmost respectability and it transpired that Starbuck had persuaded the father of a sixteen-year-old pre-Deb called Lucinda to let her spend the weekend in Cambridge: he believed my flat to be part of the University Arms, within whose portals no fair maid could ever have been seduced. Lucinda, straight off a chocolate box in a pleated green dress I can still remember, arrived first. Starbuck soon followed, accompanied by the very sexy thirty-seven-year-old wife of his tutor, a distinguished critic of Proust. This unlikely trio went into what had become Starbuck's bedroom about eleven on Saturday morning and failed to reappear until lunchtime on Sunday.

It was, for me, a depressing meal, and I consumed my light ale and cold sausages in bitter silence. Both Lucinda and The Older Woman (who looked very like Simone Signoret in *Room at the Top*) wore the sparkling glow of total female sexual satisfaction. I had never entertained extravagant views of my own beauty and desirability but when it came to competing with Starbuck, surely beside him even Boris Karloff (who had, in-

cidentally, attended the same school as me), surely even he
would have looked like a Praxiteles Apollo. And yet . . .

Starbuck was good at other people's moods, it was the salesman in him, and he soon took me aside and learnt the whole
lamentable story. It was fairly complicated, and centred on a
girl called Virginia and unrequited love. Virginia, and this was
the key to the whole story, was twenty-four, four years older
than me which at that age is a lot. She had gone down from
the university with a distinguished degree before I had even
taken the scholarship, and her life in between had, by my
standards anyhow, been cosmopolitan and exotic. She had
done post-graduate work at Berkeley in California. She had
spent a summer in Mexico *with a famous poet*; she had worked
for international organizations in Rome and Geneva, and now
she was back doing yet more post-graduate work in Cambridge.
All very grand, and apart from this she was also spectacularly
good-looking.

Starbuck was unimpressed by this catalogue of virtues.
'They're all the same in bed,' he remarked profoundly.

The main problem with Virginia was her best friend, Belinda,
also a clever, sexy girl completing her Ph.D. at Newnham. The
previous year I had enjoyed a certain amount of success with
various undergraduates in this college, and Belinda, in a spirit
which anticipated Women's Lib, had decided to cut me down
to size. On every possible occasion she had sung Virginia's
praises, always adding as a rider that I would have no chance
with her, no chance at all. She was not interested in callow
young men and would not be wasting her time with undergraduates after the kind of mature men she had dangled on a
string. And more, much more, in the same spirit. I was excited
by the challenge, but pessimistic. Belinda, and particularly the
story of the famous poet, had pretty well convinced me Virginia
was in a different league, the one where you drank dry martinis
straight up, instead of nescafé or light and bitter mixed.

Starbuck's face, even uglier than usual after the athletic
demands of the previous twenty-four hours, wore an expression
of deep interest. This was the kind of thing that brought out
the professional in him.

It had all turned out unexpectedly, I continued. Virginia had duly arrived and with a Roman sun tan in drizzling Cambridge had proved to be if anything more desirable than Belinda had made out. On her second day in the university we had met by chance at a party and emboldened by drink I had invited her to accompany me to the first night of a play for which I had review tickets. To my surprise she had accepted, even though she had spent some time first working through an engagement book which already seemed full. It was even more surprising when after the play she invited me back to the small house she was sharing with Belinda for coffee. After this had been ritually consumed I sprang on her, reasoning that there was nothing to lose and in all probability I would never have a second chance. Her resistance was no more than token and over bacon and eggs the following morning – with Belinda crashing round the kitchen in a fury – I felt deeply contented. So much for the famous poet whom I had discovered in the course of small hours intimacies had been capable only of buggery, and that rarely. Virginia herself had more conventional tastes.

But at this point something had mysteriously gone wrong. I had received a pleasant but terse card embossed with the seal of Newnham informing me that it had all been 'absolutely super' but that enough was enough, and she did not wish to see me again. Cursing Belinda, whom I correctly assumed to be the instigator of this *volte-face*, I had spent most of the next ten days trying to change Virginia's mind once again, but with no success at all. She refused either to see or speak to me, and my long poetic letters written deep into the night had remained unanswered. I was sick with misery and rejection, and Starbuck's insouciant successes made me feel even worse.

'You know bugger all about women even if you are good at writing articles,' Starbuck commented, putting on his deplorable pale blue blazer, and kneading his 'Cherokee' with a filthy hand. 'Come on.'

'Come on where?'

'To see the silly cow, of course.'

'I've tried. She looks out of the window from upstairs and if it's me then she won't open the door.'

Starbuck gave me the look of a man who had got through a lot of closed doors in his time, usually as a preliminary to selling large amounts of plastic bananas.

Belinda and Virginia lived in a two-storey artisan's cottage which the Hampstead wife of a television don had at one stage begun to convert into a pottery. Before this operation was completed she divorced him on the grounds of persistent, indeed almost habitual adultery, and the cottage was accordingly something of a mess. As we drew up outside it in Starbuck's hearse he delivered his instructions.

'Keep your head down until they open the door. Give me a minute to do the spiel, and then follow me in sharpish. We don't want to give them time to think too much, dig?'

I dug. Belinda, as always the watchdog, looked out and opened the door, probably under the misapprehension that Starbuck was an undertaker who had mislaid his corpse, and come to the wrong number. As soon as she opened the door she was beaten, and after the statutory minute for the 'spiel' – God knows what he talked about, plastic fruit possibly – I swiftly joined him on the step. His blue suede bootee, I noticed, was firmly placed between door and lintel, and as I arrived Belinda capitulated.

'You can come in for a minute but there's no drink,' she said grudgingly. 'Anyway we're just leaving. We have an appointment for tea in King's with . . .' she paused for added effect, 'with John Barton.'

I had already noticed she was wearing an unusually *chic* tweed suit, which looked as if it had come from Jaeger. Mr Barton, then as now, was a good name to drop, particularly in theatrical circles. As a fellow of King's with a beard which looked as if it occupied a good deal of his time with mirror and scissors, he was, like Starbuck himself, a hard man not to notice around the place, and was much admired by aspirant lady novelists in Newnham. Still it took more than a mere Barton to up-stage Starbuck.

'That long streak of piss who thinks he's Shakespeare's ghost?' my pandar replied chattily at Belinda's haughty back going up the bare stairs. She was in a poor geographical position to riposte, and shrugged contemptuously as best she could. Starbuck swivelled his neck round and contorted his chimp face into a grotesque wink. My instinct was to turn tail and run for cover.

This emotion grew stronger as we reached the first floor. The big room was a mess of books, underwear and an unmade divan. There was a heap of make-up strewn on top of a tea-chest, and a half empty bottle of Miller's excellent sherry standing next to it. This, Virginia's room about which I thought so much, had not yet been 'sorted out'. It had the air of a bedsitter in Belsize Park whose tenant had just departed at midnight carrying the best of the furniture with him. In the middle was Virginia, also in her best suit, working on her already beautiful face in front of a broken mirror. Those were the days when girls wore powder and lipstick, and one had to be careful of stains on shirts.

Virginia grunted in an unwelcoming manner, and I said a weak 'Hullo'. Starbuck wandered carelessly round the room, and Belinda stood with hands on hips in the attitude of an exasperated host who wants his guests to get the hell out. I cursed Starbuck for letting me in for this, and the silence continued a while. It seemed clear that the first one who broke it would probably be the loser, and Belinda cracked. Her *petit-bourgeoise* instincts got the better of her, and she said defiantly: 'As you see we aren't ready to receive outsiders.'

This ploy was intended simultaneously to excuse herself for living in such slum-like conditions, and make us feel uncomfortable at compounding their difficulties by intruding. Apart from being wasted on Starbuck, who was totally unembarrassable, it gave him the lead in he had been seeking. Perched on the edge of the divan, he nodded his head gravely in the manner of a technician faced with a tricky problem only years of training had equipped him to handle.

'Even if you have smashing furniture you'll never be comfortable in a room without carpet,' he opened. Neither of the girls replied, but Belinda sighed histrionically, as one about to expire from boredom.

'Now if you have carpet, *good* carpet of course not any

old tat, you can live like a prince with just a few old boxes.'

Since that was the only furniture the girls possessed I thought Starbuck was sailing over close to the wind. It was impossible to gauge what he thought he was doing; if anything he was making things worse. I had decided to take what Bertie Wooster invariably calls 'the manly course' (when about to leave Aunt Agatha's via a providential drainpipe) and say it was time to go when Starbuck began again.

'I know just the carpet you need here, pure wool, none of that fibre rubbish, and going free too as a matter of fact. I could bring it down in the hearse tomorrow evening, and get started with the underfelt. That's got to be done really well, of course. Very shortsighted to skimp on *that*, I can tell you.'

Belinda retained her scornful silence and Virginia – how I loved that thick chestnut hair – continued working on her lipstick, but all the same there was a perceptible if slight stirring of interest. Starbuck then embarked on a long and boring story about an uncle of his, Uncle Jeremiah that was, not Uncle Fred of course who drank, and his commercial interests, which included a small chain of cinemas in the Midlands.

'A few weeks ago,' Starbuck said, 'you could hardly call them cinemas, they were more flea-pits, you know. But when Uncle Jeremiah gets to work he does everything properly, thorough that's what he is. New screens they've got now, new *fauteuils* and new *foyers* of course. You could take anyone there now, royalty if you liked. Do you know how much the carpet he had to buy (wholesale of course) – over five thousand square yards, *five* thousand.' Starbuck shook his head at this aerodrome of carpet. The girls were still silent, and I admired Virginia's nyloned calves with nostalgia. If I could only get her alone . . . Starbuck had become philosophical. 'Even the most thorough bloke makes mistakes sometimes, inevitable isn't it? And the bloody fool (excuse me ladies) who did the estimates reckoned it would need five-and-*a-half* thousand square yards, so Uncle Jerry's left holding the baby. Wholesaler won't take it back, won't consider it. So there is it, fills half a bloody (pardon me) warehouse, doing nobody any good. Uncle Jerry asked me if I'd shift it for him as a matter of fact.'

The girls were now interested, not wildly so but Starbuck had captured their attention. Virginia had abandoned her lipstick, and Belinda was perched on the edge of a junkstore desk they had bought for ten shillings. Starbuck was building up for the kill.

'Of course it's worth money, quite a lot of money, sold off in job lots, but think of the time it would take. I mean you can't spend your life flogging bits of carpet, can you? I wonder how much you'll need here. Do you know how long it is from the door to the fireplace there, by any chance?'

Both the girls said simultaneously that they did not, and the very fact of their speaking at all indicated a shade more progress. It was the moment for the *coup de grâce* and Starbuck administered it like Dominguin at his peak. Reaching into the inside pocket of that awful blazer he produced, to my amazement, a wooden folding ruler of the kind used by carpenters. He stretched it out to its full yard, eyed the room professionally, and got down on his knees. From another pocket he produced a pencil and small book, preparatory to making notes. Then he asked Belinda to shift one of the tea-chests about six inches so he could measure more exactly. She did so as if hypnotized, and Virginia put down her handbag to aid her. Starbuck had won. In three minutes we were all on our knees measuring, and there followed a session on the stairs, and a long discussion of what colours would be most suitable. Around five-thirty Belinda changed into a sweater and jeans; by six we were well into the sherry. Mr Barton's tea party that Sunday lacked two of its guests. We dined off baked beans, Starbuck did the washing up, and in the course of it whispered a few sentences to Belinda. Shortly after they left together in the hearse and Virginia and I began again where we had left off a fortnight earlier – and thereafter we virtually lived together for eight months until she very sensibly left me to marry a Sorbonne professor who was also a millionaire.

Belinda returned home the following morning in a gay mood, and though I often wondered whether she had joined Lucinda and the Proust critic's wife in Starbuck's large bed I never dared ask. There was a long and complex correspondence about carpet in the following months, but none ever materialized. This did not inhibit Starbuck from taking Belinda to bed on several future occasions, when he was able to fit her in.

Some months later when I inquired after Uncle Jeremiah's health and commercial prosperity Starbuck offered me a reefer and looked blank.

'Mixing me up with someone else you wet git,' he said. 'I've only got one uncle, Alf that is, and he's in Strangeways for something naughty he tried to pull off with a couple of greyhounds. Switched 'em round see. He's out of harm's way for a while, the silly berk.'

In later life Starbuck prospered.

CHAPTER 6

Zakki, the Pope and the Six-Day War

♣

COMING in over Amman, even in my frame of mind, was an experience of near hallucinatory beauty; it was purple and yellow and away towards the flat horizon, reddish – the whole suffused with a light of totally clear yet soothing yellow. Such, I thought, must an atom explosion look when seen from a great distance.

In preparation for the Pope's Holy Land visit – a trip I had spent the last ten days resolutely trying to avoid describing as 'historic' though with only sporadic success – my time had been spent tracking down musty *Monsignori* in equally musty surroundings: like sex, chastity has its own unmistakable odour. There had been the Ecumenicists, invariably northern European priests, in those days thinner on the ground than latterly. There had been desiccated superiors of numerous English-speaking colleges, most of whom rightly regarded me with more or less well-camouflaged suspicion. What my bosses in London wished to know was *why* Pope Paul was breaking a precedent of several centuries to leave Italy and visit the Holy Land? When asked this apparently rational question most of the men of God winced charitably, pointing out in their different styles that the ways of Mother Church were very different from those of, say, the Mother of Parliament. While a British Prime Minister could base a decision to travel to Moscow or Washington on practical and anyway ostensibly rational political considerations, the Vatican was a very different matter indeed. Here there were such questions as the Grace of God, Divine Inspiration and so forth to be taken into account. At this point we would all look solemn.

I was in no situation to cast doubts on such Godly assertions. Already, minutes after arriving in the Holy Land, I had allowed Zakki, chauffeur extraordinary and reckless despoiler of moral standards, to lead me astray. I had abetted this Arab amoralist to cheat a colleague from the *Christian Science Monitor* (God help me), whose conscience rightly made him refuse an extortionate demand of twenty-five Jordanian pounds a day.

Less highmindedly I threw my shabby, heterogeneous gear in the back of Zakki's '55 red Chevvy without further argument, and told him to start driving. Crouched Fangio-style over the dirty plastic-rimmed wheel he screamed off up the Boulevard, leaving rubber tyre traces behind him. It was a driving style to which I soon accustomed myself.

'Englishman, sir?' enquired my new driver. He was judging doubtless from my general air of shabbiness, and in particular my scuffed desert boots.

'Yes.'

He told how he had fought with Glubb, Wavell, Auchinleck and Montgomery. Most Arab drivers over forty-five purport to have served with such martial luminaries – I even once met one who claimed to have been an intimate of T. E. Lawrence in Riyadh. Zakki was just as unconvincing.

In London, which already seemed very remote as he exuberantly bucketed his Chevvy across the potholes of this brown half-finished town, old Middle East hands had issued blood-curdling warnings about Arab perfidy.

'Treat them with the utmost caution, old boy. When they assure you, hand on heart, that they're telling the truth, forget it. They all lie through the teeth. When they swear lifelong friendship and brotherhood it means they're about to pinch your baggage or your watch. And never pay for anything without haggling.'

My reservations had been made at a place called the Philadelphia, but when I told Zakki this he raised both hands towards Allah in despair (thus, I noticed with alarm, leaving the Chevvy chauffeurless for thirty yards) and said the only place to stay was the new super-hotel, the El Urdan. I was aware of this, and also that a bevy of highly efficient London

secretaries and various local contacts had been trying for some
weeks to find a room, or even an attic, in this superior establishment, all to no avail. Briefly we stopped to have a coffee,
and Zakki produced a ragged infant, one of the six or so small
boys who were to be presented to me as his sons in the next few
days, and sent him off to stand guard on car and baggage.
Gloomily I watched a line of British army half-tracks clank
down the centre of the street, manned by olive-skinned troopers
who might have been British boy soldiers had it not been for
their veiled head-gear. Zakki was engaged in leisurely conversation with the café's proprietor intoning doubtless the Arabic
equivalent of: 'Never give a sucker an even break.'

Why had I not listened to my elders and betters?

An hour later I was getting out of a marble bath in a suite in
the El Urdan normally occupied by King Hussein's Grand
Vizier. Zakki, singlet, second-hand trousers and tennis-shoes to
the fore, had arranged it with the Manager in about twenty
seconds flat, marching to the head of a queue of opulent-look-
ing potential clients, all of whom were being told there was no
accommodation whatsoever, and nor would there be before the
Pope's departure. Getting into the bath was a blonde girl of
eighteen, whom I had talked to on the 'plane and whom Zakki
had added to our entourage when we had passed her forlornly
dragging two bulky cases along the street. By modern standards
she was perhaps a shade over-lush, but she would have driven
Fragonard into a frenzy, and it was amusing to learn her father
was a Major in the Salvation Army.

My researches in Rome, though not naturally providing
the concrete answers my superiors lusted after, had led me
to dispatch a cable suggesting among other things that Paul
VI's unexpected pilgrimage was in the nature of a spiritual
legacy – though by reputation a conservative, so my lofty argument went, the ecumenical and revolutionary fervour of Pope
John had profoundly influenced him, despite the reservations
and in some cases downright hostility of such notable reac-
tionaries as Cardinal Ottaviani.

Through inexperience and haste I had sent some of this article from Rome in cable-ese. A desk-bound ignoramus in London had 'hardened', as the saying goes, 'spiritual legacy', so the story eventually read as if the late Pope had left a will, which included a condition that Paul should set off for Jerusalem posthaste. The newspaper shot off a cable of congratulation to the Philadelphia Hotel, where they believed I was staying. Here Zakki, who was not the man to miss out on things like that, collected it for me.

Under normal circumstances I would have been highly pleased but from the date stamp I calculated this communication had apparently taken twenty-two hours from London to Amman, which meant they might as well have sent it by pigeon.

Zakki and I turned our attention to communications.

Two days before The Arrival it was totally impossible to penetrate the Amman Cable & Wireless Office at all. All day Jordanian loafers, like Bowery Bums miraculously finding themselves presented with complimentary ringside tickets for the Moore-Marciano fight and marvelling at their good fortune, stood in entranced groups watching *Match* photographers attack their rivals from *Stern*, while CBS men grappled with competitors from ABC. Even Zakki's influence was insufficient to get the car within a hundred yards of this crucial building but a confusing trek along refuse-strewn alleys gained us admittance through the back door. In this grimy main room six telex machines, any of which would have commanded a good price as antique examples of Victoriana either in the *Marché aux Puces* or the Portobello Road, were stammering uncertainly into the indifferent air. Two men in white nylon shirts, apparently their operators, were peacefully occupied drinking coffee accompanied by glasses of water, and playing tric-trac. Most of the floor, I noted grimly, was strewn with unsent cables, as if preparations were being made for some marathon paper-chase. From the main counter outside hysterical voices in a dozen languages screamed contrapuntal arias of imprecation, backed up by an orchestrated, generalized growl of frustration and rage – this was the sound, I thought, the mob in Paris must have produced while plucking up their courage preparatory to storming the Bastille.

With an imperious clap of his hands Zakki had the chief clerk summoned: there followed the inevitable kissing, and within twenty minutes I was able to inform London of such arrangements as I had made. They replied at great length, mainly with a series of intelligent and highly relevant questions, the answers to none of which I knew. Cutting the connection I concluded an arrangement with the clerk guaranteeing that all my cables would be sent off ahead of any others that might be waiting (here he glanced deprecatingly at the mounds of cable forms mouldering in various piles) as long as I remembered to write the word 'ZAKKI' in large capitals at the head of each sheet. He suggested we leave as we had come – through the back – as, with a thumb directed towards the front counter whence issued a noise as of lions waiting for raw meat, 'bad men fighting out there'.

'Jerusalem, damn quick?' inquired Zakki hopefully.

On the way we stopped briefly for refreshments at an odd, deserted establishment, half-restaurant, half-night club, constructed in yellow brick and surmounted by an insubstantial-looking cupola perched on the stagnant shores of the Dead Sea. Its air of desolation vividly recalled Cromer or Sheringham, one of those once fashionable English East Coast resorts latterly fallen into desuetude. It was the kind of place that would have appealed to Mr Graham Greene. When, six years later I revisited this eccentric establishment with my colleague Patrick Brogan, we discovered some symmetrical-minded gunner had dropped a mortar shell through the precise centre of that gimcrack dome.

The trouble, I reflected as Zakki screamed joyously in third gear round the City walls, was that the logistics of transmitting the story had entirely taken precedence. In London Cardinal Heenan had generously given me an hour of his time trying to explain the significance of the innumerable religious communities in Jerusalem – there are over two hundred – and had presented me with a totally impenetrable book on schisms. At a press conference given by King Hussein, looking very tiny and very Sandhurst, I had excountered an Archimandrite from the Lebanon who had explained at length in the most execrable

French that the Trinity was in fact a quadrilateral – with himself, as far as I could make out, the Fourth Person. I had studied the *Guide Bleu*, but almost exclusively with an eye to discovering if there were any side roads so Zakki and I could get to Jerusalem before the main cavalcade. And finally I had begun H. V. Morton's *In the Steps of the Master* but gave up hurriedly, suspecting his prose style was as infectious as smallpox, even though it would have been amusing to find out how the news desk at home would have reacted to a message referring, say, to 'the chestnut-locked, gentle-voiced Carpenter y-clept Jesus of Nazareth'.

I told Zakki to take me to the Garden of Gethsemane – no bad place, I thought, for some solitary contemplation. Here I met a tanned, quizzical man wearing a dashing fur hat recently acquired in Tashkent. He was the artist, Feliks Topolski, and his attractive combination of Pan-like sprightliness and obvious good sense moved me to confide my problems. There would be, I explained, at most four hours, and probably less, to describe the Pope's arrival and get the story to London. Some of my competitors, I suspected, would craftily send their own graphic accounts hours ahead – indeed some might well have completed and despatched their versions before the Holy Father had as much as put a foot outside Bernini's Vatican City colonnades. Should I, for insurance, also send a holding story ahead of time?

Topolski, who evidently disliked seeing young men acquiring premature vices, vetoed the idea. 'Empty your mind now,' he lectured in a finely wrought metaphor, 'so your eyes will be clear to write exactly what you see without prejudice.' This honourable statement impressed me so much that I noted it down. We then paid a rapid visit to the depressing Church of the Nativity in Bethlehem (which a few years later I saw in even more depressing conditions framed by a troop of Israeli tanks, their crews sitting on their gun-barrels, posing for snapshots) where we met a furtive photographer from, inevitably, *Paris-Match*. He had been conscientiously engaged in 'bugging' the Holy Crib with a camera that could be operated from a distance of fifty feet electronically. When the time came the Italian cameramen employed more direct tactics, simply sinking to their knees before the Pope to implore a blessing, and pressing the button as he raised a hand in benediction. All in all it seemed a good night to get very drunk which we did in a small restaurant not far from Zakki's house close to the Wailing Wall. Despite repeated attempts since 1967, I have never succeeded in finding it again, and presume the Israelis have demolished it in the course of their master plan to transform the most beautiful city in the world into a reasonable simulacrum of a Chicago suburb with some quaint old ruins stuck in the middle.

Zakki drank rarely and the combination of arak, and whisky, and more arak led to an alarming personality change. A new, highly militaristic Zakki emerged, who after re-fighting the North African campaign from Tobruk to Algiers, confided his plan for unifying the City. The Mändelbaum Gate, he reckoned, was highly vulnerable. 'One company of Arab Legion – attack before dawn – fan out and bring up the tanks . . .' He drew diagrams on pieces of paper, and ordered another bottle, spitting on the ground, which in this restaurant was not regarded as a solecism. There was nothing much wrong with Zakki's basic tactics, though it occurred to neither of us that a man with a black eye-patch on the other side of the City walls might have already worked them out for himself. One of those classic prophetic ironies the Greek dramatists were always hammering away at so mercilessly.

By the end of dinner Zakki had decided Arab Legion reinforcements were an unnecessary luxury – he, Topolski and myself would form our own commando using the private arsenal in Zakki's home – 'I got one Lee-Enfield .303, two Stens, and a German Schmeisser machine pistol from El Alamein,' he boasted.

'Those damn Jew sentries are all asleep. We go through and rape ten, twenty of those dirty Jew women. Come we go now.'

After some persuasion we settled for a valedictory coffee. Because I was cold, he knocked up a local shopkeeper and for one pound bought me an ankle-length Bedouin coat of white sheepskin, which some years later enabled my wife to be a trendsetter on the Boulevard St Germain.

Zakki drove much the same, drunk or sober – his motto was *In 'sh' Allah*, basically an expression of fatalism, though it also contains a strong suggestion of nudging Allah in the ribs to ensure he is keeping his eyes open. Whether Zakki or Allah was chauffeuring it was all the same to me; I stretched out in the back and slept.

I awoke on the floor of the Chevvy, which was still skidding. It stopped finally with a comparatively minor impact that did no more than shatter the glass on our near-side headlight. Zakki got out cursing, and I saw we had bumped into the back of yet another of those cheap American cars of the fifties so beloved of Jordanians. It in turn had crashed into a lorry which had been deserted, presumably after a break-down, and left parked in such a way that it occupied about two-thirds of the road. The car ahead of ours, which seemed to have lost almost its entire bonnet, had not been lucky, but its driver had. The offside door was open, and having either been thrown out or crawled, he was sitting with his legs stuck out in front of him, his back braced against the bodywork. It was not a prudent position to adopt, and had Zakki swerved he would probably have killed him. As it was his regular moans sounded like those of a terminal case, and when I shone a torch on him and saw the colour of what had originally been a white shirt I wondered for a second whether someone had let him have it in the chest with a shot-gun.

When we started to clean him up a bit, however, it was clear the blood had come from multiple facial cuts caused by the shattered windscreen, and his nose which was probably broken. I dabbed gingerly at a cut above his eye and he began to speak very blurred and deliberately, as if drunk. Then I got a whiff of his breath and though my own olfactory sensations had been considerably deadened by about three-quarters of a bottle of Vat 69 it made even me reel. Zakki too got the same message simultaneously; we exchanged awed glances. This man was not simply tipsy or moderately inebriated, he was royally, paralytically, sodden drunk; probably the consequent absence of all tension or reflex had saved his life. After the crash he must have bounced, inert as a barrel of lard. Zakki whistled admiringly through his teeth. A Frenchman would have said reverently: '*Chapeau.*'

We dragged him into the back seat of Zakki's vehicle and retrieved his possessions, which consisted of an old briefcase, two empty whisky bottles and an almost full one (he was evidently a Johnny Walker fan) I wondered before Zakki backed up whether we should make some effort to get the wrecked car off the road. Our passenger stirred briefly and produced a voluble flow of Arabic before reverting to total unconsciousness, which lasted all the way to the hotel.

'What did the man say?' I enquired of Zakki, as he wrenched his Chevvy into first gear.

'He say "fuck the car. Time will pay." '

'What does he mean "Time"?'

'Dunno,' said Zakki, 'he crazy, drunk fellow, Mr Dave.'

When we supported him, swaying erratically, into the lobby of Amman's showpiece hotel – happily fairly empty at that advanced hour – our passenger created a minor sensation, particularly among the servants, many of whom assumed he had been shot. Perhaps this was the first casualty in the long anticipated war against Israel, they whispered together. There seemed no chance of raising a doctor, and we got him up to my room in the lift.

After a spell under the shower and the application of several strips of sticking plaster he stopped moaning. I produced a spare shirt – his was evidently irreparable – and leaving Zakki to complete the salvage work took my typewriter down to the bar, which to my fury had closed. When they eventually joined me our passenger, though scarcely the image of a debonair man-about-Amman, at least looked no worse than a fighter who had recently been badly outclassed over fifteen rounds. He carried his precious whisky and briefcase, and I decided his bulbous nose was at the worst badly bruised, and not broken. It had the look of a nose that had been bulbous, through natural causes, for some considerable time. Zakki who had wasted no time breaking into the bar appeared with ice, glasses and soda-siphon. I said I had no more than five minutes. They exchanged some sentences in Arabic, and the battered stranger raised his glass in a toast (the soda-water, I noticed, he had testily declined).

'He says you saved his life,' said Zakki.

'Tell him any time.'

'He say he bring your shirt here tomorrow.'

'Tell him forget it.'

It was now ten minutes before three in the morning, no time for a prolonged exchange of Arab courtesies, much as I normally enjoyed them. Our friend, however, topped up the glasses from his trusty bottle, and taking from his briefcase two identical wedges of stapled cable forms each at least six inches thick deposited one on the table before me with the air of a conjuror who had just pulled off an impossible trick.

'He says it's a present for you,' Zakki contributed. Immediately it became clear what that opaque remark about 'Time' paying had signified – our alcoholic friend was the *Time* magazine Zakki, or one of them. They had sent him to file from Amman with two sets of what was evidently their complete background file on the visit, and they had done a spectacular job. A dozen or so professionals with local expertise, excellent contacts, and probably some research assistants had been hard at it for at least a week. They had interviewed every religious leader of note in Jerusalem; half the Jordanian cabinet and general staff; and also King Hussein himself. They had the names, ages and potted biographies not only of everyone in the Pope's entourage, but of everyone His Holiness was going to meet. Apart from historical and sometimes archaeological background on every stopping place on the tour, they had quoted in full all biblical references to them, plus precise citations (Matthew, XI, 2/5, and so forth). There was an interesting statistical essay comparing the increase in prices of everything from hotel rooms to fragments of the True Cross. Some poor bastard had even drawn the job of counting the exact number of steps the Pope would have to mount on his journey up the Via Dolorosa to the Holy Sepulchre mass.

'Is good?' Zakki enquired.

'Is manna from heaven,' I said.

After all we could scarcely be said to be *competing* with *Time*.

At literally the eleventh hour the Pope was almost diverted to Beirut: bad weather conditions, and I thanked God and Topolski that I had taken his advice about not describing anything before actually seeing it. Forty edgy minutes late the Papal Caravelle finally broke through the sullen cumulus. At the top of the gangway His Holiness hesitated as if disorientated – clad entirely in white the Pope looked cloud-like himself, a wisp of cirrus in a mackerel sky, so insubstantial the biting east wind could easily sweep him away. He was so fragile, skeletal almost, so unprotected. One wondered how he would cope with the circus awaiting him.

It was a highly charged moment, even for one whose religious attitudes existed in a hinterland somewhere between indifference and sporadic curiosity. It was also – and one saw this at once – genuinely 'historic'. Unhappily as soon as one tried to express this in a newspaper the emotional depth would be dissipated, and not entirely through one's own lack of skill. The medium itself would turn it all into just another story, a big one admittedly like a war or a volcanic eruption, but still nothing more than a freak, momentary whirlpool in the ineluctable flood of events. My role was no more than neutral observer and paid technician yet, surprisingly, as one watched the frail figure – now apparently blessing the tarmac – suddenly there was a sense of shock, that spine-tingle of excitement and awe that an authentic participant like St John Stevas must be experiencing.

But it was a brief luxury. The eldest of all the sons – 'In three years he join Arab Legion, and kill dirty Jews,' Zakki said proudly, was waiting with a Lambretta motor scooter I had hired for him, and which he had polished till it shone like a diamond. I drove, having no death wish, and he rode pillion carrying the typewriter. The nearest parking lot, where Zakki and the Chevvy were waiting, was nearly a mile away. He drove straight to the cable office; I typed in the back. On the top of each sheet I remembered to print 'ZAKKI' in capitals, even before the key words Press Urgent. After an exchange of kisses with the head man (I never discovered their precise relationship), we were let through the counter.

Then another case of 'Jerusalem, damn quick'. This meant sacrificing the Pope's first stop, which was scheduled to be on the bank of the Jordan (and very nearly turned out to be actually *in* the river, because of the cursing photographers trying to get close-ups). We arrived very early, the Lambretta bouncing insecurely on the roof. Abbas, the eldest son, was wearing a tweedy jacket of black and white *Prince de Galles*, first cousin to a chequer board and highly conspicuous. It stretched beneath his knees and came inevitably out of the same wardrobe as his father's pin-stripes. A lot of police in British style navy blue were checking credentials on the Lion Gate entrance, and seemed on the verge of sealing the City completely. But they were no match for Abbas. He swayed, feinting leftwards, changed pace, side-stepped right, and was a black and white flash in the crowd. Any football coach would have signed him on the spot.

The best vantage point was a café where the via Dolorosa turns sharp right and climbs in steep steps to the Holy Sepulchre. I set up my typewriter, declined a hookah, and stepped into the tiny shop opposite which had an eye-catching display of Vat 69. I had already handed over two Jordanian pounds when a rising shriek of Arabic made me jump. The shopkeeper jumped too, and sheepishly handed one pound back.

Abbas, my typewriter tucked under his thin arm for safety, was also guarding my interests. Abbas made the Arab motion of spitting. No doubt whose son *he* was. For the next three hours I sat typing and still have the notes; His Holiness was *late*.

Old Jerusalem is a wine-press fermenting with concentrated religion. Every third passerby wore the uniform of a Holy Man of some persuasion or another. The City absorbed them all effortlessly. Although the religions and sects all carried their own differing prohibitions one felt then (but no longer) a sense of total liberation. It was only possible to guess at the hot eroticism simmering beneath those black veils. This was a city of sudden shocks, and biting smells. The streets were a maze of vaulted corridors, the little houses and shop fronts breathing spicy and sometimes fetid odours into each other mouths.

When was *He* coming?

As the afternoon wore on the crowds did not grow appreci-
ably, though the excitement did. It came close to mass hysteria
but unlike its equivalent at a football match or political rally,
there was no hint of latent danger. Those waiting for the Pope
were like good-natured children enjoying a party in too con-
fined a space. Above them (unlit) Japanese lanterns swayed as
if improvised by some earnest Spock-reading mother. Opposite
was a monastery which became, a few years later, an improvised hospital for civilians wounded in the battle of Jerusalem.
But all that misery was ahead: on the Day of the Pope we still
lived in an age of innocence.

When *was* He coming?

I listed the Pope's titles – he had enough to choose from:
Vicar of Christ; Supreme Pontiff; Patriarch of the West (soon
to greet his coeval of the East with the famous ecumenical kiss
of peace); Bishop of the Eternal City – though the Vatican
City, unlike the one we were in, had never given me the slightest
impression of being even cosmopolitan, let alone eternal. It was
plain Roman, and despite Bernini and Michelangelo distinctly
American Express/Cook's Tour Roman at that. The *muezzin*
walked past, looking selfconsciously Holy, though redundant
having already delivered his dawn invocation to God. I had
acquired a translation of that dissonant wail (invariably tape-
recorded nowadays) and Allah's titles were well up in the papal
league. He was God the Eternal; the Perfect; the Supreme;
the Unique; the Alone; and, unlike his Christian counterpart,
the One without a Son.

He *was* coming. At last.

The anticipatory murmuring from the Damascus Gate was
now like distant surf, the sound of giant rollers breaking on
Bondi Beach as if they've come from San Francisco without
stopping. Momentarily the café gamblers stopped the con-
vulsive jabs of tric-trac. The itinerant coffee seller syncopated
the rhythm of his clashing brass cups, not for advertisement
now, but out of sheer excitement.

For a while the afternoon had been dying fast and flash! –
suddenly all the lanterns shone in red, gold and blue. 'Aaah,'
said the tric-trac men in wonder. It looked like a masterpiece

of stage management but knowing Jordanian technicians it was certainly just an error. They had probably come on spontaneously after someone had spent hours fruitlessly fiddling with incomprehensible wires.

God had sent us a miracle.

Despite the crowds His Holiness, still all in white, stood out. In a forgivably purple vein a colleague described him 'riding in triumph into the Holy City'. He was riding all right but the New Testament associations of the image were misleading. He was being propelled by the crowd so that his feet, which could not be seen, probably only made contact with the ground every few yards. Again one thought of him in terms of lightness – what slender shoulders to bear such a heavyweight myth. When he reached the café and the ninety degree turn, he stopped floating abruptly, bogged down in a human traffic jam.

Ahead and above the central group I found myself face to face with him. The Holy Father was shoved forwards and in turn I retreated, making space backwards up the hill, not unlike the female partner in a fox-trot, a very awkward one. We staggered thirty yards like this, infinitely slowly, but it could not go on – the Holy Sepulchre was still half a mile away and the Pope looked ready to expire. A gold-hatted policeman started yelling orders.

We wheeled into a vast room (the entrance hall of a convent, it emerged). The nuns, totally unprepared, suffered a kind of collective seizure and sank to their knees. The Pope fell into a wormy, oak chair. Beside him was a Cardinal, whom I mistook for Tisserant, and addressed in French, calling him '*Excellence*' instead of '*Eminence*' in my excitement. He looked blank. I tried in Italian and his face lit up like a lantern. Obviously not Tisserant. Was the Holy Father ill, I enquired. Could he make it up the steps?

His Eminence said the unaccustomed flight had tired him, and would I tell the policeman to clear the crowds. The cop answered 'Yes, sir', saluted, and rushed off. A second earlier he would have thrown me out. Now he thought I was official.

The Cardinal said that His Holiness would not be able to

continue unless the crowds were controlled. '*Sono pazzi*,' he said, the huge ring shimmering as he gesticulated '*Tutti pazzi*.'

'*E molto difficile*,' I replied weakly, as the gold-hatted policeman returned. Behind him he locked the big door with a museum-piece key. Among the kneeling nuns I saw a familiar, reverend figure – the man from *Match* who had bugged the Bethlehem crib. The Pope's official photographer, who in the best Vatican tradition had succeeded his father in the job, was missing.

I looked nervously at the Pope, sunk in his chair, and though apparently he had not noticed his thin hand rose in reflexive benediction, swift as a pro blackjack dealer flipping one off the top.

Before the Mother Superior finally gathered her wits and led him to another room to rest I had ample time to study his face. It was a look I later recognized on the faces of acid trippers: absent but happy and absorbed. His deep-set eyes were strained as if he were accustomed to wearing little, granny glasses. It was chilly by now but there was sweat where his domed forehead met the little skull-cap. His nose was acquiline, ugly and somehow tough; it conveyed a distinct impression of sensuality, as did the heavy lower lip. Pope John XXIII had nick-named him 'Hamlet', because of his notorious capacity for indecision. Yet he looked a man of certainties – again I was reminded of a professional gambler. A man to watch, had I met him elsewhere clad in a black suit.

The nuns shuffled out on their knees backwards, and I followed. There was no point in seeking an audience; His Holiness was mentally somewhere else, and I needed a telephone. The crowd had thinned and I realized why. All the gates had been sealed two hours earlier: the Old City had become an island, thousands of journalists outside could not get in to see what was happening – those few inside could not get out to say.

Outside the Damascus Gate I spotted Abbas, prominent in his black and white checks. My plan had been to head directly for the St George Hotel where a series of calls had been booked. Abbas handed me a piece of the Hotel paper with 'St George KAPUT' on it, and we rode off God knows where. It turned out to be the Mändelbaum Gate, and outside was the old Chevvy and Zakki, without his family for once. They were all out scouting for me, he explained. The St George was indeed 'kaput' – their switchboard had jammed altogether under the unaccustomed pressure; the Post Office was just as bad.

Out of the corner of my eye I had seen a cavalcade of estate wagons piled high with film equipment standing in a queue before the border post. They were plastered with notices saying PRESS and BBC. Under the lights stood one of the best known figures in England at that time, Richard Dimbleby, television commentator supreme, without whose presence no Royal funeral, coronation, or Summit Meeting was complete. But this Dimbleby, yelling at a group of slovenly Jordanian soldiers and officials, was very different from the Dimbleby whose pleasant face was known to millions. He was evidently suffering from the same kind of problems as me, only multi-plied because of TV crews and air-freight schedules. He was making little progress.

'You go, use Jew telephone, bloody damn quick,' Zakki said. He had worked it out already.

'They'll probably shoot me.'

Zakki laughed. 'I talk to them,' he said. It wasn't clear whether he meant the captain of the guard was his first cousin, or whether he would simply distract their attention while I slipped through on the blind side of the television vans. Several cameramen had now joined Dimbleby and it seemed there might be violence.

'OK, Zakki. There's nothing to lose.'

'Go quick . . .'

Zakki had done the equivalent of about six days work, had bought me presents, had insisted on paying for meals because I would be cheated – I reckoned I owed him at least thirty pounds, perhaps fifty. All I had on me were three five pound notes – the rest was in travellers' cheques. I handed it over, but Zakki waved it aside, urgently. I shoved it in Abbas's hand.

'Quick *now*.'

I sneaked across No Man's Land expecting a bullet in the back at any second. The last voices I heard from Jordan were

Dimbleby's saying 'This is quite outrageous' and Zakki, whose sentiments were different. 'Fuck those Jew girls,' he called.

The next day I realized I had been very lucky. There were happy telegrams from London – the congratulations should have been addressed to Zakki. One woman reporter's story had disappeared altogether somewhere between Jerusalem and New York.

'Still, darling,' she remarked brightly, 'it was a ball on the Via Dolorosa. Four hands up my skirt at the same time, and all belonging to different guys.'

When the Pope visited the Dormition on the Israeli side I met Naomi Shepherd of *The New Statesman*, and she hospitably took me home for supper with Yehuda, her husband. A neighbour who was at the university dropped in, and we spent the next eighteen months almost getting married. When I looked at Ruth's beautiful face, I sometimes recalled Zakki's views on 'Jew women'. It was easy to see why Englishmen like St John Philby, and Lawrence, and Glubb had proved vulnerable to the fidelity and almost canine devotion of some Arabs. But there was that 'dirty Jew' aspect, as well.

* * * *

The first El Al flight out of London after Nasser precipately closed the Straights of Tiran was carrying just eleven passengers; among them were seven familiar faces, which I acknowledged, and an eighth which interested me – so much so that it nearly stopped me dead in my tracks. Contrary to popular belief air hostesses are often physically rather prosaic. This one was a beauty, black hair and remarkable olive green eyes which met mine unwaveringly with no discernible trace of interest.

Among my colleagues I was distressed to see Don Wise stretching his long elegant legs across two empty seats. I have nothing against the man who has often entertained me with his wit – notably his celebrated remark that the Vietnamese language sounds like ducks fucking, a masterpiece of graphic precision. What concerned me was that pretty women, I had observed, found him even more entertaining than I did myself. Accordingly I stationed myself in a position which I calculated was likely to be the girl's first stop when she came round with the pre-take-off chewing gum. In such company one had to move like lightning.

When she arrived I exchanged her gum for a visiting card bearing an invitation to dinner at a Tel Aviv restaurant called *Le Bateau*, a masterpiece of bad taste in blue velvet with seats the shape of boats. Israeli girls, particularly those who have spent their formative years in Wild West hick towns like Beersheba or Hadera, often have a weakness for vulgar luxury. She examined the card gravely in a slim, olive hand, gave me the same unwavering stare, and passed on. Oh well, I thought, she's probably got Moshe Dayan and Topol fighting over her already – you can't win them all.

We were over Mont Blanc, half way to the Rome transit stop, when she reappeared carrying – superfluously it seemed – the gum tray. She offered it to me gravely and I gingerly picked up my card which now sat in the exact centre of the confectionery. If this was a brush-off it was a pretty laconic one. But on the back she had written: 'Why Not?'

Hadassah, as I discovered, was a girl who liked to ponder her decisions and did not go back on them. Her father's family had come to Palestine from Bombay in the 1920s when the immigration rate was so pitiably low that the idea of a State of Israel, Balfour Declaration or not, seemed entirely chimerical. (The numbers soared after 1933; Hitler was the best recruiting officer the Zionists ever had.) Hadassah *père* had eccentrically married a Hungarian Jewess, and the racial melting pot had produced something that made one gasp each time one looked at her face, or indeed at any part of her.

I gasped, and for the first time she smiled. Perhaps this war was not going to be too bad.

Hubris. By the second night we were a long way past the *Le Bateau* stage and were contentedly finishing dinner under a vine trellis in a restaurant in Jaffa, which is marginally less inhuman than Tel Aviv proper. After coffee we were going back again to her apartment which was conveniently near to the Hilton where I had checked in as a formality so there would be someone to take messages. I was holding her long hand and looking at an eccentric ring she wore made from an irregular chunk of malachite. She was smiling, she had been smiling all day; I think we both realized that the situation was evolving, without strain.

'So already you think my face is funny?' Hadassah said. I was going to explain, thus adding to our already considerable knowledge of each other's biographies, when the antique wireless broke into a flood of guttural Hebrew. There was something about the tone that stopped me short and made me listen though I could not understand a word. Hadassah stopped smiling and made a sighing noise, almost a moan. She stood up.

It was incomprehensible, heartbreaking but one day and one night had convinced me that she did not say things without ample reason. It did not enter my mind to argue.

'Shall I get them to call a cab?'

It was unnecessary. All over the room people were getting to their feet, a dozen intimacies were being shattered simultaneously. A man I took for a pro fighter came over and without ceremony began talking to Hadassah in urgent, guttural Hebrew. He looked at me enquiringly.

'He can come,' she said.

The brutal face dissolved into a sweet smile, and in a parody of the Chicago Capone voice he said: 'We're gonna take you for a ride, baby.'

The pug turned out to be a cab-driver by profession but I noticed he did not bother to start his meter. Instead he drove very fast and expertly through the back streets of Tel Aviv following a clip-board list of addresses. At each house a man or woman was waiting. By the time they dropped me outside the Hilton there were ten passengers in the car. The pug laughed, that rare laugh of a man who is genuinely looking forward to a fight.

'She'll soon be back,' he said, winking. 'You can go out on the town – in Cairo or Damascus.'

I thought it was war; instead all I had was the story of the general mobilization, and how the Israelis had collected all their reservists in the course of one night. Hadassah, as I learnt later from 'somewhere in Israel', was an Air Force lieutenant when not dispensing chewing-gum. Losses of this kind were then a kind of occupational hazard but never had one hurt so much or the sense of dispossession been so insistent.

War, of course, had been inevitable from the moment that U Thant had inexplicably fallen into the schoolboy trap of believing that Nasser meant what he said, and pulled out the UN troops. Nasser's political genius had been exciting my deep admiration for a decade but immediately it looked as if the old fox had been caught in a trap too, a rhetorical one he had made himself. The Israelis, from the cab-driver upwards, wanted nothing better than a cast-iron excuse to arrest the evolution of the UAR military build-up. Their only concern, and mine, was the frightening vulnerability of the Tel Aviv population to air attack.

So it was war, but when? A pretty Hilton receptionist, who was later fired for being found in a cameraman's bedroom, 'phoned me the next morning very early. My suite was near the top of the skyscraper.

'We want you to move right down,' she said. 'Air-raid precautions. I know you won't want to but it's much more convenient for sneaking girls up from the lobby.'

'The only girl I want to do any sneaking with is in your bloody army,' I said. 'You really think they'll bomb us?'

'You're crazy,' she said. 'But you know the Egyptian pilots – they might fly into us by mistake.'

Blitz humour, a blitz atmosphere – schoolkids filled sandbags, old men dug shelters. It was also a period of frenzied frivolity. Mandy Rice-Davies, now married and more Zionist than Golda Meir, ran a nightclub. I had first met her during the memorable Profumo summer under cross-examination from Griffiths-Jones – a kind of spiritual ancestor of Argyll of *Oz*, and the one who had asked the *Lady Chatterley* jury whether they would like their maidservants to read such a book. The QC had demanded why she had included the name of a Hollywood film star in her truly formidable list of satisfied clients, trying, in his elephantine way, to imply that her motives were malicious.

'I put 'im down because I never liked 'im,' Mandy had replied without hesitation. It was probably the only entirely unhypocritical statement in the course of the whole squalid process. I had loved her ever since.

So there was gossip at her club, and more gossip at the rather grander one run by a delightful pair called Dov and Henrietta, who also possessed a chalet conveniently placed next to the British Ambassador's beside the Hilton pool. It was possible – and even logical – to go straight from the club to breakfast by the pool, a background briefing and table tennis with Michael Parkinson. No one ever seemed to sleep; no one knew what was happening.

A military attaché trying to find out about troop movements took his family for a picnic near Lake Tiberius. His trained eye saw nothing of interest and they lunched in a wood. Afterwards his teenage daughter retired behind the adjacent bushes, and returned much embarrassed. 'Gosh, mummy,' she said, 'I've just been peeing on a tank.' They had spent an hour in the middle of a camouflaged tank squadron and seen nothing. All troops travelled by night.

I devoted my spare time to teaming up with a French photographer called Jean-Paul, whose simple ambition it was to seduce an Israeli policewoman, and gradually, in the face of all reason, one began to feel it might not happen, an impression foxily boosted by Moshe Dayan at his famous press conference when he said it was too late for war, though too soon for diplomacy. As he spoke the Israeli Air Force pilots were receiving their final briefings. London, like Nasser and a few million others, were deceived; the Israelis had started partial demobilization, rather ostentatiously. My colleague in Cairo, Phillip Knightley, and myself were both instructed to pull out. He left on the Sunday; I reserved a place on the 8.50 Rome flight on Monday June 5, a date of some historic significance.

I arranged to travel with James Cameron, who was representing *The Evening Standard*, but there was no sign of him. Perhaps he had sniffed something; I simply concluded he had overslept and boarded the flight which was unusually punctual in the company of a distinguished American woman writer, and

the President of the Bank of Israel. Just ten minutes after we
took off the captain announced the war had started.

We pleaded with the captain to return to Lod; a reserve pilot
himself he was on the verge of tears, but would not risk his passengers in air space thick with Mirages and Migs. We drove
from Fiumicino to the Israel Embassy, where the Ambassador
was happily a close friend of the American writer. He could do
no more than guarantee the three of us places on the first flight
carrying supplies back to Lod. I had left all my bags at the airport and was too depressed even to go to the *Albergo Nazionale*,
my usual Rome haven. Instead I got into a poker game that
started in the *Stampe Estera* and ended thirty hours later in the
pent-house of a broke Roman aristocrat.

The bets were so large that he insisted we say 'Up five lire'
when we meant to raise fifty thousand, frightened his beautiful
wife might overhear. We stopped only when the Israeli Embassy
called to say there was a flight.

The war dissolved into a series of images. The Mitlah Pass
at midnight, where the Israelis had taken out a mile-long
Egyptian armoured column by the simple expedient of 'brewing
up' the first and last vehicle, and then leisurely destroying the
traffic jam in between – the tarmac on the road was still the
consistency of putty from napalm, and around us gutted tanks
stank of destruction in shimmering moonlight. There was the
mad white horse on the last day of the war, the property of a
Syrian officer who had prudently fled on foot. It was careering
panic-stricken along the rim of the Golan Heights among the
Israeli tanks plunging on towards Damascus (some time after,
it should be said, the UN ceasefire). The nightmare drive in a
Ford with a broken silencer against the mainstream of Israeli
tanks and infantry in buses pouring against us to reinforce the
breakthrough, Guderian style. The photographer Steve Brodie,
a handy man in a crisis, and perfectly prepared to pit our Ford
against a Centurion travelling at thirty mph for the right of
way, drove like a maniac, brushed aside tough MPs who wanted
us off the road altogether. Despite Brodie's heroic driving
we both missed our editions: the suicidal chagrin of the following Sunday when we found out. Alan Williams, the writer so

magnetically drawn to wars and volcanic eruptions, working off his frustrations on a group of Orthodox Jews parading round the Wailing Wall, already rechristened the Western Wall, as if it were a delicatessen in which they had just acquired a controlling interest. 'You remind me,' he remarked to a spotty, lard-faced youth wearing the black uniform of the Warsaw Ghetto two centuries ago, 'of an over-masturbated pig. And you wouldn't even fight.'

As usual with Williams' insults it was the accuracy that hurt. I had missed the attack on the Old City in which Don McCullin used up another of his lives by going through the Mändelbaum Gate with the first combat wave. He was probably ahead of them. By the time I got there bulldozers were demolishing the little houses around the wall, in one of which I had drunk coffee and arak so long before, and played with Zakki's sons. One of the most disgusting images of any battle is a house which has lost a wall, so you cannot avoid having other people's fractured intimacies thrust on you – their unmade beds, a vase of flowers, lives laid bare to strangers. An Israeli lieutenant, who had never previously visited the Old City, announced that the destruction was to 'create an access road'. I was too sickened to challenge the lie; he may even have believed it.

I decided to walk back on my own and cross via the Mändelbaum Gate, though nowadays there are a dozen exits available. On the way I met Jean-Paul's partner on the *Life* team. He looked very ill.

'Will you come to the funeral?'

'*Funeral?*'

Jean-Paul had been killed by a booby-trap in Sinai, trying to get to the action by a side road. They had only succeeded in identifying him by his jungle boots, and Saigon ID bracelet. I went on in despair hoping at least he had finally succeeded with one of those policewomen. By the Gate a company of Arab Legion soldiers – the Legion who had fought so tenaciously, were squatting under the ferocious guard of a Druze platoon. Among them, surely it must be Zakki, older, tubbier, and infinitely sadder behind a now grey moustache. He was staring blankly ahead, thinking of what – his destroyed house? Abbas?

His old plan for the Mändelbaum Gate, now thronged by the ostentatiously Orthodox. Perhaps he was reflecting what he and his Legion comrades would have done to them and their 'Jew women' had the battle gone the other way. It did not bear thinking about.

My impulse was to go and chat, to give him his thirty quid. But those Druze guards in their green berets hated the Arabs infinitely more than the Jews did, and they were palpably itching for brutality, for any excuse to pay off old scores.

This was not a time to draw attention to Zakki – he should be left with his thoughts. For both of us the war was over. Santayana's epigram about those who forget history being condemned to relive it, is neat but wrong. One relives it all right, without choice, even if one's memory is bound to the past with links of iron.

CHAPTER 7

Chairman Khruschev

♣

THE background briefing for what I came to think of as the Mad Moscow Trip was mercifully terse.

'Watch your vodka intake. Keep your paws off the Russian girls or we'll leave you to rot in Siberia. Get lots of pictures of The Chairman – he prefers them in colour. Now, any questions?'

'What's the story?'

'Well, there's bound to be lots of stuff, cossacks and tractors and so on. Just file when you can. The Chairman's been very close about his plans. We don't quite know what he has in mind, actually.'

'When are we leaving?'

'VIP Lounge, London Airport, Oh Eight Hundred tomorrow. Don't keep him waiting.'

So there was only time to buy a fur hat on expenses, invite some friends for last minute drinks, and then Estonia, or possibly Lithuania, was thirty-two thousand feet below, somewhere through the cumulus.

The Chairman was in the next seat. This financial emperor of world journalism, recently ennobled with a Macmillan peerage which envious rivals (themselves still mere commoners) liked to claim had cost more over the counter than any other since the days of Lloyd George, was sunk in an attitude of ferocious concentration recalling Rodin's Thinker. His lips moved deliberately as he read. The gigantic lenses of his horn-rims hovered perhaps six inches from the page, giving the impression that he might well devour the book at any moment.

He had bought it – with my money – at the airport. It was

called *Dames Are Deadly!*, and the dame on the cover had a stiletto buried to the hilt in her pantie-girdle.

Our stewardess was impressed by his celebrity.

'Will the Lord be taking champagne?' she whispered.

The Lord, as henceforth he became in my mind, came suddenly to life, as if she had proferred a stock market tip.

'Dave and I never touch alcohol this early,' he said. 'Is this aircraft equipped with apple-juice, honey?'

He gave me a nasty sideways look as though my hangover was showing like a woman's petticoat.

'I've known many men ruined by the Demon Drink, son. Especially journalists. Beware the Demon.'

While we drank tinned pineapple juice he delivered a brief homily on the subject, inspired it seemed by folk memories of revivalist meetings in the days when he had – unsuccessfully – tried to make his fortune growing wheat in his native Canada. His not unpleasant, gravelly voice still had an echo of the spaces of Saskatchewan in it. His harsh look recalled the ascetic who had toiled eighteen hours a day acquiring his millions.

'This is gonna be a tough trip, son. We gotta get in training. We're gonna do something really memorable.'

It would have been nice to know what precisely, but he had already returned to *Dames*. Whatever our mission it was evidently too confidential for me to be entrusted with details, even though I was temporarily well regarded in the Lord's copper-tinted monstrosity of a headquarters. For this unusual situation I had to thank the Pope, and perhaps even more, Zakki.

Several nauseous pints of pineapple juice later I found myself following my proprietor out of the plane into the thin, already autumnal Moscow light. He blinked and fumbled like a subterraenean animal forcibly dragged above ground and waved vaguely at a reception committee drawn up in a broken square. They remained impassive, as if constructed of *papier mâché*. It was my introduction to the Soviet bureaucratic physiognomy. A set of beefy not unhandsome faces, all chin and cheekbone, which looked as if they had been slapped together by a sculptor who had quit before adding the final touches. The prefabricated airport buildings looked similarly provisional.

None of the men moved, but a dumpy woman dressed in violent green shoved her way forward.

'Welcome to Moscow. I am Vera, your Intourist interpreter.'

'Hi there, Vera,' said the great press lord, 'Just call me Roy.'

She never did, nor did any other Russian. His transatlantic preference for informality filled them with suspicion, sometimes even with fear. The Lord was some kind of a boss, that much they could see. And to their hierarchic minds it was an axiom that bosses, whether of socialist or capitalist origins, only squeeze your shoulder fondly and enquire after your children's health when they have something nasty in mind. Marching orders for Siberia perhaps, or in the Lord's case the offer of a post as editor of the *Great Neck Globe and Weekly Courier*, probably the least prestigious of the 204 newspapers he owned in those days.

Accordingly, no smile flitted across Vera's serious face. 'Come,' she said ominously, in her accentless, robot English. 'A reception waits.'

It was in a long beige room which though apparently perfectly clean conveyed an overpowering impression of dustiness. There was a table decorated with wax-textured white gladioli which looked as if they were normally kept under deep-freeze in a mortuary; a dozen imitation cut-glass carafes of what I took to be water; and a large number of banners bearing messages I could not read, and pictures of soldiers holding machine guns, farmers driving tractors, and smelters smelting. A few years later they enjoyed a brief camp vogue and postcards reproducing the style could be purchased at progressive bookshops anywhere between Greenwich Village and the Via del Babuino. There were also small bowls of sweets and chewing-gum tasting of candlewax dusted with licorice. The twelve square men formed a line along one side of the table with the anxious clumsiness of a platoon of recruits falling in. Four waiters filled glasses, very slowly: I smiled tentatively at one, and he met my gaze unflickeringly and expressionless, exuding all the human warmth of a hippo. Vera led the Lord along the line of square men performing introductions and I nervously gulped at my water tumbler. Immediately I experienced a burning at the base of the throat rapidly followed by a gratifying, expanding release of tension in the pit of the stomach. I gulped down the rest of the tumbler's contents, jabbed hippo in the ribs, handed him the empty glass, and said imperiously: 'Seconds.' His manner became, I noticed, at once more alert and respectful, like any common or garden capitalist waiter in the Savoy Grill in the process of being disabused of the illusion that one was an easy mark. Backs in socialist societies, I deduced ached for the lash as much as in others. For the next sixty minutes there were speeches about international solidarity, old alliances and the perfidy of the West Germans. I had violated one of my three directives within five minutes of putting my feet on the soil of Mother Russia, but for the first time it was possible to entertain the idea that the trip might be enjoyable. The proprietor, despite his sermon was also palpably more relaxed. He had said something about Coca-Cola to Vera after choking on his first glass but had been either misunderstood or ignored.

By the standards we were later to accept this was a perfunctory party and within ninety minutes we were in Zim limousines heading through the barren countryside towards the capital. Just before our departure a strikingly handsome and notably unshaved man of about thirty-five had joined the party, downed several tumblers in alarmingly short order, issued an echoing rebuke to one of the waiters who accepted it cravenly, and when the party broke up appeared carrying what was unmistakably a bottle, wrapped in brown paper.

I watched him with interest and doubt. He might have been a dissolute second secretary at our Embassy sent to deliver some tendentious briefing, but it seemed his Russian was too perfect. His suit, though it looked as if it had been slept in, was unmistakably English – a fourteen ounce Huntsman Prince of Wales tweed. The shirt was certainly American, probably Brooks Brothers, the shoes scuffed suede. I made a note: 'Perhaps he is some kind of Soviet Basil Seal?'

My Lord, it was a relief to see, was shovelled by Vera into the first limousine, while one of the wooden faced speech-makers directed me to the second. Here the man with the bottle joined me, settling comfortably with his feet over the front seat. The driver objected, but was silenced with a volley of Russian abuse. My companion placidly unwrapped his bottle, and winked at me.

'Real Polish vodka, baby,' he said, with a strong American accent. 'None of this goddam Russian crud.'

Thus my introduction to Oleg Feofanov, now the editor of *Sputnik*, the Russian version of *Reader's Digest* and biggest circulation magazine in the world, then – well then his role was never precisely defined. In practice it consisted of staying very close to me indeed, and encouraging me to break all the precepts instilled into me in London. In theory, I suppose, he was my personal KGB man, whose job was close surveillance. He certainly carried it out. In fact, it was evident that his primary concern was to enjoy himself as much as possible, preferably twenty-four hours a day.

Oleg was the first and best of a series of Iron Curtain bohemians who have crossed my path. There was Janis in Warsaw who said he had slept with a thousand women, and whose other interests were vodka and West German ballpoint pens in that order. In Bratislava Milos did little except drink, denounce the Russians – and this just after the invasion – and reminisce about the days when he had been head of Czech intelligence. It was in this capacity that he had achieved brief, world-wide fame by arresting Dr Hewlett Johnson, the notorious 'Red Dean' of Canterbury, mistaking this reverend comrade for a former Bishop of Bratislava who had been a Nazi collaborator. In Prague his brother under the skin, Jiri, pushed women, foreign currency, and even pot with equal skill. He once, excited by alcohol, invited me to join him in a midnight expedition to paint anti-Russian slogans on walls – and this was the week when Soviet troops shot at anyone who moved after eight pm. In Washington there was a Rumanian 'cultural expert' called Klaci, who was to be found from breakfast onwards in a bar called Joe the Bum's, and whose posting seemed at least as inexplicable as that of our own Guy Burgess, whom he much resembled.

The last three, I believe, are now all in prison: Oleg prospers, judging by the drunken telephone calls that sometimes arrive at odd hours in the morning, usually around Christmas or the New Year festivities. He is a remarkable man and, as I dimly began to understand in the back of that car trailing through Moscow's unprepossessing urban sprawl, the possesser of a quality rare in Russians. Oleg had style.

It was derived, I soon found, largely from the better known Bogart movies.

'Baby,' said Oleg, after I had sampled his vodka. 'You carrying any Bourbon?'

'One bottle of Scotch for medicinal purposes and emergencies only, and if you mention it to Thomson he'll have me shot.'

'Tough guy, uh?' Oleg obviously approved of this, but was disappointed about the whisky, even though this did not inhibit him from getting through most of it in due course. His preferred tipple, it emerged, was bourbon or rye.

'Four Roses,' he intoned nostalgically, 'Colonel Calvert, Old Grandad' – it was his personal litany, a reminder of the sacred mysteries, the verities by which he attempted to circumnavigate his erratic course. He repeated the list frequently when recalling the sadly curtailed period of his life when he had been posted to Canada.

'Toronto, Ontario,' he would recite in a variant litany, 'Vancouver, Nova Scotia, Calgary, Alberta – now Calgary, you could really find yourself some dolls in that joint, baby.'

And then he would call, or rather roar, for more drink, reinforcing his demand by banging his empty glass against the carafe or bottle already on the table. The glasses often broke when he did this but I never saw a waiter complain.

We were now in the centre, and looking at the inhabitants, who occasionally scowled back, it occurred to me that Oleg was the only Russian I had yet seen who seemed anything but acutely miserable. It was scarcely a warm day but crowds queued sullenly at ice-cream stalls, as I learnt they were equally wont to do in blizzard conditions. My first impression of Red Square was a pair of burly men fighting on the pavement, employing the ineffectual bar-room swings of the very drunk.

'If you think this is the Hilton, forget it,' said Oleg, as we entered our hotel. 'No goddam class.'

He was right. The lobby had all the charm of an LNER waiting room at the height of the post-war fuel crisis. We got off to an inauspicious start when my boss, perhaps through ignorance of local customs, was detected trying to lift a copy of *The Daily Worker* from a stand without depositing the requisite roubles. My room was beige, and nut-brown and green, with an evidently pre-revolutionary mural depicting the death of a stag. The stag looked suitably forlorn but certainly no more depressed than the huntsmen, though their faces wore an expression of bestial cruelty absent from that of the animal. An aproned porter, whom Oleg had been abusing, dumped my bags balefully on the dun counterpane of my vast double bed, thus slightly redistributing the coating of dust covering its surface.

'You have an electric razor,' demanded Oleg, who was fingering his stubble in front of the mirror.

'Never use them.'

'I have the new Remington Super-Jet,' said Oleg proudly.

'Well, why the hell didn't you use it today?'

Moscow was beginning to get me down. Oleg, always the diplomat, appeared with two greasy toothmugs containing the last of his vodka. He clinked his against mine, and winked.

'You know how it is, baby. A man doesn't want to sleep at home every night.'

I asked if he were married and the handsome, disreputable, stubbly face split into an evil grin.

'Now you're talking,' said Oleg. 'My next wife will be the fifth.'

Lunch was not a success. It took a shade over three hours to be served with *bortsch*, fatty beef and the ubiquitous *kasha*, then tinned fruit. The Lord was restless. At one stage he had Oleg, Vera and myself all quartering the hotel hopelessly trying to procure tomato ketchup. Our failure seemed to make him suspicious.

'Holy Joe,' he kept repeating, 'a hotel that doesn't have catsup. You *sure* you asked the manager?'

We assured him that no potential catsup avenue had been left unexplored, but he went on muttering to himself. Between *bortsch* and *kasha*, a gap of around an hour, he produced a Morocco notebook with gold edges and started to write immensely fast memoranda, in spidery copperplate. After the tinned fruit, which fortunately seemed to please him, Vera briskly opened her plastic briefcase and withdrew some duplicated sheets with a flourish.

'Schedule,' she announced, using the American pronunciation.

It looked as if Intourist had arranged things so that we would be occupied twenty hours a day for the next two months. Subjects for our excursions, it appeared, included an automated dye-plant in the Caucusus; a housing project in Armenia; an ice-cream factory in Georgia; a trade union sanatorium in Sochi (Black Sea). This was the last item on the list; perhaps after all our hosts had a sense of humour.

The Lord stared myopically at his list for a while, thick lips moving as if in silent prayer. He then tore his notes from their binding and passed them to me. They were headed: 'London cables – Urgent' (underlined three times).

I asked whether he wanted them typed, and taken to the cable office, wherever it might be.

'You just hold them. It says we're seeing *Pravda* tomorrow.'

He prodded the schedule with his thumb as if making everything perfectly clear. Then he consulted his watch, which always seemed to make him happy.

'Holy Gee. We're expected at six, and it's two after now. Let's go, son.'

Even though the grisly remnants of lunch were still on the plastic cloth before us, two after six it was. Wearing the look of someone who would dearly like to visit what she would have called 'the ladies' powder-room' Vera led the way, a shade unsteady on green high heels with peep-toes. This reception was offered by the Journalists' Union in a 'Banqueting Suite' elsewhere in the hotel. When we arrived it was easy to see why our lunch had been so prolonged. In the main dining-room there had been three middle-aged, white-smocked ladies to deal with perhaps fifty clients. Here there were ten waiters plus six similarly dressed ladies putting the final touches to a table set for twenty-four. No other guests had arrived.

Nor did they for forty-five minutes. Meanwhile the Lord took a place at the empty table, sent Vera off to buy post cards and stamps, and wrote twenty or so in half an hour. This task completed he produced *Dames Can Be Deadly* from a side-pocket of his blue serge, and began to concentrate ferociously.

Oleg had been overcast during lunch, but cheered up as soon as he saw each place had been laid with four glasses and three bottles: one bottle of red wine, one of white, and one of vodka. The fourth glass, Oleg explained, was for the champagne that would be served from a side table.

'This suite's got plenty of class,' he decided.

The room itself was strange; it might have been an *avant-garde* design for a roadhouse bar situated on a London by-pass in the year 1932. The walls were of glass and allowed one to stare, and be stared at, by the crowds in Red Square some thirty feet below. Oleg pointed out the entrance to a subway station on the corner with some pride.

'Men's room down there – you know, public toilet – you gotta go and see it. All the guys down there faggots, every goddam one.'

It seemed as though he was playing the classic Moscow *agent provacateur* of spy fiction. When in the course of time Oleg's character filled out, it became clear nothing was further from his mind. He was referring to the homosexuals in a spirit of simple boastfulness. What he adored about capitalism was its anarchic extremes, so different from the regimented mediocrity that prevailed in his own society. He longed nostalgically for the 'classiness' of Hilton foyers, the sleazy squalor of Times Square. When we came across some unexpected baroque element in Soviet life, worthy to be compared with his North American dreams, he took innocent pride in them and demanded appreciation. Oleg really was a truly lousy propagandist for the Soviet way of life.

For some time he regarded the subway with satisfaction, and then returned briskly to business.

'You know Alexei Adjubei's coming,' he said, almost with awe. 'The old man will have to make a speech. Perhaps *you'll* have to make a speech.

He dissolved in giggles at the prospect.

The Lord was instructing Vera to procure a store of iced apple-juice for *our* consumption and looked at me meaningfully: apparently he already knew Nikita Khruschev's notorious son-in-law was expected.

'They tell me Alexei's a great human being,' he said enigmatically. 'You know where the little boy's room is located?'

Oleg nobly led him off and I was making a note – *Cables?* – in my book when the glass doors opened and the reception, looking like an unusually well-drilled undertakers' convention, trooped in. Twenty men in dark suits: no Lord.

Vera propelled me forward and began introductions. She did not seem very good at it. Some of the bleak faces grew even bleaker when they saw my proffered hand. Others expressed incredulity. Could this crumpled stripling be the great capitalist press lord? By the time the genuine article had reappeared fumbling cheerfully with his fly I had met them all. The editor of *Pravda*; the editor of *Novosti*; the chairman of the foreign publishing committee; the secretary of the scientific and cultural committee, though God knows what he expected us to contribute in either of those areas, and so forth. With Vera's assistance I had lied about our circulation, and admitted to Satyukov, the *Pravda* editor, that no, his newspaper was not widely read in London. It seemed odd that he was not already aware of this cultural *lacuna* on the part of the British. The Lord greeted the company by raising both hands above his head in the manner of a victorious boxer. The editor of *Novosti*, a man of six feet four whose face might have been hewn out of a Victorian mahogany wardrobe, stooped to pin red badges in our lapels.

Oleg, who wore a similar badge, was pleased about this.

'Now you can drink with me in the Journalists' Union bar,' he confided. 'It's gotta lot of class – I'm assistant secretary.'

Then they made speeches, which were the same as the ones in the morning, or practically. In any case there was the same obsession with West Germany which, in the circumstances, it was easy to comprehend.

After each speech we clapped and drank toasts to co-existence

in wine and vodka, and during them we ate caviare and salted
fish and more caviare. After about an hour of this there was a
silence, broken only by the sound of the Lord refusing a cornucopian platter of fresh apples, oranges, grapes and bananas to
ask Vera testily whether they had any canned fruit with
carnation cream.

'They would like if you make fraternal speech,' she replied
artfully. The Lord's countenance cleared, and ponderously he
got to his feet. Here, one saw at once, was the veteran of a
hundred Elks' Conventions and Rotarian Blue-Plate Dinners:
a very accomplished after-dinner speaker. He stuck a thumb
in the top of his waistcoat in a pose which was vaguely Glad-
stonian. He beamed, and cleared his throat, and beamed again
at the wooden and by now flushed faces.

'Friends, I wanna tell you a little story,' he began. 'For me
it exemplifies the differences between our two great systems –
capitalism and socialism.'

Vera, furiously making notes in shorthand, rose to translate
them in a nervous croak while the Lord rinsed his throat with
a colourless liquid that was clearly not apple-juice. I wondered
if some embittered research assistant who had once nurtured
ambitions of an All Souls' Fellowship but had said the wrong
thing at his *viva* had worked for weeks preparing for this
moment. Perhaps the old man had committed appropriate
remarks to memory; certainly he had no notes.

'This capitalist worked in a glass-walled office so he could
be sure all his workers were working, and one day he got a
new secretary. Boy, was she stacked.'

Vera dealt with the first section confidently enough but then
bogged down. She looked appealingly at Oleg, whom I had
felt vibrating gently – but silently – beside me. He obliged with
a translation, while the Lord glared irritably at poor Vera.

'Oh shit,' said Oleg softly but with ecstasy. 'Just listen to the
crazy old bastard.'

'*Stacked,*' emphasized the Lord, regaining his theme. 'And
how.'

'So at the end of the first week he fired her. "Sorry, baby,"
said the old capitalist, "but you gotta go".'

Vera translated; the wooden faces listened with concentration (several, I noticed, were making notes, including a man Satyukov had introduced with ill-concealed contempt as one of his *Pravda* reporters).

'The girl was sad, the girl cried, the girl said: "My work's great, isn't it? Why are you firing me?"'

Vera translated: the *Pravda* reporter changed his pencils.

'So the capitalist was embarrassed, and you know,' – the Lord leant forward confidentially – 'even a capitalist gets embarrassed sometimes. Finally the guy said "It's not your work it's your tits".'

Again Vera looked perplexed, and Oleg barked a two-syllable word down the table. Vera, blushing fiercely, rattled something off.

" What's wrong with my tits?' says the girl. 'No one ever complained about them before."

' "Everyone keeps looking at them, that's what's wrong," says the capitalist. "None of these goddam workers do a day's work any more."'

Oleg nudged me, and refilled my glass.

'So the girl sees the light,' continued the Lord.

'She grabs hold of her jumper' the Lord grabbed frenziedly at his own waistcoat.

'She gets hold of her falsies – and she throws them in the out-tray.'

To assist Vera, and add impact to his tale, the Lord then picked up a pair of huge apples from Alma-Atta, the central Asian town famous for them, and did a rugged mime of pitching them in an out-tray.

Oleg started to hiccup.

'So what do you think the capitalist did?' asked the Lord rhetorically, beaming round with the air of a man who knew his audience was totally captive.

'What do you think that old capitalist did?'

Vera, now gathering strength, translated.

'I'll tell you. He tore his dentures out of his mouth' – (the Lord mimed this act) – 'and he threw them into the out-tray along with the falsies. Then that old capitalist said: "Now you can have a good bite of 'em. That's what you've been wanting to do all week." '

The Lord removed his glasses and polished their bulbous rims while the punch line was translated. Then he put them back on again and beamed. The Banqueting Suite was momentarily as hushed as Lenin's Tomb. Then, from somewhere near the depraved glass doors, a deep bellow of laughter swept across the silent table.

Briefly, there was a good deal of localized disapproval and the *Novosti* editor said what was evidently the Soviet equivalent of 'Tut-Tut', but in a distinctly threatening tone. All heads turned towards the door.

A big, overweight man was propped up against the wall positively bellowing with mirth. He wore a suede jacket, open-neck silk shirt, and his long yellow hair was thinning rapidly on top. He looked like a prematurely debauched bull.

He began to clap, and all the disapproving faces started to smile, at first a bit nervously, and eventually with more conviction.

'You know who that is?' asked Oleg.

The big man strode up to the Lord.

'Alexei Adjubei,' he said in good, Americanized English.

The Lord clapped him playfully on one massive suede shoulder.

'Just call me Roy.'

Shortly after this historic meeting the Lord mercifully announced he was going to bed. His last instructions, hissed conspiratorially as he blundered off, were that I should watch 'that Adjubei' like a hawk. It was not an easy brief.

When at seven the following morning the Lord woke me up eager for a full report it was hard to separate dream from reality. Certainly we had been to at least three separate parties where everyone danced the twist. And I had complimented a brunette on her twisting abilities and she had turned out to be a prima ballerina from the Bolshoi. And Alexei had done a cossack dance on a table, amazingly without falling off, and then there had been something about a shirt . . .

Gradually it came back. Alexei had announced he had always wanted a pink shirt, *a propos* of nothing, and slowly it had got through that mine was pink, a button-down one from New York.

'Give the guy your shirt,' Oleg had whispered.

'What *here*?'

'Yeah, he wants a pink shirt.'

So with a grand gesture I had stripped it off and passed it over, and he had given me his, and then there had been speeches about natural sympathy between the Russians and the British, and the Sword of Stalingrad . . . Retrospectively it all seemed highly unlikely, but there on the floor under the hunting scene was, unmistakeably, Alexei's shirt. The label said *Gentiluomo, via Condotti, Roma* – so much for the dictatorship of the pro-letariat.

The bath, it turned out, did not work, but this made little difference as it was already occupied. Oleg, with the pillows from my bed comfortably supporting his head, was stretched out luxuriously, his stockinged feet propped against the soap-tray. He woke only long enough to say something obscene though complimentary about the hip action of the Bolshoi brunette. He would not, he added, be taking breakfast.

The Lord had virtually completed his but was complaining to Vera about the absence of prunes.

'Nothing like them for keeping regular,' he was confiding. Vera was listening with an expression of loathing and fear that had not left her face since the fiasco of the capitalist and his well-stacked secretary. He turned his bulbous eyes on me and announced:

'Would you believe it, they don't stock prunes here, *prunes*.' He shook his head incredulously at the eccentricities of the Russians.

'Prunes would do you the world of good, Dave. You look awful. You stay close to Adjubei?'

Once satisfied of this his face took on a look of cunning and he sent Vera to buy some postcards.

'Wanted to talk confidentially,' he explained, and winked. And then with extreme urgency.

'What did that Adjubei have to say about the old man, about Chairman Khruschev?'

The answer was plenty, and most of it abusive. The burden had been that when the ball-busting old sonavabitch was around, no one, except of course the stinking old alcoholic himself, could take a drink or enjoy a little innocent relaxation without being treated like a dog. There had been a good deal about an actress whom Alexei regarded highly, and good deal more about the particular vileness of Khruschev's normally hair-trigger temper during periods of abstinence enforced by his doctors. This, it seemed, was one of them.

The inspiration came.

'He said he felt, er, free at the moment because Khruschev was out of Moscow.'

'Anything about K. wanting to see me?'

There was no choice but to admit this had not been one of the topics on Adjubei's extensive agenda. We accordingly left for the editorial offices of *Pravda*, the first step on the day's schedule, in an atmosphere of heavy gloom but at least, finally, it was now clear why we were in the Soviet Union at all. The likelihood of the second most powerful man in the world—perhaps indeed the most powerful – falling over himself to receive a mere Canadian multi-millionaire with a newly-acquired English peerage seemed unlikely. The point may even have crossed the Lord's mind. Vera indefatigably tried to interest him in the sights of Moscow but he hunched sulkily in the back of our limousine; his lips moved occasionally, but he was only talking to himself.

In the circumstances the *Pravda* visit might have gone worse. As soon as he sniffed newsprint the Lord brightened perceptibly; presumably he associated the smell with money. He was also fascinated by the fact that most of the compositors were women and earned, he calculated after fierce cross-questioning, about eighty per cent less than their male counterparts in his London empire. This interested the Lord deeply. So much so that he played little part in a solemn seminar arranged for us in the editor's office. Instead, he jotted figures in his little book, and added them up endlessly. Finally he looked up happily, and interrupted a solemn lecture by the foreign editor about the distribution of his correspondents throughout the world, a matter which the Lord evidently found of scant interest.

'Pavel,' he called boisterously, 'I gotta proposition for you.'

Satyukov, the *Pravda* editor, smiled weakly. There was something about the set of his teeth and the expression in his eyes which gave him an uncanny resemblance to a ginger rat.

'Pavel,' the Lord continued, 'with this nice little monopoly you got here there's a lot of money in *Pravda*, darn sight more than in the London *Times* if you want my opinion. You know what I'm gonna do when I see Chairman K?' The Lord slapped his knee happily.

'I'm gonna make him an offer for it.'

The faces round the long editorial table grew even blanker, it seemed, than before. The Lord was pleased to have made an effect.

'Hey son,' he said to the foreign editor. 'You say you have a telex line to London?'

The foreign editor confirmed he had.

'Give him those cables, Dave,' ordered the Lord. 'Let's see how efficient their communications are.'

The idea of *Pravda* paying for his cables – most of which were esoteric instructions to his merchant bank which must have had the Moscow cryptologists busy for days – kept the Lord smiling all day. Only after a very bad dinner during which he had exhaustively expounded his simplistic ideas about the basic similarity of socialist and capitalist systems did a brief cloud cross his wrinkled brow.

'Get off to bed now, honey,' he told Vera, as a preliminary to confidences.

She clumped dutifully off and the Lord sighed.

'You'd think K. would have been in touch before now. I met him when we had that publicity stunt here a couple of years back, and I *wrote* him I was coming.'

We went upstairs in sombre mood. From my bedroom came the sound of Louis Armstrong singing about what he had found on Blueberry Hill. Oleg, who had been strangely invisible all day, was stretched out on the bed, playing my transistor at full blast and drinking my Scotch.

'Next time you got to bring rye,' he greeted me.

The man in the next room was beating on the wall with his shoe so I turned the music off.

'Tell me, Oleg, do you think Khruschev is really going to give the old man an interview?'

'He's sure as hell crazy,' Oleg said cheerfully.

'Who? Chairman Khruschev or the Lord?'

'Both,' said Oleg. 'You never know what he'll do next, old Nikita.'

The subject was not important enough to interest him for more than a moment.

'Listen, I gotta date for you.'

'Forget it, maybe tomorrow.'

Oleg combed his hair, used my *Eau Védiver*, and headed off. He left the transistor but took the scotch.

From the outset, as I have indicated, the Moscow venture had been pervaded by an unreal, surrealist quality, but at five am the following morning it lurched decisively towards total confusion and insanity. The 'phone whined at me in the darkened room, and I groped my way towards the instrument which had been placed for maximum inconvenience beneath the dying stag. I very nearly took it off the hook and returned to bed, assuming the caller to be a vodka-sodden Oleg or Alexei, babbling of ballerinas. But the voice was a strange one, redolent of north London, a hint of cockney behind the carefully modulated, genteel vowels. Whoever owned it had probably attended London University, or possibly some technical college. I had an immediate image of a man in a birdseye serge suit from Burton's, worn with a shetland pullover and an array of multi-coloured ball-pens in the breast pocket. He might well have an interest in greyhound racing as well, and what conceivably he was doing on the telephone in Moscow before dawn was simply beyond my imaginative range.

'Sorry to bother you at this early hour,' said the voice matily.

'There is a special military flight for Tzelinograd scheduled to depart in ninety minutes. Comrade Chairman Khruschev is on an inspection tour of Kazahkstan, and will meet Lord Thomson there tonight. Perhaps if you would be kind enough to be in the lobby in, say, forty minutes . . .'

'Where are we going did you say?'

'Tzelinograd is in Soviet Central Asia.'

I said I would rouse Thomson, and the mysterious voice rang off with a bracing 'Cheery-oh'. The Lord, in blue striped silk pyjamas and without teeth or glasses, looked even more subterranean than usual. He was deeply suspicious at first, understandably suspecting me of inebriation, but once he had grasped what was happening he moved with remarkable speed for a man of his years. 'Get to it, Dave,' he said, working on his teeth. 'I knew Nikita wouldn't let an old friend down. We're just like that.' He brought thumb and index finger together, simultaneously raising the other fingers on high, rather in the manner of a baseball umpire.

'Where d'you say this Kazahk place is?'

'Kazahkstan, it's called. I think it must be around fifteen hundred miles from here, maybe a bit more. It's bang in the middle of the country. Where Tamberlane the Great came from.'

The Lord, who wore his historical knowledge lightly, clipped his sock suspenders together and nodded in an informed kind of way.

'You mean one of those old time Czars.'

I was tempted, as so often on this trip, to reply: 'Up to a point, Lord Copper' the answer used by the wretched Mr Salter of the *Daily Brute* when his proprietor made minor errors about matters like the date of the battle of Hastings. As a schoolboy I had believed Evelyn Waugh's *Scoop* had been a work of fiction; now I knew better, and realized it had been straight reportage but lacked courage, particularly at that hour of the morning.

'That kind of thing,' I said.

The Lord nodded, satisfied.

'Thought so,' he said, putting on an Anthony Eden hat.

'This is going to be a great adventure Dave, a Very Great Adventure. They'll write about this in the history books.'

In the car out we prepared a list of questions to put to the Soviet leader at dinner that night, but we were being over optimistic about Russian travelling methods. We had our own 'plane all right, indeed I think we had about three, but the next twenty hours were spent in a haze of take-offs and landings at different airports, most of them little more than rough strips surrounded by nissen huts, and prefabricated hangars, and huge sad bunches of silent peasants carrying wooden suit-cases and large piles of sausages and rye bread. Everyone except us was weighed down with food, which was very sensible of them. Adjubei, who had arrived two hours after us at the air-port but still in plenty of time before the actual flight departure, threw his weight around all day with the grace and gentleness of a Prussian drill sergeant, and though the officials he berated looked terrified to the point of hysteria, food they could not produce. Oleg, who had also arrived late, sat hunched under a huge chart of depraved design showing Aeroflot's internal routes. Vera, who as usual looked like hell, remarked briskly that the Russian line was bigger than Pan-Am and TWA put together. It was not one of Oleg's propaganda-minded morn-ings. 'Bullshit,' he said, loud and clear and went to forage – in vain – for vodka. Pavel Satyukov, exhibiting the rat-like cunning he had obviously applied to creep to the top of the *Pravda* hierarchy, got into conversation with a citizen in flat cap and braces, who looked oddly like a Yorkshire clog-dancer. This ruse won Pavel an apple, which he devoured ravenously and furtively in a corner.

In the course of that day I began, through the haze of jet fatigue and hunger, to see how the Lord had acquired his millions. He alone remained unruffled. Oblivious to the sights around him – which were largely identical patches of cumulus, or identical nissen huts – he spent the day working through a thick pile of annual reports and balance sheets. These, he told me, were of companies on his potential take-over list, and since he was away from the office, he reckoned this was an ideal opportunity to mull over them undisturbed. While everyone else was, by evening anyway, on the edge of despair the Lord, strapped into his seat, seemed to grow happier and happier. By ten o'clock, his balance sheets around him, he had begun to whistle a tune I finally identified as 'The runaway train ran over the track and she blew'. This had probably been top of the Canadian hit-parade when he was fifteen or so, and it turned out to be oddly prophetic.

Tzelinograd, as far as one could judge in the dark, was a kind of shanty town, not unlike a very large construction site. This was not surprising as the famous Virgin Lands scheme, which had been Chairman Khruschev's own disastrous baby, had only been going since the middle 1950s and, as we were shortly to see, was still in that state of disastrous muddle apparently endemic to all Soviet attempts to make their agricultural system remotely competitive with that of the West. A kind of emergency banquet had been laid on for us in a large corrugated iron hut reserved for distinguished visitors, during which we drank fermented mare's milk, the traditional Kazahk tipple. Considering its vileness, and his liking for bland supermarket foods, I thought the Lord dealt with it in an exemplary manner. There were the usual speeches about co-existence, and he made his speech about the secretary and her falsies, and it got to be two in the morning. Everyone, I noticed seemed very worried, and a lot of telephoning was going on in the background. Finally, just as we were about to go to bed, Vera and Adjubei told us there had been a change of plan, and we were to meet Khruschev on his private train which was going to make an emergency stop at a nearby station to pick us up. We caught the train after a hair-raising drive through the dark and at eight-thirty the next morning we were having breakfast with Nikita Sergeivitch himself, who was gluttonously consuming curds out of a small bowl decorated with a chirpy looking yellow canary. I, for one, found the whole thing very hard to believe, but the Lord took it all in his stride.

It had been clear from my first night out with Alexei and Oleg that something was going badly wrong. Alexei, who was pathologically indiscreet, drunk or sober, had told me at one stage that he was shortly going on a very important visit to West

Germany – a country he hated – and the trip was obviously
worrying him, as well it might. It was almost certainly intended
to re-orient Soviet policy towards an accommodation with the
Federal Republic at the expense of Comrade Ulbricht, and it
seems to have been a virtually private initiative of his father-
in-law's. From an American contact before we left Moscow I
had learnt that Palmiro Togliatti, the veteran leader of the
Italian Communist Party, had been trying to arrange to see
Khruschev for some time about this and had not, it seemed,
been successful. He, like every other communist leader in the
world, was worried about the Soviet scheme to bring all the
world parties together and unite them against China. It had
occurred to me that if Togliatti was having difficulty making
contact with Khruschev our own chances must surely be slight.
From Oleg I had learnt that the 1963 harvest had been an
unmitigated disaster, and there were indications that this year's
would be not much better. It all added up to an atmosphere
of intense strain and worry, and someone better versed in the
nuances of Soviet affairs than either the Lord or myself, might
have been able to deduce that a new power struggle was going
on. In fact, when we saw Chairman Khruschev that morning
he had something under eight weeks of political life left to him.
Why he saw us at all – and, incidentally, allowed the gravely
sick Togliatti to die empty handed – puzzled me at the time,
and has for that matter puzzled me ever since. His cavalier
approach had disastrous propaganda consequences first on the
Italian and then on the world communist parties, and yet he
saw us. For some obscure reason he must have believed we
were important.

Certainly we did not look it. Even the Lord's superhuman
stamina was beginning to wilt, and my air of total bewilderment
must have been obvious enough. 'Tovarich', said the Lord
expansively as we went into the private breakfast suite, and
Chairman K embraced the Lord several times. Neither of them
really had figures designed for convenient embracing and it
occurred to me, while amateurishly taking the obligatory pictures, that they looked as if they were demonstrating some new
comic dance, a version perhaps of 'Boomps-a-daisy', only with

bellies colliding instead of bottoms. There was a lot of caviare and, inevitably, vodka toasts (on that trip, I acquired so deep a loathing for the drink that although I can get down virtually anything if necessary, and often have, vodka I cannot touch). Khruschev had three little carafes containing different varieties, or perhaps vintages, of this abhorrent tipple, and made some sour jokes about his doctors' restrictions. Everyone looked very frightened except the Lord, who was occupied in making gestures.

The main one involved a large parcel I had been miserably lugging around since our departure from London. It turned out to contain a lot of not very good silver plate, which the Lord grandiosely unwrapped and showed to his host for all the world like a carpet salesman in Beirut vaunting his wares. I had a strong impression that the First Chairman was disappointed in his plunder, and he examined it only perfunctorily, though he did hold a couple of plates up to the light to check the hall-marks in what seemed an unexpectedly knowledgeable way. Then something rather disastrous happened. The Lord commented on the large electric clock which dominated one end of the private suite, and Khruschev explained it showed Moscow time, accurate to the second. The Lord countered by demonstrating his wrist watch of which, by ill chance, he was inordinately proud.

I had already been bored by this object, which was of gold, on several occasions. It was a very early model of a type later to become common which used a tiny electric battery instead of the conventional movement. Some sycophant or fellow industrialist had presented the Lord with this fat and ugly thing which bore a florid dedication on the back, and also operated as an alarm clock. This the Lord demonstrated a couple of times, and Chairman K suddenly showed interest. He tried it on – unfortunately it fitted very well – and listened for the tick, which was either completely nonexistent or extremely soft, I forget which. He was very reluctant to surrender the watch, and affected to believe it was a gift. The Lord, alarmed that his toy was in danger, indicated very clearly this was not his intention at all, and in an attempt to mollify this leader of two hundred and twenty million souls offered him a ball-pen inscribed with the name of his Television Company in Scotland. Khruschev pouched the pen without apparent ecstasy, and reluctantly returned the watch to its rightful owner. The Lord attached it to his wrist with great care before embarking on further small talk, but it was clear the atmosphere of *bonhomie* that had characterized the opening of the proceedings had been shattered, perhaps irretrievably. I scribbled 'Give him the watch' on a bit of paper torn from my notebook and slid it across to the Lord behind a large pot of gladioli, but the Lord only crumpled it up irritably. The Chairman said he had work to do and *might*, the word was ominously emphasized, fit us in later. We were ushered out and returned to our own suite.

It had been a bizarre encounter. The train, one was able to see in the light of day, was of an antique pattern, presumably Czarist. It was full of red plush and gilt mirrors and looked like a kind of ambulant Edwardian whorehouse. The luxury was oppressive; it was like travelling enclosed in one of those oval, velvet-lined boxes which held the gold, Fabergé Easter eggs the Czars collected so assiduously. Khruschev, I wrote in my notebook, fitted as snugly into this hyper-elegant setting as Genghis Khan at the Court of Louis *Quinze*. We sat in our mad train, waiting miserably, for several hours. Through our rococo windows stretched the steppes, endlessly empty, endlessly identical, a few hundred miles of the almost nine million acres Khruschev had insanely decided must be intensively cultivated. At one stage the Lord had himself tried his hand at wheat farming, before he decided there was more cash – a lot more – in newspapers. He was sceptical (quite rightly as it emerged) about the quality of the corn we could see stretching to the horizon. At breakfast the First Chairman had boasted that his agronomists had cut down on fallow land so that in some areas all but twelve per cent of the steppes were cultivated every season. The Lord explained at some length that in Western Canada, which was anyway dryer than Kazakhstan, they sometimes kept up to half the land fallow to retain moisture; the yields were so much higher it was worth the sacrifice. Khruschev had an almost Hitlerian capacity for being convinced by cranks and it was a matter of objective fact that despite fifteen years of pushing various forms of agricultural collectivization, in 1964 fifty per cent of the meat and fruit, and almost all the eggs and vegetables that got to the Russian consumer, stemmed from private enterprise. The Lord, who was nobody's fool when it came to assessing efficiency and profitability, had grasped this anomaly with remarkable speed, and kept saying the First Chairman had better change his agronomists. I was mainly concerned about our interview. Adjubei was worried too, and so was the official interpreter, Viktor Suchodrev, my friend with the north London voice who had been responsible for that dawn call in Moscow. They dropped in to our suite periodically, and the conversation invariably got around to the famous watch which apparently was still bothering the First Chairman. The Lord would not be moved. It was *his* watch, and he was holding on to it.

And in the end he won. For the first five minutes of the famous interview (I noted down it was 16.24 local time, three hours earlier in Moscow) Khruschev's clock bothered me, and every time the Lord leant forward so that his cuff rolled back and his own chronometer was showing I feared impending disaster. After that Khruschev was so obviously enchanted with the sound of his own voice there was nothing to worry about. We asked our set questions, and the First Chairman used them as a basis for a series of answers which, if the interpreter was as good as he seemed, were of incredible brilliance, though they added nothing new to Western knowledge of what the Soviet leader was thinking. In his biography of Khruschev, written a couple of years later, Edward Crankshaw re-told a famous story of how Mr K, doubtless after a few drinks, had once rounded on a group of the usual toffee-nosed Western diplomats, and asked them a rhetorical question. They, he pointed out, had been educated in the finest universities in the world, while he had been a barefoot boy who had begun herding cows. Why was it he could run rings round them?

All through the interview, hearing him explain to the Lord in what way Capitalism and Socialism were different (the Lord was an exponent of the idea that the systems were drawing closer together) I found myself asking the same question, without finding an answer. The only thing that worried me was that the man, evidently suffering from either alcoholism or its withdrawal symptoms, should have thought it worth three hours of his time to answer sophomoric questions. Yes, he believed in nuclear disarmament. No, he did not think Goldwater was an embellishment to the American political scene. And so on. There was a bad moment when the Lord, who was not as well informed on the situation then prevailing in Cyprus as he might have been, said that the British Government would be delighted to withdraw their troops from the island. The First Chairman looked interested – the Lord, remembering some scrap of dinner-time gossip with R. A. Butler, the British Foreign Secretary of the period, had forgotten, or simply did not know or care about the British sovereign bases on the island: Butler had evidently been talking about the British contingent to the UN Peace-Keeping Force, which was something very different. In the end there was a long sparring match about whether or not the *Sunday Times* should be allowed to be sold in Moscow.

I took several thousand words of notes, and looking at them now my impression is the same as at the time: how could Khruschev have combined such brilliance with so inadequate a knowledge of international affairs that he believed this formidable but strictly capitalist Canadian and his inexperienced factotum were of real political importance, as he obviously did. Perhaps it was yet another example of the Soviet leaders' inability to understand the way things work in the West – Burgess, Maclean and Philby had failed to fill the gap (though Burgess had won acclaim and a *dacha* by correctly forecasting that Macmillan, not Butler, would succeed Eden).

In any case it did not matter. Eight weeks later Khruschev was put out to grass.

When I asked if I could interview the spy Kim Philby, Khruschev laughed, and promised to make arrangements for me to approach Philby himself. 'He is a free Soviet citizen – it's his choice,' Khruschev said. He also told the Lord that he thought I was underpaid; under the socialist system, he claimed, no young man would be expected to work as hard as I did. Perhaps he thought it would get me a raise, but he was wrong. That night, when I started getting nervous about communications and talked of telephoning the interview through to London at once, the old capitalist reverted exquisitely to type. 'There's no point, Dave,' said the Lord earnestly, 'in getting scoops if you spend all the money on international 'phone calls. You don't make profits that way.'

It was hard not to admire the Lord. He was as unmovable as the plains of Saskatchewan. And, of course, he got our story to London via *Pravda*'s telex – and gratis.

* * * *

The morning after the news of Khruschev's death reached France I was in a bar called The Laughing Gull on the water front at Sète. One of this town's main claims to fame is that Paul Valéry is buried there – the attendant at the cemetery, an idle man, has trained his mastiff to lead literary pilgrims to the right grave, thus enabling its master to bask undisturbed in his shady *loge*. Sète is not, all in all, an inappropriate place for a cosy chat about death, and Khruschev's had some special local interest. Sète is one of the most strongly entrenched communist strongholds between St Denis and the Mediterranean.

'*Khroutchev*,' as the French spell him, was already demonstrating that his myth was likely to endure: the very fact that his name was being mentioned at all on a Sunday morning in a bar with off-course betting facilities underlined that. Sunday is the hallowed day of the Tiercé, a gambling event of such magnitude that few Frenchmen would consider passing the hours immediately before the races exchanging views on a topic so intrinsically frivolous as the merits of a recently defunct world statesman, particularly a foreign one. Instead, they concentrate on weights, handicaps and jockeys to a point where even money and sex, the conversational standbys of the week, receive only the most perfunctory attention. Poincelet and Piggott are acceptable and even obligatory subjects; Nixon and Pompidou are certainly not.

The two citizens nearest me were drinking respectively deep

red and vivid green concoctions – 'Tomate' and 'Perroquet'. A few year ago if you ordered a 'tomato' the waiter put a slug of Grenadine in your pastis; and if you were a 'parrot' man he laced your pastis with mint. Now these Midi variants on a traditional alcoholic theme come processed and ready-mixed in the bottle. So too, I noticed, did my neighbours' opinions about the deceased First Chairman of the USSR.

Just as the Gull clients had leant heavily on advice from the media experts when assessing their horses so my neighbours' thoughts about that villainous old man had evidently been conditioned by what the papers (and particularly television which I had missed) had been churning out in the last few hours. Indeed if one had edited their exchanges to excise such colloquialisms as *'merde alors'*, and then written out what was left in sub-mandarin prose, the result would have been strikingly similar to the long and bland obituary that *The Times*, cosy in Printing House Square, was probably setting into type at just about that moment.

Tomato reckoned that the Twentieth Party Congress had been the turning point: *'La rupture avec Stalin,'* he quoted from some headline or another. Parrot thought Kroutchev had been 'cool' over the Cuba missile crisis (for which he had of course been responsible), and talked of the end of the Cold War. Neither mentioned the invasion of Hungary. As this was a period of Franco-Russian *détente*, or supposedly anyhow, it is likely that the ORTF, France's Orwellian state-controlled television system, which is nothing if not sensitive to governmental preoccupations, had played this episode down. But there were admiring recollections of the First Chairman's performance with his shoe when addressing the UN General Assembly. Here television was on safer ground because the UN was as unpopular in France as ever; I supposed they must have made some play of the incident. The old boy was a fine shoe banger, and the UN seldom provides much drama.

Eventually their conversation, joined occasionally by other punters, was clearly running down. Khruschev's final epitaph, as seen from Sète, was as follows.

TOMATO: He was a real joker (*'rigolaud'*).

PARROT: A real good type (*'un brave type'*).

So Tomato repeated *'Enfin, c'était un brave type'* for emphasis, and they contentedly returned to serious matters: the Form Book.

It was something of a shock. So much, I thought, for the media; for all those expensive cameras and editorialists, pundits and popularizers. If the results of their joint efforts had been to create an impression so wildly deviant from reality – *'un brave type'*, indeed – then my neighbours would have been better off reading comics, and the kremlinologists writing them. And I too, in a tiny way, must share the guilt. Writing from Moscow I had helped, if minutely, to propagate the 'cuddly Mr K' stereotype, largely because he had spent so much time embracing people (rarely, it should have been added, to their apparent delight). Worse, I had falsely given the impression that the occasion described in the last chapter had been light-hearted and friendly with an underlying seriousness appropriate to a meeting between great men mulling over grave matters. In fact, it had been in many ways comic, though largely in the manner of a *comédie noire*, such as Dr Strangelove. I had indicated an underlying seriousness, which simply had not existed. Perhaps I had been overwhelmed at my insight into what kind of man it was who was holding the future of some considerable section of mankind in his none-too-steady hand, or rather at the end of his spatulate thumb. Of course, I told myself in extenuation, there wasn't nearly enough time to write it properly. But when was there ever?

Later, reading an English obituary, the Sète experience came flooding back, provoked by one phrase. The obit. writer, evidently an adherent of the *'brave type'* school, remarked in passing that the deceased's eyes had been noticeable for 'their shrewd peasant twinkle'.

For the benefit of this probably honest if misguided writer, for Tomato and Parrot, and to try and purge my delinquencies at the time, I would like to record that Nikita Sergeivitch Khruschev's eyes were not of the twinkling variety. Unless, that is, you consider that a laser beam twinkles. His gaze was, however, very striking for the following reasons. In the first instance his eyes were preternaturally small, button-like at best and when he bellowed with laughter, which was very often, rolls of fat intruded across the lids so that they were in danger of disappearing altogether. But they never did completely. Two tiny black stones were always on the alert in the centre of that blubber, and with the exception of a close stare I once exchanged with a wild boar on a hunt in Sardinia I have never known an expression so malevolent and frightening.

Important politicians are almost always funny in some way, often through no fault of their own. A certain lack of self-consciousness is virtually a prerequisite for the job, and making a fool of oneself in public periodically is one of the prices politicians pay for power and fame. This is probably why Edward Heath's features fall so naturally into the sheepish look of a child who has caused the adults to laugh at an unconscious *double entendre*. The old pre-presidential Nixon used to have a similar look; typically he invariably followed it with a series of snaky little glances in all directions as if searching for the source of laughter in the next room so he could arrange for it to be swiftly smothered. I have seen a normally phlegmatic man dissolve into tears of laughter when seeing De Gaulle for the first time in the flesh (and, to be fair, have seen others cry with patriotic pride as well). Harold Macmillan, with typical urbanity, pre-empted the whole area by simply caricaturing himself permanently. He, if you like Tomato, was a *'rigolaud'*.

Khruschev brought peculiar physical gifts to the political circus and they should have made him a wonderful clown, perhaps the clown of the century. There was his irregular and totally bald head, irresistibly turnip-like. The weird duck waddle which was emphasized when viewed from the rear by the short-cut jackets of the Roman suits he had flown in from the Via Gregoriana. The endless bombast, drunk or sober, reminiscent of a thousand silent comedies of little men – Mr K was barely an inch over five feet even in elevator shoes – trying to be big. So much like Chaplin in *The Great Dictator*.

But despite all this there was nothing funny, nothing even mildly humorous about the man. (Probably Hitler in the flesh failed to be much of a joke either.) One could see why his immediate entourage were so acutely nervous. Though he was, in later life anyhow, always apparently just in control of himself, he seemed perpetually on the edge of letting go. (This impression was probably heightened because at the time of our visit the Kremlin doctors were rationing his vodka intake, and had forbidden it altogether before breakfast.) 'When will K start yelling?' I scribbled down. And another note taken at the time: 'Lunching with K is like being in a cage with a starving wolf tethered by garden twine.'

You only needed to have seen that gaze once to know what the wolf would be doing if it ever broke loose. I have inspected psychopathic murderers in the Pen and known some exuberant army officers whose pleasure was hunting men, or a kind of men called 'Gooks', from helicopters as one might pot ducks. Towards the end of his career I even got a look at Sonny Liston which left me in no doubt, things being what they were, that for a hundred dollars he would have been prepared to kill anyone with his bare hands, perhaps even for fifty. But compared with Nikita Sergeyevitch's gift for making the prickles rise on your neck these men were just beginners.

One day during our absurd visit Khruschev delivered a speech on the resounding success of his pet project for producing wheat in the previously uncultivated (and probably uncultivable) Central Asian plains of Kazakhstan. This speech was remarkable largely because it was delivered in the Palace of Culture in Tzelinograd, the capital of Kazakhstan, and was attended by around ten thousand workers, all of whom knew perfectly well that 1964 would rival 1963 as the worst harvest year since the idea was launched in the middle fifties. All the same they applauded his lies, perhaps out of habit, perhaps out of fear. There was no holding Khruschev when confronted with a captive audience like this – talking to the people had always been his personal speciality – and at the 150-minute mark he was still going strong.

Waiting backstage with a motley bunch of the Khruschev secretariat it was hard to tell whether one was suffering more from boredom or exhaustion. No one, not even the *louche* Alexei Adjubei, was prepared to take a bet on how long the

First Chairman would bellow on. Finally, the First Secretary's Chief Bodyguard appeared strolling briskly from behind a section of stacked scenery.

I had got to know this character, whom I called Joe, pretty well, and as bodyguards to political leaders go he was way above the average. (With the exception of one former légion-naire who made his own absinthe in his garden at Puteaux, de Gaulle's gorillas lived up to the nickname better than any other single group I ever encountered. They made the FBI men at the White House seem positively genteel.) I decided, in a moment of temporary insanity, that it would liven things up if I played a joke on Joe, and accordingly went into a heavy cowboy routine. Spinning professionally on one foot, John Wayne style, I drew a pair of imaginary six-shooters from the hip, and started blasting away in his general direction.

'Bang Bang,' I said.

Joe's reflexes appeared to be in very satisfactory condition. He swivelled, jumped sideways landing in a crouch, and simultaneously his hand, which I had not seen pass inside his jacket, appeared from underneath it. Mercifully Joe's hand was empty. The index finger, however, was levelled at a sensitive point around my middle.

'Bong, Bong,' said Joe. 'Bong.'

When a Russian sees a joke, no matter how childish, he likes to leave no one in any doubt. Joe spent some time in baritone laughs but no one else was amused. Alexei Adjubei, not nor-mally noted for his discretion, led me solemnly behind some more scenery. There he began yelling with fury, and continued or several minutes. Ashamed at my foolishness I tried to stam-mer out that of course I would never have considered such levity had I not been sure Chairman Khruschev was engaged in exhorting the workers, well out of earshot. Alexei took the point, and grinned. Then he looked grim again, and made an unmistakable gesture with his finger, passing it in an upward loop across the line of his fleshy pink throat.

'Bad to joke with,' Alexei gestured towards the curtains, through which we could hear Khruschev's amplified ranting. 'With him.'

Alexei considered for a while and then continued, groping for words.

'Never make joke with becker about bread.'

'Becker? Baker, do you mean?'

Alexei grinned again, this time mordantly.

'Yes,' he said. 'Never with baker.'

Years later I tried to find out from an upper-class English/Russian interpreter whether all this 'baker/bread' business had some kind of proverbial significance. He knew of no such proverb, but wondered whether it might have been one of the peasant saws the Khruschev clan were so fond of. If not, what did he think Adjubei was on about, I asked. My friend pondered for a while.

'Something about taking professionals seriously when it comes to their own subject, I imagine. Sounds like he didn't much care for his pa-in-law, thought he was too interested in shooting people, that kind of thing.'

'That's roughly how I took it.'

'You should have asked him,' said the interpreter. 'It might have had some historical importance.'

Of course, but now it's too late and Alexei is beyond the reach of questions. First he lost the editorship of *Izvestia*, and then came what must have been a killing blow for that cheery cosmopolitan. It was announced he was to be editor of a weekly magazine in Vladivostok and one wondered what he must have done to the bureaucrat, or perhaps the man's wife or daugher, who devised this ghoulish sentence. Vladivistok somehow had a personal ring to it; it indicated beyond doubt that there was some quite specific Adjubei-hater behind the machine. Worse soon followed. There were reports of a manslaughter/drunken driving charge; and Alexei has never been heard of since.

The news of Khruschev's fall reached me in the Adelphi Hotel in Liverpool on polling day in the 1964 British General Election, the first one Harold Wilson won. I passed the news on to him and reacting, as he always did, in careerist terms, he said: 'Bad luck for you.'

And so it was, desperately bad luck. If it had not happened, or had even happened three months later, I would have achieved a world scoop by interviewing Kim Philby in Moscow. I would also probably have learnt Russian, worked on *Izvestia* as a reporter, spent a lot of doubtless drunken and sexy nights with Alexei and numerous girls from the Bolshoi. Professionally, the First Chairman's fall was a disaster for me, and I was a young and ambitious man.

But even through that youth and egotism, and here Tomato is my message, I could not find it in my heart to be anything except relieved. For weeks one had been obsessively involved with a domestic election which to us had seemed of overwhelming importance but even that night, among the champagne and the slide-rules as the first results came in, it got through to me that over there in the Kremlin, not here in Liverpool, everyone's destinies had been manifestly and quite decisively altered. I slept that night, Tomato, and it was not because of Harold Wilson's victory, nor even because of its contingent champagne. That night I slept because your '*brave type*' was safely under wraps.

CHAPTER 8

The Whisky Ambassador

♣

His Excellency the Scotch Whisky Ambassador was standing on the steps of the Foreign Press Club in Rome preparatory to leaving for the north, where he was to judge a series of 'Signorina Scotch' beauty contests. He was attended by a kilted Pipe Major, in from Glasgow to serenade the winners, and invited me to join them on this testing diplomatic mission. HE has held down a series of bizarre jobs in his life, but none had been so ideally suited to his talents as promoting the exports of Scotch to the land of *espresso*.

Reluctantly, I confessed to a previous engagement. There had been floods, so it seemed, in Florence, but no one appeared to know their extent. I was off to find out.

'It's all over,' said HE. 'I heard it on TV.'

For obvious political reasons the Government had been anxious to minimize the worst disaster that had struck Florence since 1557, and their task had not been difficult. Romans find all things Florentine antipathetic, or boring, or both. If the government radio said there was nothing to worry about that was good enough for them. And it was certainly good enough for the members of the *Stampa Estera*, a club whose members included few enthusiastic flood investigators.

Mussolini's personal forays into journalism had not been very distinguished, but they had at least taught him how to handle the foreign press. His formula was simple but it had worked very effectively for over forty years, long after *Il Duce* himself had ended hanging by the feet in Milan. The dictator had reasoned that if the foreign journalists accredited to his country were given a centre that combined admirable communications and sources of (official) information with subsidized bar prices they were unlikely to inconvenience anyone by nosing around too much. There were also perquisites like free opera tickets and cheap first class travel, but few correspondents made use of this latter facility, except on occasions for holiday trips to Porto San Stefano or the lakes. They were not as a mass great travelling men; indeed some of the older members found it hard to negotiate a few marble stairs which connect the bar with the main telex room, and younger, spryer correspondents would carry their cables for them. The *doyenne* in the early 1960s was a splendid lady who once conclusively resolved a literary argument by saying that she had slept with both Hemingway and Fitzgerald, and as far as she was concerned they were both lousy.

She was doubtless telling the truth. She had been holding down her stool, with one unavoidable break during hostilities, for over forty years; twenty-year members were regarded as *arrivistes*. Few members of the *Stampa* ever left, voluntarily that is, and there was a general tendency to regard colleagues who found themselves reluctantly promoted to better paid, more prestigious jobs in Washington or Paris with deep pity. Given this knowledge I was not surprised to discover that even four days after the Arno had erupted into Piazza Gavinana at what I later discovered was fifty miles an hour it was impossible to find anyone who had actually driven up the *autostrada* to see what had happened. Apparently one foolish young man had attempted to get there the day after the floods but had of course got bogged down, and thereby missed his deadline, the ultimate sin. The others had been perfectly content to rewrite the notoriously venal and hilariously inaccurate official State-controlled wire agency, which had described the catastrophe in terms of a little local difficulty. In any case, everyone assured me, all the fun was over by now, and there would be nothing to see. As I left I felt rather a fool, four days behind the story. All the same it had been impossible to make telephone contact with Florence, and this made me dimly suspicious.

A hundred kilometres north I picked up a young air force mechanic – *un Marconisto* as the Italians chauvinistically say – who lived twenty miles from Florence, and was very worried. He had been given a compassionate leave pass to visit his aged parents after three days in Naples trying in vain to make contact with his village. This sounded bad, but at the *autostrada* complex called *Firenze Sud* everything was normal, even down to a Christmas tree, just about seven weeks premature. They reckoned no special provisions were needed for Florence that could not be obtained on the spot. Things were 'back to normal'; the television had said so. All the same I bought six cans of lager, to everyone's amusement, and they turned out to be all I had to drink for over two days. For perhaps five miles on the by-road going in everything seemed normal except some deepish patches of water, and an abnormal amount of military traffic – for the first time that night the troops were being mobilized in large numbers. Then suddenly on the ring road the traffic came to a complete halt; finally I dumped the car on a verge and walked. It was about two miles from there to Piazza Santa Croce, where I finished, and the walk took just three hours. Firstly, the mud was simply a thin, universal skin; then for a mile it was ankle deep, and after that knee high. There was no one on the streets but people called to each other from windows, disembodied voices for by now it was dark. Most of them were asking questions of their neighbours, usually about whether their water and electricity had come back on. Always, the answer was no.

I arrived in Piazza Santa Croce following a light in the sky – at first seen over the house-tops I had thought it was a giant fire. In fact, this piazza, which I later learnt had filled up to a level of twenty feet in the flood's first three hours, was the only illuminated patch in a town of nearly half a million people. Some soldiers had set up searchlights using a mobile generator which illuminated great rippling dunes of fetid mud. In the centre, which had been partly cleared, the only silent crowd I have ever seen in Italy was queuing before the water carriers, their shadows reflected by the searchlights, one of which suddenly went out with a noise like a very big champagne cork popping. I could make out that some of the mud dunes had cars stuck in them, like truffles in *pâté du périgord*. There were also the carcases of several horses. Hell, I thought, will be exactly like this.

When I had left the car I had entertained extravagant ideas

about the Excelsior Hotel, and even Harry's Bar. In the event
I found someone with a dry third floor in the Borgo degli Albizi,
and woke at dawn simultaneously shivering with cold and
sweating. From the top floor I could see that over the Arno,
which was out of direct vision, there was a halo of yellowish
fog, a great chunk of fallen cumulus, that looked as if it had
come from an incinerator, and smelled the same. Later when I
saw the mayor, Piero Bargellini, who lived nearby behind the
Santa Croce Basilica, I noticed that he and his secretariat, all
of them wrapped in damp blankets, were suffering from the
same sweating/shivering syndrome. It was not cholera, though
as the city was a mammoth laboratory of disease it might well
have been, but an odd kind of flood 'flu which everyone seemed
to catch, and stayed with me, more or less, for two months.
Despite this wherever one went Florentines were silently digging. When Bargellini gave me a list of emergency materials
required he put shovels and water pumps at the top, above
water, food and blankets. Trying to get a message to London
was evidently hopeless. Bargellini had made contact with Rome
once in four days on an army link that had broken down after
fifty seconds, and not one of Florence's thirty thousand telephones were working. The mayor mentioned, with mild wonder,
that the city engineer had said at least fifty million cubic
metres of water had erupted through the city, often flowing at
over forty miles an hour, in less than a day. I earnestly treasured
this statistic for so few were available; all of the mayor's records
had been destroyed, and there was no one way of telling how
many Florentines had been born since the flood, let alone how
many had died. A venerable stable boy who was standing forlornly in the Piazza della Repubblica added a figure so precise
it suggested horses were more highly regarded than people. In
the Ippodroma delle Cascine one hundred and fifty thorough-
breds had been drowned though they had saved the famous
sprinter *Steno*, he informed me. The troops were presently burning the petrol soaked cadavers if I felt like watching. Personally
he had preferred to go for a walk through the mud, and I agreed
with him.

When I finally made contact with London from the hill town

of Pistoia, forty miles away via winding side roads, my erudite and aesthetic colleagues babbled, lunatically as it seemed at the time, of art treasures. What, they demanded, has become of Pisano's bronze doors on the Baptistery; to the friezes of Ghiberti; to Cimabue's crucifix, recently moved, they recalled, to the Santa Croce Museum (with disastrous consequences); to Michelangelo's sculptures in the Bargello; to the musical instruments in the Museo Bardini? They seemed irritated when I in turn told them about old people dying of shock and cold, and perhaps even of thirst, in those tiny streets behind the Piazza della Croce, still impassable after five days because there was a need for water pumps, and shovels, not to mention the bulldozers these comic, undirected troops had so signally failed to provide. Two days later the City Council decided they would do a better job looking after their own, and wisely took over from the dispirited soldiery, most of whom had arrived unprovided with field rations, and were lining up with flood victims – forty thousand were homeless, Bargellini said that weekend – at the Red Cross soup kitchens beneath the reproduction of the Michelangelo David outside the Signoria. Of course, they were anyway half right in London, insofar as old women are infinitely replaceable, while Cimabue crucifixes happen only once every five hundred years. It simply did not look that way at the time. Probably I had been infected by the collective paranoia of the Florentines, except that paranoia is an irrational belief that one is being persecuted, while to believe that Florence was *not* being persecuted when one looked at that city five days after the water had receded seemed, and still seems for that matter, to have been the crazy response. Still, another two days and the worst was over, though the smell of mud laced with naphtha – widely used for central heating systems that had exploded under pressure – clung for many a long week.

Visitors started coming in, among them Edward Moore Kennedy, the Junior Senator for Massachusetts, who arrived by private helicopter and whose stay was brief. He was there to publicize a generous gift from a foundation set up to commemorate his elder brother, and he began by posing for five cold photographers beside the frowning David reproduction.

He then gave a press conference in the United States Consulate, and seemed distressed it was so sparsely attended. His remarks, though simple enough, required translation, and I found myself interpreting them to a group of haggard and finally incredulous local journalists. This was at a period when Chappaquiddick was a community whose celebrity stretched no further than its own inhabitants, but none the less he made a poor impression. It seemed that if the Kennedys could pay to charter their own helicopter, they might have been able to afford someone to brief the great man, or even buy a map. For the Senator, who referred to Massachusetts in virtually every sentence, was under the impression that Florence, like his native fief, was a seaboard community. This, Kennedy said, was why Massachusetts and he as its representative understood what the Florentines were suffering with such passionate sympathy.

Mildly, I pointed out that despite appearances to the contrary, Florence was not by the sea, and that it might be better to amend this section of his statement to remove ambiguity, or even offence. The Senator, who like everyone else was suffering from a heavy cold, snapped at me to get on and do the interpreting as it was. I did as I was told, to first the confusion and later the fury of my Italian colleagues. Here was planted a germ of scepticism about the clan Kennedy which I was to remember a couple of years later when hearing Robert Kennedy's views about such subjects as winning the black vote while simultaneously presenting what his aides called 'a hard on Welfare posture'. Still, I suppose Florence got the Kennedy cash, and they needed it too badly to afford to be oversensitive about its provenance.

Florence found a lot of foul weather friends and aid started arriving from the most unlikely places, including Aberfan, Moscow and Tel-Aviv. Even the Italian Government finally decided it was a disaster zone, and various politicians from the capital arrived on inspection tours during which they were booed by the people queuing for hand-outs of emergency supplies, and were, given the circumstances, lucky not to be lynched. My friend Phillip Knightley came in from London, which gave us enough breathing space for him to visit the hydro-electric dams of Levane and La Penna, thirty-five miles up river, south of Florence. Interviews there, and others in Florence, proved that the city officials were warned of the impending flood eight hours before it happened, and that even after the disaster, dam gates had remained open pumping more water into the city during the period that the flood was at its height, and even for three days afterwards. The city administration took no emergency measures during their eight hour warning period, and warned no public services, though somehow or other the goldsmiths on the thirteenth-century Ponte Vecchio were tipped the word, and appeared to clear out with their stock hours before the flood waters burst over the top of the bridge. But this was simply a routine story of inefficiency and corruption, which might have happened anywhere in Italy.

So Italians, except of course Florentines and others in the north left standing on the roof wondering whether the rising water would stop below the guttering, reacted with little enthusiasm, with the inimitable Italian *dolce fa niente*. Floods were a bore: floods had happened every year since defoliation became serious. If you were crazy enough to live on a river. . . .

In Nairobi once I had met an Italian from Bologna who devoted just over ten months each year to wandering round the world's most agreeable places. He financed this expensive mode of life by hiring out amphibious vehicles at ridiculous prices during the floods that came every year, the floods the authorities always affected to treat as a complete surprise – an amazing aberration on the part of God, which no one could be expected to foresee. Hence no preparations.

'It is painful,' said the Italian with the White Highlands tan. 'But every winter between October 24 and December 7 I have to be in Northern Italy. Ah, the exigencies of commerce . . .'

Never had Scott Fitzgerald's remark that money is like a fin seemed more appropriate.

There was a furore, a tardy one, when the Italian Left finally caught on to the story, *our* story, the one Knightley had picked up in Levane. But they were only interested in Florence as an excuse for castigating the Government. The city itself sank, almost unnoticed, beneath the political polemic.

It was essentially an international story because Florence, like Jerusalem and Paris, is one of the cities that belong to the world. A lot of Scandinavian and American hippies showed up spontaneously and worked hard (hippie popularity, I noticed, was shortlived, and two years later the police were harassing the long-hairs lying around the Ponte Vecchio as fiercely as ever). An English university student arrived in a battered jeep with a water pump in the back. He had been worried, he told me, about Cimabue (with good cause).

He had come intuitively, and so had most of the hippies. The inadequacy, and lateness, of the media reaction may have been a positive help. Starving Biafran kids, Anatolian earthquake victims, the raped women of Bangla Desh – once processed by television they lose their reality and turn into plastic background noise. The constant pressure of events and their indifferent but heavyweight coverage – brilliantly christened 'Newzak' by Malcolm Muggeridge – often promotes no more than indifference. Real battle scenes never look as dramatic as those staged with smoke-bombs and tomato ketchup. During the India/Pakistan conflict I was travelling and within a week heard people in France, England and Australia react to harrowing television shots of refugees in almost identical terms. 'Hopeless people,' they said in effect. 'If they want to kill each other let them get on with it.'

In Europe anyhow, charity is now widely regarded as the government's responsibility – a consequence of welfare socialism. The idea that good works are a kind of spiritual debenture stock, guaranteed to yield a cast iron twelve per cent in heaven, has long been dead. In America this does not hold true. Apart from being naturally generous – and conscious of tax deductions – they have become so used to picking up everyone else's tab for so long that it has become almost reflexive, even if congressmen bitch periodically. (There is no more ironic sight available to modern man than the 'grunts' in Viet-Nam cutting a poker pot all through the night to help 'this Gook kid' suffering from third degree burns their buddies in the sky have inflicted.)

Anyway we had done our best. A full team had moved in,

including Colin Simpson, who knew the location of every *chef d'oeuvre* within five miles of the Uffizi, and the superb international photographer, Romano Cagnoni, who had spent his youth in Tuscany. (He remarked, while photographing some maltreated frescoes, that at eighteen he had persuaded a girl to join him in this very church for a joint prayer to God and the Virgin Mary: the idea was to get permission for them to go to bed with each other.) *The Sunday Times* had launched an appeal fund with great success and we were going to rush out a special colour magazine. On the final day I went to the British Consulate on the Lung'arno Corsini to say goodbye to the people there, including a brilliant doctor from the Treasury in London, who had done so much to help Florence, and also myself.

Outside was the Whisky Ambassador on his way to BEA in the via Tornabuoni, the most beautiful airline office in the world. Here, it emerged, he had a cache of, naturally, whisky. And what was more, some Highland seismograph must have been operating in his mind when he had left it – instead of dumping the crate, logically, in the cellars, it was well above the flood line on the third floor.

Even the Italian predilection for pretty girls and Scotch had not been strong enough to survive the flooding. They had been forced to postpone the beauty contests: Signorina Scotch remained, as yet, uncrowned. At this stage the city was still highly inaccessible: HE had obviously endured a rough journey over land and water, his usually impeccable suit and shoes were wet and muddy.

'What on earth are you doing here? There has to be an easier way of getting a drink than this.'

His Excellency reverently poured a rare malt Scotch which I had selected from his cornucopian crate.

'I like this town,' he said finally. 'And I never believe that rubbish on television. I thought I'd see what had really happened.'

'Haven't you been reading my stuff?' I asked, aggrieved.

'Of course, it's much better than the Italian press.' (This was a backhanded compliment if ever I'd had one.)

His Excellency had been a reporter in his time and was as great an expert on, for example, the Mafia, as on Scotch. He was also a sensitive man and nobody's fool. He sensed my irritation, and passed a placatory glass.

'You must have learnt there's no way of knowing, *really* knowing I mean, unless you've seen for yourself,' he said. It was slightly reminiscent of Topolski in Jerusalem.

A bit later, when we had published our magazine and I had been shown the Zefferelli film of the disaster with Richard Burton's plangent, Celtic commentary, I reflected that the Whisky Ambassador had been right. Zefferelli and Burton had done an honest professional job; so had we. Yet neither came within range of describing what the Piazza della Croce had really been like under the searchlights, those silent Florentines queuing, those dead horses.

CHAPTER 9

Prince Philip

♣

'AND how,' they would invariably ask, having established one was English, 'is Her Majesty the Queen?'

At an age when by rights I should have been immersed in Middle English texts or pondering the reiterative imagery in *Paradise Lost* I was more often than not traversing the European continent, my rucksack on my knee. If I learnt anything from these incessant pilgrimages it was that drivers seldom offer lifts out of disinterested altruism. Generally they wish either to demonstrate their Fangio-like skill behind the wheel, seduce their passenger, or simply chat to pass the time.

'She is in excellent health,' I would always reply, which as my relationship with the lady was, to put it mildly, slender, might perhaps be thought presumptuous. On the other hand most of my angry and less hypocritical contemporaries would probably have answered to the effect that they neither knew nor cared, though it would be nice to think she had fallen down one of those bloody coalmines she was everlastingly inaugurating.

Anti-monarchism in England has never seemed to me any kind of a runner – after all, someone has to receive the Emperor Hirohito. It is a commonly accepted and totally misleading myth that Royals work like dogs at a job they hate. Their programmes are rarely taxing, and nothing makes them happier than to be curtsied to by some dim alderman's wife, or have their limousines surrounded by cheering natives, particularly the latter. Those who point out that the Royal Family's cultural standards are more or less identical to those of, say, the Honorary Secretary of the West Purfleet branch of the Women's Voluntary Service, do not seem to have much of a case either.

In general, the dumber the monarch, the better for all concerned. The last documented example of a constitutional ruler
involving himself in a really serious affair of state was George
VI browbeating Clement Attlee, who should have known better,
into removing Hugh Dalton from his provisional post as Foreign
Secretary to bring in Ernest Bevin as a substitute. The latter knew
nothing of any country except his own, and never developed.

The King's objection to Dalton appears to have been
based on the fact that his father had been Canon of St
George's Chapel Windsor, and he took it as a calculated
insult to the Royal Family that the son of so impeccably respectable a figure should have called himself a socialist. Better by
far if George VI had concentrated on his passionate interest in
military uniforms and decorations – a characteristically Royal
and entirely wholesome preoccupation.

My pro-monarchist feelings have progressed unabated since
the age of eight when I was taken to Wembley Stadium to wit-
ness one of those curious entertainments where rival regiments
compete to see who can manhandle pieces of obsolescent field
artillery over artificial obstacles in the fastest time, and normally
dignified horses are made to perform equine dance steps to the
accompaniment of military bands. There are always lots of
kilts and drums too. It is the kind of occasion eight-year-old boys
and Royalty find entrancing. This all took place in the days
when policemen were friendly neighbourhood bobbies, not
fascist pigs, and on our way to the exit we found a double line
of them looking unusually smart. Two enormous sergeants, acting in unison and speaking out of the side of their mouths,
shoved me forward so I was wedged between them.

'You stick there, son, and keep quiet, and you'll see something you'll never forget,' one hissed conspiratorially.

He was absolutely right. In due course two young girls in
military uniform appeared, and solemnly shook hands with the
waiting guard of honour. Princess Margaret Rose, as she was
then called, not only looked like her namesake, but smelt
rose-like too. Princess Elizabeth, a burlier, more wooden figure,
made a slighter impression, but the complexions of both girls
staggered me. It was widely publicized during the war that the

King, wishing to share the austerities of his people, insisted that
the Palace menus should feature only the same statutory rations
as those consumed by his subjects in the Old Kent Road or the
Gorbals, a diet which would now be unacceptable to an unemployed garbage collector. Accordingly, the post-war British
were a pasty-faced, spotty, sickly looking lot. Either one egg and
a pint of milk weekly changed their dietetic effects startlingly
in the rarefied atmosphere of Buckingham Palace, or those
princesses' skins were a triumph of cosmetic art.

My second Royal encounter, some fifteen years later in the
North of England, was equally satisfactory. My professional
duties for the *Manchester Guardian*, as it then was, had involved
an appearance at Bolton Road Safety Week, which the Queen
Mother was inaugurating. My task was undemanding and having noted details of the Royal lady's peculiar green dress with
sleeves that appeared to have been inflated with a bicycle pump,
and distinctly Sitwellian hat, I strolled contentedly off in search
of the refreshment tent and a telephone. I was so deep in the
haze of enveloping boredom endemic to provincial newspaper
reporting that quite unconsciously I evidently stepped over a
rope barrier. To my horror I found myself about five yards
directly in front of the Royal guest, who was floating along on
her balloon sleeves some way ahead of an obsequious posse of
local dignitaries, and their wives, doubtless well-leavened with
bodyguards. God alone knows who she imagined this bizarre
young man could be – assassin? Plain-clothes detective in disguise? (If so it would have been one of the most imaginative
disguises ever achieved by that invariably uninventive branch
of the police). The *Guardian* has never been a dressy newspaper,
and though I was wearing what I regarded as my formal attire,
which meant I had a tie on, the rest of my outfit had been
purchased in bulk some years earlier from my Cambridge tailor,
Jack Carter, who ran a secondhand clothing establishment in
Portugal Place within convenient distance of St John's. I
remember his assuring me with pride that the scuffed chukka
boots with odd laces that adorned my feet had once been the
property of Lord Rothschild, no less.

Anyway it takes more than an incident like this to throw a

real pro and the Queen Mother, without missing a stride, bestowed on me a smile of radiant warmth, as if she had un-expectedly stumbled across a dear friend for whose company she had been pining during a prolonged separation. Perhaps she recognized the Rothschild boots.

Two strikes to Royalty.

A periodic London chore was to listen to the Duke of Edinburgh exhorting gatherings of industrialists about the need to boost exports, think technologically, galvanize their workers, and toil. The industrialists would applaud vigorously and then drift companionably off to discuss methods of galvanizing their workers at the Caprice or the Mirabelle. These pep-talks gener-ally took place in the already over-congested environs of West-minster, and the streets surrounding the chosen *venue* were invariably so jammed with chauffeur-driven Rolls-Royces that it was seldom possible to get within half a mile in a humble taxi. This was annoying when it rained, which was often, and had I been set a word-assocation test triggered by 'Prince Philip' my response would almost certainly have been 'wet'. This implied no criticism of the Duke himself; it was simply that most of the time I heard his speeches – or speech really, as they were all remarkably similar – I would be aware of water running down my collar.

The Prince's relentlessly down-to-earth style was dull, but the industrialists who were his target seemed happy with it. His predecessor Albert, after all, had adeptly – though certainly with conscious guile – reflected an epoch of earnest hypocrisy by being more earnest and hypocritical than the best of them. (On the whole I prefer him, as it seems highly unlikely Philip will leave a memorial to delight and amuse Londoners one hundred years hence.) Our contemporary Prince, bustling with technological mateyness, is following the same tradition, and the years he spent at Gordonstoun, a school which possesses an unparalleled capacity for turning out perpetual school-boys, have obviously also left their mark. (I shall never forget Philip's cousin, the ex-King Constantine of Greece and another *alumnus* of this strange institution, slouching at dawn across the tarmac on Rome airport, after the failure of a *coup* so risible that it had been aborted by a handful of semi-literate peasants' sons. Constantine was firmly holding on to an officer's swagger stick, a kind of sceptre-substitute I suppose, and looking irresistibly like a boy who had just been dropped from the House fives team.)

If in England the Prince was no more than a mild but perfectly acceptable bore, once outside the saloon bar *ambience* of his adopted country there seemed evidence of a distinct deterioration in his personality and behaviour. Peripherally connected with a couple of foreign Royal progresses I observed that his manners contrasted unfavourably with the impeccable, if waxen style favoured by the Queen. Occasional conversations with those whose *métier* it is to describe how Her Majesty's latest Hartnell creation brought ecstatic smiles to black faces revealed a distinct coolness on the subject of the Prince Consort. An Australian photographer, with Antipodean bluntness, assured me his ambition was to impale the Duke on a stick introduced after the New Guinea fashion for porkers.

Early in December 1966 I was innocently occupied in a Paris hotel bedroom attempting to make sense of a work called *Literature and Philosophy*. This was not an attempt to mortify the spirit, but as preparation for interviewing the author, Monsieur Jean-Paul Sartre. They called me from London. The message was that an exclusive interview, one of the few ever, had been arranged with King Hassan of Morocco, and that I was to go there at once.

'Where exactly?'

'Morocco, of course,' said the man in London irritably. 'You must know where his nibs hangs out.'

I suspected he had only the dimmest idea of Morocco's geographical location, and had almost certainly lost the scrap of paper on which his overworked secretary had noted the *venue*.

'You mean Casablanca, I suppose?' This was obviously not a name he recalled. There was a silence.

'Marrakesh possibly? Or Fez?' More silence. He had suffered enough.

'It must be Rabat,' I said kindly.

'Of course, *that's* it,' said the man in London triumphantly. And he added I was to tie up with a very fashionable young London photographer, who was already on his way, in a hotel called 'the Tower or something'.

'You know I'm supposed to be seeing Sartre all day tomorrow? And Simone de Beauvoir?'

'Bugger Sartre. Tell him you'll do him on the way back. And there's another good Morocco story – the Duke of bloody Edinburgh's going to be there.'

Now Sartre is not like that, not like that at all. He was unlikely to be pleased by the news that an Anglo-Saxon capitalist newspaper reckoned he was less interesting than an anachronistic feudal monarch of fascist tendencies. Nor was he. Sartre has his own feudal aspect and it had taken two months of negotiations with secretaries, editors, collaborators and disciples to fix the rendezvous in the first place.

Still, King Hassan would certainly be more amusing. I knew little about the man but had always associated him with Emperor Seth of Azania in Evelyn Waugh's classic *Black Mischief*, the one who running short of ready cash had printed his own banknotes featuring a portrait of himself in the robes of an Oxford BA wearing a top hat. I recalled that when the French had decided to exile his father, King Abdullah, and sent a frigate to Casablanca to collect him, the old boy had turned up with sixty concubines. I had seen photographs of the son, a stiff, cocky looking man not unlike Hussein of Jordan, though Frenchified in the same kind of way as his Arab brother was Anglo-Saxon: while the one had done a stint at Sandhurst I supposed the other had studied at St Cyr. The Duke of Edinburgh's role was a mystery – perhaps he was going to deliver a speech about British exports.

The hotel in question turned out to be called The Tower of Hassan, an exotic establishment built in Hilton Moorish. I arrived very late, and was greeted by a large staff of porters in Hollywood Arab dress. Colourful though they were there was no doubt that my photographer, who was neurotically pacing the lobby, upstaged them all. Apart from his shoulder length hair, a rarity in those days, he wore patched blue Levis and a magenta shirt with a ruff down the front. This fashionable embellishment was partly concealed by the three Leicas hanging round his neck; he probably took them to bed with him. His twitches I recognized at once, and though he was exclusively a coca-cola and pot man they bore a striking resemblance to alcoholic withdrawal symptoms. His daily retainer was probably about the same as my weekly wages but he was twitching because so far he had taken no pictures, and he was worried there might be a better job going somewhere else. He greeted me with relief, though without warmth.

Arriving early he had immediately 'phoned the Royal Palace to let the King know he was ready and waiting; at the least he had expected a dinner invitation. He had been handicapped as he spoke not a word of French, nor indeed of any language except Mile End Road cockney, leavened with hippie slang he had acquired photographing starlets. The call had not been a success.

'Some frog berk gave me the right run around,' he said. There were no messages at the desk so I gave him some *kif* purchased from the hall porter at an exorbitant price and went to bed, hoping for better things in the morning.

In the next few days I got to know virtually everyone of importance in the capital from the Foreign Secretary to the Grand Vizier to the man who dispensed coffee in the Palace's VIP waiting-room, one of about a dozen. Everyone, that is, except the King. London, as usual, was little help. The famous interview, it emerged, had been 'fixed' because someone had met a man at a dinner party who owned the public relations company employed by the Moroccan Government. All I had to do was mention his name; it was perfectly straightforward. I mentioned it several scores of times and in return received coffee, bland smiles, visiting cards, invitations to various receptions, and on one occasion – from the Minister of Tourism – a handsome Morocco leather writing-case embossed in gold with 'Or 22 Carats' written on it, in case anyone was in doubt.

The photographer held out on *kif* and belly-dancers for five days, which was well above par for the course, and then quit after an obscene telephone call to London. He was anxious about the proximity of Christmas, which he always spent with his mum.

I sent a cable full of words like 'disaster', and added a request for three hundred pounds. I then packed my bags, booked a Paris flight on Air France, and sat back waiting for orders to pull out. Unlike my photographer friend it was a matter of some indifference to me where I celebrated the Christmas festival, as long as neither London nor Rabat was on the list. To my astonishment after a twenty-four-hour silence I receive instructions 'to stay for the Duke'. That meant three more days at least.

I passed them largely with an American fellow resident of the Tower, a tough-looking man who spent most of his time wearing a kind of uniform consisting of impeccably cut riding breeches and a monogrammed Sulka shirt. At first I had taken him for a male model, the kind who advertise virile products like pipe tobacco and sports cars (he actually owned a white Maserati) but he was in fact reputed to be either an international gigolo or a CIA agent. It was hard to imagine why he had selected Rabat in December to pursue either of these demanding occupations.

When I discreetly enquired he replied vaguely that he was 'into minerals' – a fashion-conscious figure he liked to be one jump ahead with his idioms. I enjoyed touring around in the car but conversation languished, largely because of the Christian name shorthand of the rich. I was constantly confused trying to work out who all the 'Blueys', 'Chucks', 'Fionas' and 'Clems' actually were. He knew everyone in the world with the exception, he admitted rather shamefacedly, of the King. But he *was* going to play polo with the Duke of Edinburgh.

The American wanted to 'check out' the polo terrain so we went down and were startled to find the ground occupied by Moroccan troops in roughly battalion strength. They were on their knees, fanned out across the field at two-yard intervals, a plastic bucket between each pair of soldiers. Their task, it transpired, was to root out dandelions, weeds, tufts of wort grass and any other offending vegetation which might have caused HRH to leave with a poor impression of Moroccan polo grounds. Another battalion, we discovered, had been trucked down to Marrakesh, also on the Royal agenda, to do a similar job on the golf course there, should HRH take it into his head to have a swing with a mashie. More troops were hastily erecting several marquees, and a very fragile-looking grandstand; I made a mental note to keep well away from it.

'You got to hand it to these quaint old régimes,' said my friend, obscurely pleased. 'Looks like they've detailed the whole goddam army on gardening fatigues.'

Despite these elaborately respectful preparations HRH looked decidedly sullen when his visit finally began. As it was 'unofficial' his host was Moulay Hassan, one of the Royal princes, a lanky youth whose long black hair shone with pomade and who sported a Ronald Colman moustache. He bore a striking resemblance to the South American educated heir of a German arms manufacturer who had acquired something of a local reputation at Cambridge on account of his *penchant* for throwing his riding boots at passing porters. Moulay Hassan was also an equestrian buff: he was to captain the team opposing the Duke's. The King, as Head of State, was barred by protocol from receiving the Duke, publicly anyway. For him it was the Queen or nothing. I was beginning to wonder whether the man had been assassinated years before and the fact concealed from his devoted subjects. He was apparently invisible.

The morning tour of the capital was dull enough to excuse HRH's expression of unendurable *ennui*: none of the locals paid him even the scantiest attention. Rabat's main claim to distinction is the Tower of Hassan, the real one not the hotel, and through some muddle the car I was in arrived there ahead of the royal Rolls. To kill time I mounted the endlessly winding internal corridor which eventually leads to the top. Unless someone shot the Duke, an eventuality which given the profound indifference his presence had evoked was highly unlikely, there was nothing worth writing, not even a paragraph. On the flat top of the tower, which is surrounded by a low wall, two Moroccan

couples with about a dozen children between them were enjoying an *al fresco* picnic. The children were playing a Moroccan
version of tag, and the atmosphere was refreshingly wholesome.
A bevy of local security men arrived and after politely checking
my credentials lit cigarettes; one of them started to play with the
children. Perched on the edge of the wall one could see the white
minarets, rectangular apartment blocks and grand diplomatic
villas which in haphazard concert combine to give Rabat so
insubstantial, provisional an appearance. Like Ankara, though
less squalid, the place looks as though they ran it up overnight,
and are already making preparations to demolish the whole
lot and start again. With any luck Monday night would see
me in Paris.

'What the hell are those kids playing at? And get that bloody
man out of the way.'

The voice, a very loud one, interrupted the calm. O God,
I thought, one of those beefy Scotland Yard security people
is throwing his weight around, quite unnecessarily too. Why
can't he realize he's in someone else's country? It was unusual
because the officers chosen for these trips, unlike their French
and American counterparts, are invariably the soul of modesty
and discretion. I eased myself off the wall and turned round
to see what was happening.

'Hey you. Didn't you hear what I said? You're blocking my
bloody view.'

It was no crude detective inspector but the Duke himself,
and a Duke apparently near apoplectic with rage. The Moroccans, who looked understandably bewildered, and myself,
appeared to be his targets.

The use of the personal pronoun 'my' was particularly reveal-
ing and, questions of ownership apart, it would have taken a
group of perhaps fifty people strategically spread out to have
any chance of restricting that 360 degree panorama. If ever
there was a case for punching someone on the nose this was it.
What, I wondered, was the statutory penalty for thumping a
Duke? Apart from the limiting factor that he was considerably
larger than me there was also probably a fair chance of getting
shot by some trigger-happy bodyguard: reluctantly I discarded

the fantasy and joined the Moroccans in descending the Tower.

The afternoon's polo, by comparison anyway, was a great success. The cream of Rabat society was present wearing the previous year's Paris fashions, the grandstand failed to collapse, and the Duke's side – with, it seemed to my untutored eye, a certain amount of diplomatic assistance – emerged victorious. Moulay Hassan presented him with a silver cup, and Rabat society applauded. HRH's ponies had all been highly recalcitrant, and he had been very tough with them, cursing loudly all the time. This had created a highly favourable impression on the High Society spectators, prominent among whom was General Oufkir, the government security chief. Not long afterwards a Paris court, which I attended, convicted the general *in absentia* for his organizing role in the notorious kidnapping of the Moroccan opposition leader, Ben Barka, from the pavement outside Brasserie Lipp on the Boulevard St Germain. Several defendants testified that before he was finally murdered Ben Barka had been tortured. The Moroccans adore children but when it comes to other animals, human or otherwise, they are not a sentimental people. I asked my sweating American friend for his professional opinion of the Duke's performance. 'The guy's a real bastard with a horse,' he said.

The British Embassy reception held to celebrate the Royal arrival began on an unexpectedly up-beat note. A very young Wykehamist presented me at random to the nearest person in sight. She was a strikingly attractive and intelligent woman who turned out to be the Pakistani ambassadress. When two young girls in saris who were so spectacularly beautiful that I took them for visiting film stars appeared at her elbow she smiled indulgently.

'These are my daughters who say Rabat is boring. Will you look after them for me while I circulate?'

I could have embraced all three of them. Though I had smoked no *kif* for some days my impression as I led them hastily to one of the several alcoves that gave off the main drawing-room, was of floating about three feet above the ground. We settled down with a bottle of champagne on a bench seat by a bay window, and they drank heartily, indeed with a certain midnight-feast-in-the-dorm gusto. They were certainly bored and I had the strong impression that they were ready to try anything that might inject a bit of excitement into life. My own mood was precisely similiar.

The elder one, aged nineteen, was at a language school in Oxford; the younger, only seventeen, attended what she called 'a prissy finishing school in an awful village miles from Geneva'. They were both flawless with deep almond eyes, and sulky expressions which I noted happily were beginning to clear a bit. They each talked bitterly of chaperones – my God, I thought, were I responsible for guarding the virginity of either of these luminous delinquents, I wouldn't stop short at twenty-four-hour surveillance.

'A girl I went to school with has just had a baby son, and she's *two years younger than me*,' said the little sister.

'The only men in Rabat are dirty old cabinet ministers, *really* dirty too, or married,' contributed her elder.

'Are you married?' the young one wanted to know.

It was hard to tell whether the champagne was having an aphrodisiac effect on them, or whether they were simply obsessed by sex permanently. It was certainly getting to me, not that artificial stimulants were necessary in this company. They had now moved on to the topic of His Majesty's sex life with an inventive gusto that would have appealed to Havelock Ellis. Each night, they said, he had twenty new girls: I expressed scepticism.

They were quite indignant at hearing His Majesty's capacities doubted.

'We see the girls going past our Embassy every night on their way to the Palace,' they said. 'Of course they're veiled so you can't tell how sexy they are. They put them in a coach – we call it the Passion Waggon.'

'They must do a lot of funny things,' said the senior sister, 'I mean do you think they each wait their turn, or whether, you know, kind of go altogether . . .'

The sanctified descendant of the Prophet probably had his own time-honoured and majestic devices for dealing with quantities of women simultaneously, paraded at company strength if necessary, but as far as I was concerned a mere couple at a time was one too many.

I asked whether they knew any of the men at the reception. The reaction was vehement, as if I had referred to chaperones or some such controversial issue.

'Of course we do,' said the elder one impatiently. 'I told you before, they're all married.'

She had a point. Since those halcyon pre-Burgess and Maclean days bachelors, let alone homosexuals, have tended not to prosper in the Foreign Service: ambitious diplomatists nowadays marry young, and beget children with Old Testament zeal. Few guests at the reception were under forty-five, and of those who were almost all the men either had their wives at their elbow, or wore that glazed, resigned look common to men whose wives are near enough to ensure that neither sexual adventure nor even mild flirtation could conceivably figure in the evening's programme. Bachelors, let alone studs, were at a premium. The fact that I had enjoyed the company of the girls undisturbed for half an hour was a graphic indication of the sexless *ambience*.

The principal object of interest was naturally HRH whose balding, sun-bronzed dome could be seen in the centre of a large group, happily at the far end of the room. The girls had the taste to exhibit total indifference to the Royal guest of honour. They had seen him perform at polo and been unimpressed. Besides it was well-known that he was married.

'Let's leave this dump and go dancing somewhere,' I suggested, pouring the last of the champagne encouragingly.

'Yes, let's,' said the big sister.

'Super,' said the little one, who despite the prison-like existence she claimed to be leading at Oxford had nonetheless picked up plenty of local mannerisms. I explained about my American friend, my *unmarried* American friend, whom I would telephone to join us.

The party was beginning to thin out so I set off, still floating, to track him down. Again almost anywhere else I would never have run the risk of letting that couple out of my sight but I calculated that when I got back they would be sitting precisely where they had been all evening, and almost certainly alone. Perhaps the married men were *frightened* of them. The danger with the American, who was after all a pro, or reputed to be, was that he would take on both daughters with the mother thrown in for good measure.

The agent of *hubris* spoke in a commanding voice I now had no difficulty in recognizing. Nor obviously did the Wykehamist who made a commendable effort to stand to attention while balancing his silver tray littered with bits of smoked salmon on toast.

'That's the man who spoilt my view,' the voice of *hubris* declaimed. 'I want to talk to you,' it added.

For most of the evening a long 'reception line' had snaked round the room, as if the guests were forming up to perform an outmoded dance called the Hokey-cokey, or signing on for the dole. Now every wife who had wished to tell her grandchildren she had curtsied to the Duke of Edinburgh, and that he had complimented her on her dress, had achieved this ambition.

HRH, glass in hand and restive, was looking round for some action and that marine gaze had tragically fallen on me.

Had my reflexes not been dulled by champagne and lust I might have had the wit to feign an epileptic fit, or simply cut and run for it. But an embassy official, a grown-up one with grey hair which smelt of Topper's Eucris, was at my side at once propelling me firmly towards the Presence, a hand resting gently on my elbow. It was the diplomatic equivalent of being frog-marched.

'What's your name?' he hissed in my ear. I told him, and was presented. HRH smiled benignly as he might have done at a sacrificial goat.

'Lots of free champers, eh?' he said heartily. I suspected, rightly, that this was to be his sole concession to polite chit-chat, and mistrusted his opening deeply. It was like being asked if one was quite comfortable while being settled down in the electric chair.

'Excellent,' I said. There the preliminaries ended, and he careered headlong into the subject uppermost on his mind.

'Knew you were a reporter the moment I clapped eyes on you,' he began. 'Can smell 'em a mile off.' His tone was that of those women who melodramatically divine one's zodiacal sign, an act for which they usually like to have an audience. HRH conformed to this pattern, and glanced round to make sure no one had failed to grasp his display of intuition. To my distress I noticed that the group in our general area seemed to be getting bigger.

'I've just made sure the proprietors of three bloody Italian newspapers never get into society again,' continued HRH cheerfully. It seemed a peculariarly inconsequential start, even by Royal conversational standards, but I was dimly aware he had recently been staying with some Italian millionaires, so presumably the country was still on his mind.

'Did you enjoy the polo?' I asked, turning the conversation with what I thought of as considerable diplomatic skill. 'I notice your side won,' I continued ingratiatingly.

The British Ambassador, I noticed, was hovering by the Duke's shoulder looking faintly embarrassed and concerned. *You* should worry.

HRH replied parenthetically, and given the occasion not very graciously, that if I wanted his opinion some of these Arab ponies weren't all they were cracked up to be. But this subject disposed of, he homed back inexorably to his main topic – the iniquity of Italian newspaper proprietors; the filthy lies they published, especially about himself and the Queen; the bloodiness of reporters, and, above all, photographers; and his intention of revenging himself on the lot of them by ensuring, as far as I could make out, that they would be ostracized from whatever he considered to be Italian High Society – a sanction which, it seemed to me, few of them were likely to lose much sleep over, particularly in the case of the photographers.

No Italian photographer has ever received an invitation in his life, except perhaps to his sister's wedding. Nonetheless neither has any Italian photographer ever been prevented from going precisely where he wanted. They simply either bribe or assault anyone who tries to keep them out. It was only too easy to follow the Duke's train of thought and see where a slight broadening of his original thesis was going to lead him. Fleet Street would inevitably soon be mentioned, but for the moment he was still obsessed by the evil Italians.

'Never a moment's peace. Bloody reporters wherever I went, bloody reporters hanging in the trees. You wouldn't believe it – they camped out overnight waiting to get me.'

Wouldn't I just, I thought. The crowd had perceptibly thickened. Those who liked scenes were edging in; those who found them distressing, with the exception of the Ambassador who was hovering wretchedly in the line of duty, were murmuring discreet farewells and moving off. Among this latter group I thought I caught a glimpse of the Pakistani Ambassadress – pray God she didn't take her nymphomaniacal offspring with her.

The Duke, after a pause for effect, was now going again; and his voice had taken on its most resonant British exports, modern technology *timbre*. There was no longer any need for the curious to sidle towards us, as if accidentally: the voice, the authoritative, inimitable tone of the archetypal blimp, carried forty yards with absolute clarity.

'Not that *your* people are much better than the Italians,' he was saying. 'Though of course we organize things better at home. I've seen *you* around before you got in the way today. I suppose you're going to write the same bloody lies as the Italians?'

'I don't even know what lies you're talking about.'

There was, after all, a limit, and he had gone past it, a long way past. The Ambassador was evidently close to a coronary seizure than at any point in a long career. He made a truly pathetic stab at distracting the Duke by suggesting he might like to have a few words with some Moroccan dignitary or another, but was completely ignored.

HRH gave a sceptical snorting noise, an equine kind of noise from the base of the throat. It indicated total disbelief. His reactions were frankly puzzling, because though he had been drinking he was by no means drunk. His next words, which as far as I was concerned were also his last, went some way towards explaining the evil humour that had afflicted him from the moment he had touched down.

'Of course you know. These bloody lies that you people print to make money. These lies about how I'm never with my wife. You know very well. Don't pretend you don't.'

On maturer reflection, alone in my hotel room, I worked out that some of the French *journaux de concierges*, which are fairly similar to their Italian counterparts and had probably followed them, had recently come out with a rash of 'Royal Divorce Imminent' and 'The Lonely Queen' stories. They were based, insofar as they had any basis at all, on the undeniable fact that during a considerable portion of the Queen's pregnancy the Prince had been travelling in foreign parts. There had also been, I recalled, the suggestion that he had been conducting a passionate *affaire* with some Italian aristocrat. Since stories of this kind are the staple of *Ici Paris* and *France-Dimanche* I had no more than glanced idly at the headlines in search of momentary diversion at Orly. Apparently they had really stung him.

Anyway he had earned the right to be told his life story, had earned the right several times over, so I let fly. The style was a fair *pastiche* of the homilies on 'The Integrity of the Press' that presidents of the National Union of Journalists like to deliver at conferences in Clacton or sunny Skegness.

'*My* newspaper,' I began proprietorially, 'doesn't go in for that kind of story. We don't print lies, and we also try to avoid boring our readers as far as possible. Your presence here is of no possible interest to anyone, except perhaps the Hurlingham Polo Club, so I am writing nothing about you at all. As a matter of fact I'm in Morocco doing something quite different. It hasn't got the slightest connection with either you or *Her Majesty*.'

All in all it wasn't too bad for the spur of the moment. I reckoned the 'Her Majesty' was a nice touch; HRH had referred to her throughout as 'my wife', which I dimly suspected was a breach of protocol, or anyway etiquette. It seemed that apart from the contents of the rest of the speech I had also managed to slip in an applied rebuke, a suggestion that he had been lax in observing the strict proprieties which hedge Royalty. The whole blast had gone very well, even if it was not exactly correct to say I was 'doing something quite different'. Strictly speaking I was there doing precisely nothing.

But, minor quibbles aside, it was far too good to risk letting him have the last word, so I curtly inclined my head in a kind of caricature of the way Prussian officers greet their enemies in war movies, and stalked off. Most of the other guests, rightly judging the celebration to be well and truly over, also headed for the exit. Before I got to my car, however, up popped the Wyke-hamist looking ashen and asked me to wait for a while in some ante-chamber. This I did with ill grace. I assumed there were to be threats of complaints to editors and proprietors and possi-bly even more terrible sanctions. All this was bad but it pre-occupied me much less than the whereabouts of the girls, who had vanished completely.

My brief chat with the Ambassador was very different from what I had expected. It turned out to be one of those frothy *soufflés* of obliquity, understatement and euphemism so dear to the Foreign Office heart. These are not as outsiders often think, deliberate parodies of Bertie Wooster, but a highly sophisticated linguistic structure elaborately designed to exclude the possi-bility of anyone making a statement sufficiently concrete for it to be cited later. (There are exceptions to this rule, such as Declarations of War, but they are rare.) But his drift was clear, and we parted cordially. He was a decent man, and HRH had no right to let him in for a situation like that.

I have never, to put it mildly, set myself up as a model of urbane good behaviour, and on not a few occasions have found myself sheepishly apologizing to an Ambassador for some excess or another. Later, alone, smoking *kif* in a forlorn attempt to boost my low spirits, I reflected that at least one notable first had emerged from the *débâcle*. At last an ambassador had apologized to *me*. But I needed more than that, much more, to make up for those lovely, irrecuperable girls.

CHAPTER 10

Kevin

♣

TWENTY minutes after dawn and already it was so humid my shirt stuck to my back like a hot compress. Everyone grouped sleepily on the Bangkok military airport looked unhappy. Most of us habitually wore that rumpled look of people who spend too much of their lives in jet planes, but on top of this there was a special dawn twitchiness peculiar to those who have hangovers and have spent the night in a whorehouse. Only 'Sarsparilla', an Italian journalist famed for his good nature and crazed behaviour, looked *chic* as always, and only Kevin, the new boy, looked as though his unhappiness was so acute that at any moment he would dissolve into sobs.

Under normal circumstances I would have paid Kevin more attention, and might even have divined that he was going to be very important. As it was I had watched his ridiculous, disorganized arrival with numb detachment. His green Chevrolet taxi had arrived on the tarmac about an hour late, not that it mattered. Out of it fell Kevin, a tall near-hysterical boy who looked about nineteen but turned out to be twenty-seven. He was loaded down with cheap suitcases, a portable typewriter, a pile of newspapers, and a lot of cameras slung like bandoliers across his shoulders. He wore a synthetic 'heather mixture' tweed suit, which now looked as if it had been tailored out of blotting paper. He was obviously a compatriot, the only one there; equally obviously he had only the faintest idea of what he was doing. Sarsie, whose real name was almost indistinguishable from 'Sarsparilla', immediately established that Kevin represented a London news agency, and had started his Viet-Nam assignment as he was to continue it – by making an absurd mistake. Kevin had ordered his cab to the civilian airport fifteen miles out of town instead of the US military base.

I went with the others to interrogate a Negro master sergeant, whose news was both good and bad. The Têt offensive had started four days earlier but there was still heavy fighting, or so our sergeant said, around Tân Son Nhut airport in Saigon. Landing there, he reckoned, was sure to be dangerous. The VC were laying down mortar and rocket fire on the main strip. My colleagues formally cursed this news in various languages but became noticeably perkier, like hounds picking up a faint scent. They had come from Paris, Rome, the Middle East and, in one eccentric case, Kansas City, to cover the battle. All of them like myself, had probably spent a large proportion of their interminable journeys worrying that by the time they reached Saigon the action would be over. It was an inglorious reaction, a typical example of *deformation professionelle*.

Except for Kevin I knew them all. Bill O'Reilly, who worked for a chain of radio stations in the mid-west, I had last seen during the war in Israel. He was a native of Chicago, given to periodic melancholy and dipsomania. Georges Mènager of *Paris-Match* had been in Israel too. His greeting that morning had been a laconic '*merde alors*', accompanied by a mock salute towards the battered brim of his Australian bush hat. Jean-François Chauvel of *Le Figaro* was as usual accompanied by his exquisite blonde wife, a *pied noir* he had met during the battle of Algiers. Geneviève wore a kind of caricature of a parachute jump suit which Cardin had tailored for her. 'Salut,' I had said, kissing her hand, which had staggered the master sergeant, unaccustomed to these Parisian manners. 'Georges says "*Merde alors*".'

'*Salut*,' Jean-Francois had replied, working on his pipe. 'Georges is absolutely right.'

He spoke the kind of English one might expect from a man whose father had been French Ambassador in London. Chauvel looked more like a tough Brigade General than a journalist, an impression heightened in a melodramatic Hollywood kind of way by the neat bullet hole in the lobe of his right ear. He wore a combat outfit that had come from Tû Do, the high-class whorehouse and parliamentary section of Saigon which under the French had been called rue Catinat. Next to the Chauvels, Kevin, counting his suitcases worriedly, looked like an unmade bed.

Inevitably, Sarsie soon started giving him advice, and odd sentences drifted through. 'Ten baht is a huge tip . . . Don Muang is only for civilian flights . . . when you get to Da Nang ask for Mickie Mouth – she does the best blow job in South-East Asia. Just say you're a friend of Sarsie.'

Probably Sarsie, with his silk suit and Via Veneto shoes, was the first friendly person whom Kevin had met since he had confusedly found himself on the Bangkok flight from London. The little Italian had been everywhere and was an ideal journalist insofar as his dominant pleasure was transmitting information. His equivalent in the London suburbs would have known all the train timetables by heart, and the 'phone number of a man who could get colour TV sets below cost price. Here, in the course of an interminable sweaty morning, he imparted very different lore to the grateful and bewildered Kevin – how to get Vietnamese piastres at three times the official rate; where to buy parachute boots; how to exploit the American information chief's weakness for banging his fist on the table when raising a hundred dollars on a pair of deuces; where to get combat uniforms tailored. . . . Lunch time came; still no flight – Sarsie showed Kevin how to use chop-sticks, and told him the probably apocryphal tale of the Alsatian tracker dogs donated by the British to the ARVN (South Vietnamese regulars), and immediately consumed, garnished with Cantonese rice, by the delighted soldiery unused to such gastronomic treats. By this time I had developed crippling migraine and was only slightly relieved when Bill O'Reilly broached one of his twin water canteens, the one he kept primed with white Bacardi rum. In the afternoon some bureaucrat decided we all needed additional cholera and plague shots under a new regulation from Saigon. They took us protesting in a coach to the medical centre where we met a US Medical Corps private called Di Felici who filled us all with terror. This monster, who wore a white smock and carried a needle, had a Caliban forehead with such hair as he had starting directly above the eyebrows. Most of Di Felici's skull had in fact been shaved, except for a straggly red and vaguely pubic frizz on the very top. He was scowling as we lined up for his services, and several intrepid war correspondents at the front of the line started to edge back. I moved forward to take their places assuming that if there was only going to be one needle, which looked about Di Felici's speed, shot number one was going to hurt a lot less than shot number ten. Sarsie, also frightened tried melting Di Felici's heart with a flood of nervous Sicilian.

There had been a boy called Di Felici – he pronounced the 'c' Sicilian style, as 'sh' shush – in his class at school in Palermo, said Sarsie. It was a fine old Sicilian name. I understood about half of it which, judging by Di Felici's deepening scowl, was fifty per cent more than him. Sarsie tried again in English, this time to some effect. Di Felici started to shout in anger.

'Fuck Sicily,' he said. 'You're full of crap. I'm American – you're trying to say I'm some kind of a wop?'

He wielded his needle like an ice-pick, and when the big C-130 left, an hour before dusk, we were all nursing sore arms. There were two platoons of the First Air Cav aboard, recalled from forty-eight hour 'R&R' – rest and recuperation – leave passes in Bangkok. Over half were still drunk and the humidity brought out pearls of alcohol sweat on their faces. They were unnaturally silent and it was impossible to tell whether they were worried about the fighting in the forty-eight hours ahead, or the doses of clap they had certainly contracted during the forty-eight hours that had just passed.

Kevin sat next to me and introduced himself. He was slow and nice and clumsy in his distress – I remember thinking that though he told me he came from East Anglia where his father was a schoolteacher he had preserved something of that passive almost cow-like quality you sometimes meet in Irish peasants. Probably this country boy impression, and perhaps even his name, had come down to him from a grandfather in Tipperary or County Mayo. He was made for reassuring, unchallenging countryside, fields that were green and predictable, unlike those ahead. He was still, as far as I could gather above the engine noise, at the Street of Adventure stage of journalism. His only previous visit abroad had been to Germany, where he had a girl friend. He spoke no languages, and had only been two years in London since leaving his local paper. The agency had selected him, he explained modestly, because the more senior men were married and reluctant to go. Bright blokes, I thought, and God help Kevin. God help us all for that matter.

Soon he was desperately sick, crouched moaning over a plastic bag. The Flight Master had distributed pellets of wax to put in our ears, and Kevin, thinking it was some kind of American delicacy like bubble-gum, had chewed on it a while before discovering his error. His arm hurt from Di Felici's attentions, and the Bangkok food was catching up with a stomach brought up on fish and chips. And, of course, like everyone else, he was scared. We circled the huge airport which looked like an inferno. I counted six different fires, probably petrol dumps, with black suffocating smoke beneath the orange flames. As we landed the first of the night's huge sodium flares started to float down towards the perimeter so the tangles of barbed wire took on the colour of egg yolks. I helped Kevin with his chaotic luggage and lost him as he hurried across the tarmac asking an ARVN soldier for '*la toilette*' in East Anglian French.

Saigon was horrible under its pall of smoke, the haze of burning buildings and simmering garbage. This was the beginning of a season of horror, of spilled bowels and amputated limbs and terminal screams. In the market the next day buying gear I met Kevin in search of a photographer for his accreditation identity pictures. Going back we saw a respectable middle class lady, exquisite in her *ao-dai*, the elegant half-skirt, half-trouser garment that makes Vietnamese women look like floating cirrus, screaming in rage because a young boy had been injured by a grenade outside her front door. He was demonstrating his ill-breeding by pumping the last of his arterial blood over her immaculately sandstoned steps. Finally, he had the good taste to stop bleeding and die. An American ambulance team picked up his gutted body and shoved it in one of the ubiquitous rubber bags which must have kept some small

Stateside town in employment – it was a period when they were using over five thousand such bags a week.

Kevin and I watched from a nearby bar while the lady in the *ao-dai* got to work on the detritus of her bit of the war with a pea-green hose she kept to nurture her bougainevillea. Even from the other side of the road one could smell the carbolic with which she had spiked the water as she hosed down her steps. She wore pink plastic gloves like a middle class wife in Europe or the States doing a bit of *dilettante* gardening, but being careful not to ruin her manicure at the same time. She might have been rinsing a few cups, not those pools of inchoate, almost black blood with their attendant blow-fly swarms. Kevin left his 7-Up in search of the lavatory, stomach gurgling uneasily, trying to brush off a trio of bar-girls as he went. While he was away I watched the lady at her task – probably her servants had fled in terror. One wondered whether the water and blood flowing into the bougainvillea roots would fertilize next year's flowers. The defeated sphincter muscle's contribution would doubtless help boost her display.

Kevin was badly shaken and I directed him to the five o'clock press conference in the JUSPAO building wondering whether in his East Anglian school they had talked about *dulce et decorum*, whether he had read Wilfred Owen's comment from an age when they were only just learning the technology of death. On the way he said he wondered whether he would ever learn to cope with Viet-Nam and, not replying, I in turn wondered whether any of us ever would, any of us there, that is. Presumably in Washington, where Earle C. Wheeler was soon to recommend over two hundred thousand new American troops, the whole affair looked like an equation of logistics and firepower, and when the ladies donned rubber gloves it was for rinsing coffee cups.

Kevin was still bothered by his stomach when I travelled north to the battle in Hué. It was a relief to get away from Saigon, away from the stagnant hybrid of muddy swamp and open sewer, away from the smoke and the refugees. Hué, even in time of war, is decidedly a better class of city. It is Viet-Nam's pride, its Oxford and Cambridge, its Florence, its Aix-en-

Provence, the traditional home of the Imperial family with their baroque pagodas, the religious centre, the heart of Viet-Nam's scholarship and culture. Here a French priest in the nineteenth century virtually created Vietnamese literature and poetry by transliterating the incredibly complex Vietnamese characters into simple Roman script anyone could learn. Here the French founded the best school in South-East Asia which bore, as far as they were considered, a crop of troublesome fruit: among its *alumni* the Hué Lycée numbers Ho Chi Minh, General Nguyen Giap and Diem. Once a sampan at dusk along the Perfume River, surely one of the most beautiful in the world, provoked that sense of total physical well-being and joy that one finds on a terrace on high ground in East Africa at the end of the day, in the White Highlands, in Salisbury, even in Bulawayo. But all this was before Têt 1968.

The vc had arrived during the fireworks and tea drinking and formal passages in the citadel that go with the Têt holiday in Hué, and the us Marine Corps had failed ever since to shift these seven stone warriors in rubber tyre sandals out of their fortress. The Americans had to fight from house to house and they were trained, inasmuch as they had been trained at all, to fight in jungles. Failure, frustration, the fear that they were cowards – the besetting sin for those uniformed nineteen-year-olds fresh out of Boot Camp – had turned the Marine Corps very nasty indeed. They were killing and destroying things without reason: civilians, dogs and cats, buildings. I joined Beta platoon, understrength with only forty-two men. Twelve days earlier the platoon had been involved in an abortive attempt on the citadel; there were just seventeen survivors of that morning left. The others had been killed or wounded, 'medevaced' (army jargon for 'medically evacuated') out via the Phu Bai staging point, a drafty wooden encampment perched on a morass of red mud twenty kilometres down a road pastorally flanked by green breast-shaped hillocks which made for an oddly reassuring English home counties landscape, and also provided ideal terrain for the vc mortar crews who were blasting us with total impunity from the reverse slopes. The sampans were already a matter of history, and daily Hué was being turned into a mini-Dresden, or a South-East Asian Coventry. The marines had admitted failure; there was no longer enough gung-ho to go round. A colonel, who has earned himself a footnote in the history books, produced an unconscious aphorism, the implications of which passed far above his crew-cutted skull.

'This town,' he announced to a bunch of incredulous and frightened correspondents, 'must be destroyed to be saved.'

The 'saving' part of the operation remained uncertain – the handful of vc holding the citadel seemed prepared to stay there indefinitely, and the marines' attempts to dislodge them were looking more perfunctory daily. On the other hand there was no possible ambiguity about the 'destruction' element in the colonel's bleak equation. According to the mayor, who like all educated citizens spoke excellent French acquired at the lycée (now naturally a mass of rubble), ninety-five per cent of the commercial and residential sector of the town, where there had never been more than a couple of dozen vc anyway, had been razed to the ground. This achievement we owed to B-52 strikes backed up by ground artillery. What military advantage accrued from this indifferent, though highly efficient destruction was hard to define: most marine officers looked stoney when asked this question, even phrased in the most placatory manner, and occasionally riposted by demanding whether one was a 'commie'. The least thoughtful and most cocksure justified the holocaust in terms of 'Zapping Charlie' or 'teaching the mother-fucking Gooks a lesson'. They didn't differentiate much between good and bad Gooks.

Ostensibly my partner on this trip was Don McCullin but, as usual, I lost him early on. This was because he decided the best photographs of the marines capturing the beleaguered citadel were to be taken from the vantage point of the Viet-Cong – that was, about fifty metres on the citadel side of the American front line. His idea was to take a series of wide angle shots of the marine assault platoon capturing the citadel at bayonet point, Charge-of-the-Light-Brigade style. This imaginative photographic idea posed certain problems. In the first place it involved Don finding a hole in No Man's Land, around fifty yards ahead of the marines' front line position. This meant of course that he was stationed precisely in the middle of the crossfire, which was unhealthy. When he devised this idea he was under the impression, nurtured by various gung-ho marine lieutenants, that the final assault was only a matter of hours. He reckoned this was an acceptable risk and wriggled professionally forward with his Nikons and C-rations. Most of the marines assumed that he was some kind of super-commando, and watched him – from behind the wall they were using as a protective shield – with awed respect. I ungracefully retreated about five hundred yards away from the action, also on my belly.

The Boot Camp heroes were wrong, and the marines did not storm this contemporary Iwo Jima, either that day, the next, or even the day after. Don remained where he was in No Man's Land, taking pictures of the Viet-Cong yellow and red flag flying triumphantly over the citadel's main palace. Eventually the ARVN Rangers, mini-marines in leopard-marked combat suits, did the job the US Marines were too frightened and demoralized to undertake themselves. So much for gung-ho. In the meantime some sneaking shame at being there with Don had pushed me into taking a chance, and being the first British correspondent into Khe Sanh. When I got back to Hué, confused and surprised at still being alive, the battle was virtually over and Don in one piece, physically at least – had left for Saigon to air-freight some of the greatest war pictures that even he had ever taken. My object in returning was to find out what had actually happened during the week or so when the Viet-Cong and units of the North Vietnamese Army had been in control of the venerable capital. I had heard the official 'Free World' version which I knew by definition to be a tissue of lies, because if the official spokesman in Saigon deviated momentarily into truth, it was simply an oversight.

The combination of blatant lies trotted out daily at the five o'clock press conference in Saigon, and the extraordinary Pentagon jargon used to express them, attracted all those who felt like a good belly laugh. Sometimes even the crew-cut public information officers, whose job it was to purvey this drivel with the help of visual aids, themselves dissolved into giggles. Visitors were smuggled in, as one might take a foreign guest to the Palladium in London or the Crazy Horse Saloon in Paris, to show off the local sense of humour. Not for nothing were the press conferences known as 'The Five O'Clock Follies' – they belonged to the purest vaudeville tradition. Art Buchwald, with the help of a slide rule, proved that if one accepted the MACV figures for 'enemy KIAS' – that is dead VC – the entire population of both Viet-Nams had gone to their long homes some time in the summer of 1967, and therefore no one was left for 535,000 GIs to fight. During the Pinkville Trial at Fort Benning, Lieutenant William L. Calley Jr mentioned in passing that on that horrific day on March 16, 1968 Captain Medina his superior officer had called him up by radio. He had wanted to know what the body count was, if any.

Calley's platoon, already in the wrong position and in a state of confusion, did not know where they were. But the lieutenant *had* seen some enemy, or anyway Vietnamese, bodies sprawled in a patch of tapioca. He accordingly reported: 'Six to nine bodies.' Medina, who was no fool when it came to the niceties of US military protocol, immediately signalled 'Sixty-Nine' to Task Force. By the time this figure had been processed and delivered to the Public Information duty officer running the Five O'Clock Follies it was probably six hundred and ninety. President Johnson's global decisions were based on thousands of 'facts' of this order. No wonder he never understood why it all seemed to be going wrong, and blamed the mess on unAmerican peaceniks, forerunners of the 'Campus bums'.

Whether Hué had been saved or not was a moot point, but by God they had made a beautiful job of destroying it. Giant bulldozers, driven by cursing Sea-Bees, were trying to cut paths through the rubble of what a fortnight before had been pink-roofed villas, havens of cool and comfort. Kevin, disconsolate as ever, was in a former school, now the marine headquarters. I took him on a jeep ride; it was easy to talk to what was left of the citizens as long as one spoke French. The English language they associated with bereavement and destruction. The mayor gave me a bottle of 1955 *Mouton Rothschild* and a tin of *escargots*, products of Marseille, to go with it. I opened the tin with a bayonet and the major found some freshly baked *baguettes*. Kevin was horrified by the snails; the marines called the *baguettes* 'Gook bread' and stuck to plastic Swiss Roll from the C-rations. It was the best meal for three weeks. Afterwards I gave the mayor's aunt, who had a broken shoulder, my last morphine shot, which I was bitterly to regret. Then the mayor, twittering nostalgically about the Brasserie Lipp on Boulevard St Germain, hopped deftly into the jeep to take us on a conducted tour of what was left of the Citadel, the pride of Viet-Nam. It had stood up pretty well, and it was still possible to recall those elegant evening strolls among the pagodas and pavilions. We stopped to watch a dozen young children playing with multi-coloured kites – saffron, orange, Reckett's blue. Not for the first time I wondered at a child's capacity to adapt even to the most obscene environment. But then, of course, these kids regarded war and death as normal; the eldest was perhaps ten, and they had never known anything else.

The sun was mild against a washed out blue sky dotted with kites. The only noise was the shrill laughter of a gaggle of Vietnamese kids, fooling around as if the battle had never happened. The tension, assisted by that good claret, began peeling off. I felt, for some absurd reason, like crying as the children ran around, and I assumed I must be drunk.

It was a nasty little explosion, like the crack of a big whip. The children screamed and I was already in the dust on my side of the jeep, one knee gashed and bleeding from where it had hit the gear lever as I dived, a temple swelling like a pigeon's egg from its impact with the ground. The mayor, evidently no stranger to battlefields, had baled out over the back, and we met face to face under the vehicle, both frightened. He asked me if it had been a mortar and I said it had sounded more like a grenade. Infinitely cautiously and stiffly we straightened up, ready to get away from the vehicle if there was any follow up. Kevin, I noticed, was still crouched vulnerably in the passenger seat, his forehead against the windscreen. I screamed at him to bale out, but it was unnecessary. It had been a grenade sure enough, but not pitched by the vc – it was an unexploded remnant of the battle some kid had stepped on. The other playmates were now huddling round something red and screaming where the explosion had been. Kevin seemed paralysed. Forgotten kites drifted westwards, tails and strings splaying out unregarded by their owners.

The red mess turned out to be a six-year-old boy called Nguyen Hoc. Trailing his kite he had stepped into a ditch and kicked an unexploded grenade with his left foot. That foot, and a good part of his lower leg, was now shaped like a dripping red spear. The shrapnel had stripped the whole of the left side of his body, including his face, with the precision of a butcher skinning a rabbit. Already, seconds after the explosion, the slaughter-house red that a minute earlier had been olive skin had acquired a film of grey dust and an escort of blow-flies, buzzing excitedly at the unexpected treat. Young Hoc was making a low moaning sound. The right side of his body was unmarked, and with his right hand he was still grasping his kite string. His playmates had stopped screaming by the time we got to him: by now they were twittering busily at each other, for all the world like those song-birds you see in the pet shops next to Chatelet. Perhaps the noise evoked more nostalgic memories of Paris for the francophone mayor.

We loaded him on the back of the jeep as gently as possible where he was joined by his elder sister, an almond-eyed beauty of perhaps nine whom the mayor had discovered. We covered him with my combat jacket, which was as big as a great-coat on him, and Kevin rolled up his jacket to make a pillow. The sister held his unwounded hand which was still keeping a firm grip on his kite string. As we set off it billowed behind us giving the jeep an inappropriate carnival air. On the east wall of the citadel the First Air Cav Regiment had established a helicopter pad, and as its main purpose was to fly wounded and dead out – what they called a 'medevac operation' – we drove there in search of a doctor. It took about fifteen minutes, driving very slowly over the pocked and dusty track. Every time we hit a bump Hoc gave a minuscule scream, the kind of sound an injured mouse might have made. All the time his sister talked to him in lilting Vietnamese inflexions. I asked the mayor what she was saying. Kevin was crouched forward in a catatonic trance.

'She is being his eyes,' said the mayor. 'He cannot see anything. She is telling him his kite is flying higher than any of the others, and soon it will be time to go to sleep.' There was no doctor at the chopper pad; only a Corpsman whose name printed on his khaki jacket stuck in my mind – he was P/Fc Rheingold, an unshaven pathologically bad-tempered former resident of Teaneck, New Jersey. His role that day was undertaker, not nurse. In the shade outside his lean-to headquarters a dozen bundles in rubber sacks were waiting to be lifted to Phu Bai, then on to the ghastly mortuary at Thon Son Nhut in Saigon, and finally to Arlington. You could smell them at fifty paces. In anything approaching normal circumstances I would have had strong reservations about trusting P/Fc Rheingold to mind my dog for half an hour. But he turned out to be a man of parts. First he examined Hoc, fanning himself with his forage cap which had 'Make Love Not War' embroidered on the peak, and an ace of spades – an unreassuring symbol – stapled on the back.

During the examination he kept up a stream of muttered imprecations – 'cock-sucking gooks' was his favourite and recurring phrase. Then, very deftly, he disengaged the kite, handed it to the sister to hold, and carried the gory body, which already seemed to have shrunk, into his office. In half an hour he had cleaned and dressed the wounds with amazing efficiency. He also produced coca-cola from a giant dispenser which by some technological miracle had already been installed; there was also a coffee machine with paper cups manufactured, so the trademark said, in Indianapolis. Rheingold pinned a note to the boy's shirt explaining the dosage of morphine he had received. It must have been pretty heavy because the side of his face that was unbandaged wore an expression of blissful content.

Kevin came out of his trance long enough to ask what the prognosis was. 'You gotta get him to the gook hospital over the river. He's gotta be hospitalized.'

'Will he be OK?' Kevin persisted.

'Sure, number one. These gook kids are tough. He's gonna be just great, lucky little mother-fucker. Of course, he ain't going to be seeing anything ever again.'

We left with Hoc dozing on a purloined stretcher, and carrying a rucksack crammed with coke, C-rations and a dozen emergency medical kits. After the hospital we deposited Hoc's sister where we had found her. The children had forgotten the incident and as we drove off she was ecstatically flying Hoc's kite, munching on a Hershey bar. No one talked much for the rest of that afternoon. A society in which a six-year-old who has been blinded and crippled is regarded as lucky takes a bit of getting used to.

Kevin, still shattered, left Hué that evening to file a story about the refugees. It was not a very good story, and it seemed to me he should have held on another day. Still, as he confessed late that afternoon, he had already been in trouble with his bureau because he had stayed too long in some village down in the Delta and been twenty-four hours behind UPI and AP. Twenty-four-hours! This bad day in the Delta had been one of the few he had actually spent in the field since his arrival. The after effects of Felici's needle had kept him on his back for nearly a week; then he had caught mild sunstroke, quickly followed by an extended bout of diarrhoea so acute the doctor had started by diagnosing cholera and then dysentery. In the late afternoon we parked our jeep outside a cement reinforced cottage, which had been given over to the press, which apart from us consisted only of a brace of terrified South Korean photographers who sat in a corner hissing to each other, and periodically moaning. There were still a few snipers but, except for the Koreans, it was a quiet evening. Kevin started to talk compulsively, mainly of his inadequacies as a war reporter. He said how much he wished he could be as good as various people we both knew, some of whom were indeed brilliant, and others who were nothing special. Kevin was easily taken in, and typically Sean Flynn, Errol's wild son, was one of his heroes, though Sean's major preoccupation was only very peripherally journalistic.

'I'd be happy if I could get one good story on page one, with

my picture and by-line on it,' Kevin said. Unconvinced. 'Like
they have in the *Express*.' I said in six months no one would
remember one way or the other. 'Even half a column,' Kevin
said longingly, 'even that much with a by-line.'

Further confessions were cut short when the marine transport arrived to ferry him back along the dangerous road to
Phu Bai. Disorganized as ever Kevin grabbed his gear from the
back of our jeep and disappeared in a cloud of thick dust that
smelt of napalm, or maybe something worse. An hour later it
was dark except for occasional tracer across the Perfume River,
and cold. When I went to the jeep to pick up the combat jacket
I had discarded in the afternoon I found that Kevin had taken
mine and left his virtually identical one behind. I worked
through his pockets with care but there was nothing except a
crumpled letter, a bottle of Horlicks tablets and some anti-
diarrhoea pills. He was a non smoker; my jacket had contained,
among other useful items, several packets of cigarettes and thin
cigars, plus a fifth of Old Grandad. It was a night without
tobacco or alcohol. I wrote my notes by candlelight, and long
before I had finished the Koreans were asleep on stretchers,
tossing and crying out in nightmares only too easy to imagine.

Searching for something to distract me I finally read Kevin's
old letter; it was so touching I copied parts of it down. It was a
silly note in round hand on pink paper and evoked a distant
world of girl secretaries and perhaps the odd air hostess sharing
a Victorian apartment somewhere off the Fulham Road. One
could see it all; the laddered stockings on the grimy sofa; the
girl who was always in curlers; the sluttish one who slept with
too many boys too soon and always forgot when it was her
night to buy the bread; the disapproving, capable one who
made a cardboard box with a slit in the top for telephone
money. Cherry, Kevin's correspondent, was I think the last
one.

'Darling Kevin!' she began. 'You are naughty going off like
that. All the girls at 22B are absolutely in despair!! You didn't
even kiss us good-bye . . . Monica was quite put out, and so
was little Me! Hil says it's dangerous out there, she saw a film
on TV and they're having a battle. BE CAREFUL, You Have

Been Warned. Last night Monica got one of her flashy men
(Julian he's called, really creepy in *my* opinion) to take her to
The Speakeasy and Mick Jagger was there. Trust Monica (and
of course she forgot the eggs and the Ovaltine, *as per usual*, mind
on higher things I don't think). I'm off to Basingstoke for the
weekend, what a bore, but lucky old Hil's going to scrumptious
Stratford. . . .'

And so on. Cherry was a great hand with exclamation marks,
and she had even put one next to the 'Tons of Love' at the end,
surrounded by a plethora of x's for kisses. So that was what
he had left. Bitter at the 'local', as they would call it, on Sunday
mornings, the men in heavy-wool jerseys of the kind called
Fishermen's Knit, the girls in jeans their bottoms were too
pear-shaped to fit. Dinner at candle-lit bistros where you
brought your own Algerian red (known as 'plonk'), and paid
a couple of bob to the sub-deb waitress to make a hash of un-
corking it. Necking afterwards with the car parked in one of
those quiet squares behind Kensington High Street. Kevin surprisingly hadn't talked about his car; probably it would be
ancient, with a facetious name – 'Genevieve'? 'The Mighty
Mouse'? – painted amateurishly on the bonnet. Finally I slept
on my stretcher, half listening to the heaving Koreans, half
visualizing Kevin with Cherry primly beside him, chugging
unevenly down the Fulham Road one quiet Sunday morning,
the sun reflecting on all the newly delivered milk bottles.

The best and most eccentric restaurant in Saigon is on the
ground floor of the Royale Hotel. In style it is strictly French
colonial with lime green as the predominant shade. Everything
is worn thin: the table linen, the faded blue plates depicting
Loire châteaux, and above all the face of the proprietor, Monsieur Ottaviji, whose age is unknown. It is possible to make
guesses, however, because late at night M. Ottaviji sometimes
describes how he first arrived in the country with the French
Foreign Legion in the rainy season of 1917. His face is wrinkled
like an old orange and the pouches under his eyes are so deep
he looks like an emaciated lizard in his faded silk suit of great
antiquity. The wrinkles and the swollen hands suggest that

during his expatriation M. Ottaviji has picked up some local vices, and is no stranger to an opium pipe.

'*Le pays est foutu,*' he would say in his hoarse bored voice. '*C'est la force des choses, m'sier.*'

It was a level of detachment which, I felt, could only be maintained with the assistance of narcotics, or hallucinogens at the very least. The last night I was there celebrating my imminent departure quite a few of the Têt arrivals floated through. The Chauvels, as unruffled as ever, were kidding Sarsie who was dining in some style with two young Vietnamese whores of great beauty, who seemed moreover to be identical twins. M. Ottaviji, even more mordant than usual because of a recent increase in the price of chickens, was sighing to himself while nibbling on a lobster à l'hormoricain. Kevin joined us for coffee, clumping himself down next to the frail Ottaviji like an oak nudging an aspen. He was rather drunk, and talked for a while about the local girls. I felt embarrassed, as I always had since the episode of the letter I should never have read.

'*Ah, les filles,*' groaned Ottaviji in sympathy, dabbing at the relief map of his forehead with a frayed napkin. Viet-Nam had clearly changed Kevin. It had made him suffer, but also in some strange way calmed him down. Predictably, he had been shocked by the American conduct of the war, and was worried that his agency was too hawkish. He had seen some bad things at Camp Carroll in I Zone, during its bombardment, and he told us the details.

'The country is finished, it is a disgrace, it is absurd even . . .' M. Ottaviji croaked his litany of doom as from a distance. His wife, an exquisite Vietnamese lady of thirty-five, left the cash register momentarily to join us, clinking melodiously from the gold bangles on her wrists.

Kevin, gauchely ignoring her, was about to say something when M. Ottaviji raised a withered claw to indicate he was not yet finished.

'Yet, you must remember one thing about this derisory corner of the world. It shelters us. One can live here and, I assure you, there is no where else left where one can live, except perhaps Vientiane.'

I translated this fairly tersely. 'He say's it's a dump all right but that all the other dumps in the world are worse.'

On this note Ottaviji tottered elegantly off, leaving Kevin looking surprised. It had probably not occurred to him before that anyone could actually *like* Viet-Nam, or find life there agreeable. I could see he was thinking of South Ken tube station, and the memory was likely to render him maudlin at any moment. So I pleaded an early start and said good-bye; my last words turned out to be as maladroit as all the others. I painted a lurid picture of the delights of Hong Kong, where he would soon be going for a short leave, and made optimistic noises about some special features he was trying to write. My last words to him were that I would be looking out for his name on page one. Going out into the curfew I saw Kevin standing by the bar and waving, grinning happily at our private joke.

*   *   *   *

The Times office on East 42nd Street in New York is a kind of penthouse which boasts a lot of very blue carpet, framed photographs of the Queen and Churchill, and two beautiful secretaries. At that time amenities included a blood-curdling view of the East River from twenty-seven storeys up, a super-lative telex operator called Joe, and one truly baroque touch. This was a greying negro called Fred, who wore a special blue uniform which toned nicely with the carpet, and a peaked cap on which was written in gold: '*The London Times*'. Fred's job was to get hamburgers and beer from a dive on Third Avenue, a task he fulfilled with vague courtesy. It was a miracle the Black Panthers hadn't slain this most picturesque of Uncle Toms in the elevator.

It sometimes took that elevator ten minutes to get to the top and one morning Fred and I were stuck in it together. It was a question of talking to each other, or listening to 'Winter Wonderland' on the muzak which I had once unsuccessfully tried to rip out of its loudspeaker; accordingly, we talked. Fred, plucking at his peak in constant deferential salute, showed me Page one of the *New York Daily News* – 'vc Blast Saigon Press' it read. There was a big picture of a maltreated looking jeep, surrounded ominously by bodies. 'Hope them no friends of yors, sah,' said Fred, a shade ghoulishly. Although he chose to express himself in a style reminiscent of the comic nigger in Hollywood films of the 'thirties, Fred was no fool. He knew where I had been before New York, and I suspect he sniffed a human drama.

The third name in the list of four dead reporters was 'Kevin Lorrimer, 28'. Two of the others I had known fairly well; one of them had been a senior member of Kevin's bureau with two years of Viet-Nam experience. The sole survivor, who had played dead until the vc officer who had gunned his colleagues down was changing his magazine, described how their jeep had swung round a corner in the maze of Cholon and found themselves face to face with a vc platoon. The officer had apparently been giggling while he fired, a point the *Daily News* was particularly sore about, though it did not signify anything. Knowing the Vietnamese his reaction had probably been nervous rather than sadistic.

We had arrived at the top, and I became aware once more of 'Winter Wonderland', and Fred. 'Never came across any of the poor bastards,' I told him, and pressed the escalator button to go down. Fred raised an eyebrow. 'My office is being temporarily transferred for the morning to Costello's Irish Bar two blocks up on Third,' I told him. There, against a soothing background of baseball and horses, one would have room to think about Kevin in that jeep. Why, for instance, had he been there at all? There could have been no journalistic necessity because the agency had another man on the spot, a senior reporter who would certainly have been assigned to write an eyewitness story of the latest vc flurry of activity in Cholon.

It looked very much as if Kevin had gone along for the ride. I hoped it had not been bravado because he would have felt so angry with himself when he finally realized that the little man ahead was shooting. They would have come across the vc so abruptly round one of those sharp bends that it would have taken a while to realise who they were. Then there would have been the hope, perhaps even assumption, that the soldiers would understand and respect the Foreign Press sign, '*Bao Chi*', stuck prominently on the windscreen. Finally they would have realized that the man with the deadly, pinging AK-47 made no distinction between 'round-eyes'; to him they were all enemies. Perhaps it would have occurred to Kevin in those last seconds that he was the victim of an error identical to the one so many US field commanders were making daily. I imagined him in that hopeless crouched position, the one he had adopted on the first flight in to Saigon, and again in Hué the day Hoc trod on the grenade. Cholon was the wrong place to start looking for a womb. To the Americans all 'gooks' looked the same; to this man so did all 'round-eyes'. Perhaps Kevin had some happier image, mist on the Fens or maybe Cherry and the girls at 22B. It might just have been too quick for Kevin to have had any sentient flashes at all before the lights went out.

On the side-walk going up Third I bought a *New York Times* which, I noticed, had treated the story with more restraint. Still, there was nearly a full column on page one, and Kevin would have been gratified to see that his by-line appeared in it no less than three times. There was a mug-shot of him too – fulfilling the ambitions he had revealed in Hué at the end of that horrific day. Sadly, the picture was not on the front – for that you had to turn to page seventeen, beside the Macey's ad.

* * * *

Over three years later I went to a cocktail party near the Théâtre de France in Paris and fell into conversation with a highly-strung Australian called Frank Palmos, who was touring Europe on a scholarship. To my amazement I learnt he had been the sole survivor of Kevin's jeep, which explained why he was highly-strung. Palmos had reacted faster than the others and baled out just before the shooting. He had been intelligent and sharp enough to station himself behind the jeep below the field of fire of the burp gun which had shattered the windscreen and put twenty-six bullets into John Cantwell of *Time Magazine*, the driver. He told me that the right half of Kevin's forehead had been blasted away in the same opening salvo, and he would have died at once.

I showed Palmos the above account, which I had already written and have not changed. I turned out to have been almost psychically accurate, even down to the crouching. This is part of the description Palmos recorded for me of that frightful morning.

'Kevin was, how shall I say, doing a hide-away. He put his knees up in the back of the jeep and slid his bum forward, he was pulling himself together rather than bracing himself for a heavy crash. It was as if he was hiding under blankets.' Palmos added that he and Kevin were the only nervous ones on board; the others had been confident, foolishly so in the manner of Sean Flynn. Fifty metres up the road they had passed an empty sentry box which meant that the 'White Mouse' policeman who should have been guarding it had taken to his heels, a sure sign the vc were close. The shooting had started just as Cantwell was fighting to get the jeep into reverse. It stalled.

I had thought my original ending about Kevin's name finally appearing on page one was perhaps too sentimental, and wondered about changing it. When Palmos told me the full details of that last trip I decided to leave it as it was. Just before the burp gun opened up, a matter of seconds before Palmos threw himself backwards on to the road, Kevin made a joke which in the circumstances was heroic, if bitter. 'If there are vc here and they get us it will make a helluva story – at least I'll get my name in print.'

CHAPTER 11

Bill O'Reilly

♣

KHE SANH on St Valentine's Day 1968 was, as the marines there kept saying, 'mind-blowing'. They were not only ahead of the hippies with this expression, but they were using it with unhippie-like precision. Just as someone on a bad acid trip may start wondering whether his mind will be blown or – nagging fear – whether it has already gone, so one's primary concern in Khe Sanh was for one's personal sanity. In the course of eight hours that day the North Vietnamese troops who had been besieging the garrison of around 4,800 US Marines for a month laid down a murderous fire of nearly 1,400 rockets within a section of the perimeter measuring less than five hundred square metres. The warning of discharge was a flat thump, and after that there was plenty of time to hear them coming in, shriller, straighter and faster all the time. You lay with your nose digging into the red Khe Sanh mud with plenty of time to wonder whether this was the one that would push your reeling mind over the edge, or, worse, whether if the bombardment ever stopped one would suddenly discover against a background of heavy silence that it was too late, and that one's sanity had already floated off towards one of those sullen green hills, their tips covered in cumulus, through which scarlet and yellow flashed with bureaucratic regularity signalling yet another rocket was on its way.

To help the besieged men General Westmorland had issued a specific and unpublicised order, countermanding normal operating procedures for the high level B-52 bombers. Elsewhere these monsters, carrying a forty ton bomb load and discharging it from 55,000 feet, were for obvious reasons forbidden to make drops within three thousand metres of friendly troops on the ground. At Khe Sanh 'Arclight', as the marines called the big bombers several miles up, were putting 750-pounders down five hundred yards from our perimeter, which seemed to me to be cutting it a bit fine. When the bombs exploded the bunker supports lurched, sand started to spill out of the bags, and the overall effect was not unlike being in an earthquake, though more unpleasant. I kept visualizing the results if a clutch of even the 500-pounders arrived inside the perimeter; it would have only needed a very small miscalculation, and it was a tribute to the skill of pilots and bomb-aimers that even with their tight operating margins they never made one. Khe Sanh was not a good place for chat; most of the time I made notes, or recorded sounds, usually explosions. St Valentine's Day had started before dawn, waiting for transport from Da Nang base, and my notes read as follows.

'05.45. Will there be a flight to relieve "Operation Scotland" (Khe Sanh) by noon? Met. boys unsure. Only two flights yesterday, one had 329 50 cal machine gun bullets aft. (Who counted them?) Surroundings grim as normal. Large office split up, vaguely medicinally, into sections with sweating hardboard. A sign says: "Important – Ignore This Sign". Institutional humour. One-pipped, bespectacled Lt. Butt is briefing us. He has brought cardboard cartons wrapped in plastic so we can have breakfast out of their gurgling coffee machine. Also some airmail envelopes, again wrapped in plastic, so we can write to our next of kin. A bit premature, lieutenant? Everyone else is writing busily so I shall make a will. Doesn't one need some kind of stamp and witnesses to make it legal?

'Mr Butt briefs us: "Gentlemen, one thing when the aircraft comes to a halt. Sit tight. The ammunition has priority. Once the ammo crates are cleared get out of the back, turn right at ninety degrees, and run till you hit the support trenches which are located at approximately thirty-five yards off the strip. Charley will be shooting at you."

' "Questions, gennelman?" says the loot. O'Reilly, the mad Irishman from Kansas City who like me had bribed his way on to the flight (what better definition of madness?) raises a languid hand, caricaturing a High School kid.

O'REILLY: You mentioned in, ah, passing, *ammunition*, loot.'

BUTTS: Affirmative, sir. Any correspondent who doesn't wish to fly with high explosive just has to say so.

O'REILLY: High, er . . .

BUTTS: Right, sir. Ground to ground rockets, plus anti-tank rockets, HE 66 and 72 mm.

O'REILLY (sniffing story): You trying to say Charley's got tanks there too?

BUTTS (doggedly): You signed your waiver, sir. Still time to get your name off the manifest.

SKIP (AP man who previously, like me, has not said a word): Guess there aren't any craft goin' in not carrying HE. Right, lieutenant?

BUTTS: Right.

Forty minutes of uninterrupted silence after this. All three of the waiting correspondents go twice to the lavatory during this period. 07.30 we start to talk.

Skip, the AP photographer with a face like a rock someone has been bashing at with a crow-bar, speaks as if to himself.

'I bought this stereo tape recorder in Saigon, four-forty dollars. Really nice sound. All I want to do is sit down in a whorehouse there and play *Kiss Me Kate* and *Madame Butterfly* all afternoon.'

O'Reilly and I pondered this eminently reasonable ambition for a while, nodding sagely. 'Anyone with balls, *real* balls I mean, would have checked out of this flight the moment he heard that shit about HE,' O'Reilly finally announced.

Skip sighed, and fiddled with the buttons on his flak jacket.

'Maybe Lieutenant Butts was trying to scare us, you know, kind of a joke,' I contributed weakly.

'Give you odds against,' said O'Reilly. 'I mean does the guy *look* like a humorist?'

Butts didn't, and wasn't. When, at 0900, the three of us were finally strapped into the C-123 we were separated by a pyramid of wooden crates with steel corners lashed down along the centre of the cargo plane's belly. One, about four feet from my groin, had the following information stencilled in red on the side facing me: 'Warning: Anti-Tank mm 72. No naked flames within one hundred yards.' In case the message left any unresolved ambiguities the stencil concluded with a large skull and cross-bones. The Flight Master was a Virginian called Wildhack. He wore a cocky ginger moustache, and looked genuinely unfrightened. When I asked him why we were using a C-123, instead of the normal bigger C-130s, he shrugged: 'I guess it's because of the 130 Charley took out Saturday. They make too big a target. You'll see the burned out shell on the runway when we get there.'

After the folding panel at the back of the aircraft had closed Wildhack addressed us through a microphone on a wire.

'Gennelmen, when we arrive sit tight. The ammunition goes first, then you follow. In case something not anticipated happens on touch down I ring my bell.' (He rang a bell.) 'That gennelmen is the signal to bale out *with no delay*, and get the fuck out of it. As far from the aircraft as possible. And you run *right*, away from the wire. On the perimeter we got Charley.'

With no change of expression he lit a Robert Burns with a match struck on the steel edge of one of the ammo crates. I caught O'Reilly's eyes, and raised my eyebrows in mock despair. He opened both palms to the air, the gesture of a beggar in Jerusalem pleading for alms.

In the event both Bill and I got in, and more surprisingly out again, without suffering anything except psychic wounds. Certain things I noted at the time seem even more significant with hindsight, among them the fact that none of the staff officers in the base had even *heard* of Dien Bien Phu, an uncomfortably similar situation, let alone read anything about this previous classic battle of crack troops isolated from their supply lines, surrounded by an army also under General Giap, and dependent on air support, or in other words the weather, for survival. Why Giap let the marines off the hook by withdrawing a couple of months later remains a mystery. If he had the twenty thousand men American intelligence believed, overrunning the base would have been a fairly simple operation, particularly if he was ready to sacrifice troops, as he always had been in the past. In Washington it was later suggested by someone who often knows about these things that the psychological effect of a Khe Sanh capitulation would have been so violent that President Johnson might well have found pressures for him to riposte with anything less than tactical nuclear weapons irresistible. My informant believed that Hanoi had been told this. Whatever the reason, one day the Vietnamese disappeared up the cloudy valley that leads to Laos and my colleague Jean-François Chauvel came within an ace of getting himself killed by arriving with the First Air Cavalry's 'rescue' force, who were greeted by the marines with heavy calibre machine gun bursts.

The appallingly poor quality of the officers in the heavily protected Khe Sanh command bunker took me aback, and so did the fact that a master sergeant I met in a poker game was peddling cannabis – 'Cambodian Red', 'Thai Flowers' and the famous 'Dynamite Grass' from the Mekong Delta. Quite a few Black troops I had met in Saigon smoked pot, some even smoked (though not injected) heroin. But this was the first time I had come across combat troops using dope in a battle zone, and no ordinary battle zone at that. I did not report this at the time because it seemed an isolated incident without general significance, and in any case I felt the wretched devils beleaguered in that valley deserved whatever comfort they could find. But when I got back to Da Nang, as shocked and shattered as the Korean Ranger who had taken a shrapnel burst I helped carry off the 'plane, I had become convinced that the Marine Corps were a liability to the American effort, and should be pulled out. A few days later I took this slightly further and wrote that there was no way the Americans could win the war, supposing it winnable in conventional terms, with less than a two hundred thousand *good* combat troops in the field, which meant a total commitment of something in the order of two million men, which was presumably inconceivable. After Khe Sanh it became clear that there was no question of the Americans achieving more than the most limited aims; simply containing the vc and the North Vietnamese regulars was probably the most they could realistically expect.

Retrospectively, one wonders why it took so long to see the

light. The answer, probably, boiled down simply to hardware. As a small boy the richness of the Second World War GIs had overwhelmed me in the midst of our desperate austerity. Twenty-five years later it was hard to believe that an army equipped with such cornucopian *matériel* could be beaten by guerilla troops, indeed by troops of any kind including the Israelis, the best I had ever seen.

At one stage during the battle for Hué Ambassador Harry Komer, who was officially in charge of the derisory 'Pacification Program', and in reality the CIA chief for South-East Asia, gave me a ride to Da Nang in his helicopter. On the way he told a story very unlike the one he expounded to the President a week later when he was to back up Earl C. Wheeler's request for 235,000 more troops. As we circled the CIA Air America base at Da Nang, Komer said that as a result of his post-Têt inspection tour he had concluded that all the work that had been done in the villages and hamlets in the previous two years had been undone, and that the situation might even prove to be worse than it had been in 1966. I did not report, or indeed really believe this either. In the first place Komer was suffering from exhaustion and shock and I guessed (rightly for once) that on reflection he would change his mind; the conversation was unattributable then in any case. But the decisive factor was that we were talking above an airport, and not even the main Da Nang airport either, but the CIA's ancillary base, which contained literally miles of 'planes in meticulous rows. There were many miles more on the main base, and these bases together were smaller than the vast Tân Son Nhut complex in Saigon. The Israeli air force could have taken the lot out in ten minutes flat but as long as the Vietnamese lacked air support it seemed inconceivable they could hold out against these lines of silver birds. There was to be one more experience of this order, one that saved my life as it turned out.

Waiting for transport in Phu Bai north of Hué I had been interested in a C-130 that had arrived to be greeted, with unusual enthusiasm, by a group of thirty ground staff, all of them ready with fork-lift trucks. In the hangar they had appeared from there were several hundred other fork-lift trucks, probably more, I reflected, than existed in the whole of North Viet-Nam. The C-130 can carry tanks if required, but on this occasion when it split open the cargo turned out to consist of several scores of enormous deep-freeze containers, each of them about fifteen feet high. They were for beer and coca-cola, someone explained, and it was so remarkable that the American Army had been able to, or for that matter interested in shifting that much coke to this God-forsaken air strip I spent some time trying to check just how many bottles there were, and consequently missed the next flight out. My office, unmoved by the original horror-filled cable from Khe Sanh, had sent me a service message suggesting the place 'Might Repay Second Visit'. Though I had cabled back something sarcastic or obscene, the idea of returning had fascinated me, doubtless for morbid pathological reasons. The flight I missed was for Khe Sanh, an unlikely destination from Phu Bai, and had I been on the spot I expect I would have taken it. Any excuse to escape from Phu Bai would have been tempting, and anyway a photographer friend with whom I had just cooked lunch, Robert Ellison, had taken it. Bob's plane was hit on landing by the 50 calibre machine gun at the east end of the Khe Sanh strip, which had nearly put an end to O'Reilly and myself. Bob, like everyone else on the flight, died in the flames.

When O'Reilly got drunk, which was periodically as opposed to regularly or permanently, he took the matter with befitting Irish seriousness. One night in Saigon he got through a fifth of white Bacardi in the Officers' Club above the Rex ballroom – a room in which for various reasons I never felt very happy. In general, I got on badly with the (invariably non-combat) officers who patronized the place because they believed my hair was unacceptably long, and also had a patriotic prejudice against the British who, in their eyes, had been woefully slow to get in on the act and despatch eager eighteen-year-olds to kill Gooks. O'Reilly hated the club too, though for different reasons: he could not understand why they insisted on closing the bar at eleven pm. We accordingly returned to his flat for what he called 'a small night-cap', and turned out to be another fifth of Bacardi.

The little apartment was shared among several regular Saigon reporters, but happily none was there that night. They had left behind a detritus of camera and recording equipment, of cables and books and flak jackets and even a loaded AK-47, with which O'Reilly periodically played, to my alarm. From below one could hear the whores twittering on Tu-Do, and the occasional baritone obscenity of a drunken Air America pilot who seemed to have three or four girls with him in some room. The apartment smelled of opium, and some time before dawn O'Reilly got round to saying what was bothering him.

He had just received a batch of fan mail from the States, among which was a letter from a lady in Kansas, who said she was a widow who spent a lot of time listening to the radio. She had been following his despatches for several months and found them 'very fine entertainment', but one thing had recently been bothering her, particularly in the recordings from Khe Sanh. These were full of background noise, she had noticed – bangs of various kinds, screams and moans, a veritable cacophony. The lady listener was uncertain whether or not these noises were authentic or manufactured in the studio with wind machines, strips of corrugated iron and so forth. Either way she felt that they should be toned down because they seriously interfered with her enjoyment of O'Reilly's comments. 'What are you going to do?' I inquired.

'I already wrote her,' replied O'Reilly, 'saying the sound effects editor is being fired for playing his coconut shells too loud, and it won't happen again. Also I give up, I'm going home.'

CHAPTER 12

Robert Kennedy

♣

THE big Boeing carrying the assassinated body of Robert
Kennedy to New York was late (like every other Kennedy
aircraft with which I ever had dealings). Accordingly, it was
almost dark but under the ubiquitous TV arclights the coffin
was brightly illuminated as it was let down from the plane on
an enormous lift platform, normally employed, so I learned,
to load cocktail olives, finger lickin' good plastic chicken and
other obligatory ingredients of trans-continental airborne
cuisine. For the occasion this platform had been draped purple,
and lined up in front of it the mourning Kennedy women –
God help them – wore Greek Chorus black. They looked as
always, dignified and somehow highly drilled. In mourning, as
in so many other roles, training had bestowed on them the
status of professionals. Their black chiffon hair scarves blew
in the slight wind in unison.

The reporters who like me had flown in from Los Angeles on
an earlier plane had been brought to the right runway on the
other side of the airport in a Kennedy campaign coach. We
had been herded into a cross between cattle pen and observation platform by the usual vile-tempered police and now, as
the male Kennedy mourners lifted the coffin with the same
ventriloquistic precision the women had shown, it struck me
that no one was jostling. This was odd as I was right in the
front of the pen in the best observation position. The explanation was bizarre. A cluster of TV crews had set up a line of
little monitor screens at the back for their own technical purposes, and these were now surrounded by perhaps three-
quarters of the reporters present. They had turned their backs
on the tarmac, as if making some collective protest, and were

simultaneously peering at the little monitor screens and scribbling notes.

There, a few yards away, was the real thing, yet their impulse was to watch it, and in due course report it, predigested by television. It was hard to think of a more appropriate manner to report the return of what a famous commentator a few yards away was calling 'Bobby's simple casket' to what in due course he also called 'Bobby's native soil'.

It was more or less obligatory at this period for people to remark that Sirrhan's two bullets were all the more tragic because Bobby had been killed 'just when he had found himself'. What, one always wondered in silence, had there been to find, except the money, and the ambition, and the self-deforming expertise with the media – what my colleagues writing a book about the election had unkindly christened 'The Bullshit Machine'. This 'finding himself' view was usually reinforced by references to Bobby's emotional relationship with Cesar Chavez and his *chicanos*, the million or so Mexican Americans working in California's giant and corrupt 'agro-business'. It was a eulogistic time, after all, a time for compliments, but like every other positive achievement being laid at Bobby's door, right down even to the apparently self-evident 'he was a wonderful family man', one's reaction was always: 'Yes . . . But.' And the 'But' part of the equation usually had the suggestion of something fraudulent, something that had been distorted by the media, attached to it.

Yes, out there in California one had seen the 'Stoop' labour force screaming and singing for Bobby. Yes, they had been convinced he was specifically 'their' candidate, and had accordingly accounted for perhaps half of his slender majority in the last primary, the one that had really mattered, and would equally probably have made him president. *But* what about the fact that the loser, Eugene McCarthy (whom *no one* thought was the *chicanos'* candidate) had actually started public support for this much abused minority some seventeen years previously, precisely at the period in fact when Bobby had been the most dedicated supporter of that other McCarthy, the obscene Joe. What this deranged and criminal witchhunter had thought

about the 'Stoop' labour is unrecorded, but it is easy to imagine
what would have happened to the idealistic, left-wing Chavez
had he and the Bobby of the period still been operating. Still,
after the Bullshit Machine had dealt with the question on the
little screens. . . .

Kennedy and television were, by this time, as deeply connected in my mind as I think they had been in his. Television
had been born for him and he was one of the handful of people
I have known who actually look better on it – even on the
roughest American colour reproduction – than in real life. The
screen made him look younger, though he looked young anyway, and much more handsome. It ironed out the deep-set
quality around the eyes that in life spoilt his good looks. It
concealed, or usually anyhow, the arrogance, the impatience,
the ignorance. It was his right arm, and like certain famous
actors, when one met him 'off stage' there was a distinct impression that part of his personality was absent.

Our first meeting had taken place inauspiciously in a grisly
motel suite in Nebraska. Bobby had been tired and ratty;
Ethel, in a pillar-box red suit, a kind of watered down Cour-
règes which was still far too advanced for this land of hair-
curlers, was trying to soothe him. Bobby had a gift for placing
people in mental camps labelled 'Mine' (for unconditional
sycophants) and 'The Enemy' (for everyone else), and within
seconds there was no doubt about which side of the wire I was
on. It was all to do with how hairy he was, or was not.

Through their bush telegraph Bobby had learned I was
friendly with a well-known woman writer who had recently
produced a series about him and his family for a mass circulation woman's magazine. I had read enough of it to know it
had been well done, and was very far from critical. There had
been pictures of babies and dogs and swimming pools with
white telephones and the obligatory descriptions of his tan (I
was pleased to see it was regulation deep brown) and his teeth
(which I noticed were white as starch). But somehow it had
caused deep offence, and Bobby immediately asked me whether
its author was sick. I replied that she was one of the least sick
people I knew. He was unconvinced. 'That girl's sick,' he

repeated, shaking his head, 'really sick.' I asked in what way and after a good many evasive answers which had me beginning to think she had stolen the best silver or seduced the nanny, the cause for offence was finally revealed. 'She wrote I had hairy wrists,' said Bobby. 'She *what* . . .?'

It took a couple of seconds for this to sink in and then I found myself staring at his wrists, which were very clearly on display as he was wearing his white shirt with the sleeves rolled up after one of those spontaneous games of touch-football which the candidate played two or three times a day when the TV men had time to set up their gear. The Kennedy wrists seemed unremarkable enough, except that they were well-tanned beneath a heavy coating of fur. To add to this lunatic exchange Bobby, I noticed, was also staring at his wrists too. 'Sick,' he said again. 'She ought to have treatment.'

I made a few desultory enquiries about this exchange afterwards, wondering whether perhaps 'wrist' could be college-boy slang for 'penis', or something of the sort. I remembered that in cockney slang 'one off the wrist' meant to masturbate, but apparently this had nothing to do with it. It seemed, all in all, that my friend had violated some psychological media barrier to do with hair; perhaps it was like saying he had a spot. After the make-up man has been to work these things are not supposed to exist.

Shortly afterwards, in Indianapolis there was a chance to see some more facets of the Kennedy campaign, particularly in the course of a long speech to the local Real Estate Association in the down-town Howard Johnson. Bobby used this opportunity to suggest, in a novel twist on one of his main election themes, that there was a lot of cash to be made out of rebuilding the ghettoes, and that real estate agents who took part in this noble humanitarian venture would earn their reward on earth in terms of enormous tax relief and depreciation benefits. There was a lot about the Bedford Stuyvesant project and private enterprise, and a lot more about precisely the *size* of the tax concession he advocated. A few of the younger go-getters made notes, presumably finding it impossible to keep still when percentages were being quoted, but most of this extremely prosperous gathering looked grim over their frozen sea-food cocktails. It seemed unlikely a single participant would have voted anything but Republican, even if the candidate had suggested that all poor people should be automatically drafted, or their hooves sold for glue. After this his regular Black Man's speech, delivered outside the Chrysler factory a couple of hours later, lost some of its plangent conviction, and the workers looked as unimpressed as the Howard Johnson Babbits. He said 'Hello, I'm Bobby Kennedy' to five hundred of them clocking in with their dinner pails, and one in five of them, I conscientiously noted down, looked away as if he were begging. Coriolanus, who had got into trouble because he could not bring himself to act a charade of humility before the poor, could have learnt a lot from this performance.

Despite the early *contretemps* over this matter of how hirsute he was we were soon on fairly close terms. On those endless planes drinking free Kennedy Chivas-Regal there was little to do but chat, and he was particularly interested to chat with anyone with recent ground experience of Viet-Nam. At first I thought his machine gun questions were self-protective (the best way not to be interviewed is to get the interviewer to do all the talking) but it was a technique he used all the time. He was hungry for other people's information, those he paid, and those who came for nothing. Like his elder brother and father he always hired the best help around, and used it. A man I know in Rome has supported himself for years by sending a monthly newsletter to the Kennedys on the Middle East, about which he is very well informed. I suppose they are in a file somewhere in case they are ever needed. I thought of him, listening to Bobby asking his questions of everyone, and reflected that brother Edward persuading a more gifted fellow student at Harvard to take his Spanish exam for him was operating in the same general area. According to the family ethic there was nothing objectionable about this, it was even good sense (though of course it was wrong to have been found out).

As I say there was a lot of time to think and make notes on those planes and one day I found in an old notebook a conversation I had once enjoyed with a distinguished Oxford don about Guy Burgess (would he had been there, to enliven those long days). The point at issue had been whether Burgess had been a communist through ideological conviction, or for other reasons. The don had said that Burgess had possessed a positively Keatsian appetite for vivid and extreme sensations, in ideology as in food or sex. Communism was simply the strongest taste going.

Kennedy himself, one reflected, listening for the hundredth time to the section about his three-and-a-half year stint as 'the chief law enforcement officer of this country', was a man who liked lots of emotional pepper. He loved extremes in all forms; Clay-like he wished to be the richest, the most energetic, the most ruthless, to do everything more and take everything further than anyone else. But the one area where this did not apply was ideology. He himself had little capacity for abstract thought, but in any case the exigencies of Kennedy-style vote-chasing meant ideology was out. You had to be one person for the Blacks and another for the Real Estate Association; one person in the summer of '67, quite a different one in spring '68. Consistent policies were out; instead such coherence as there was stemmed from style, and not thought. The essence of the campaign was the fix, the deal, and invariably the final compromise. Most of the campaigners shared with the candidate a taste for going to the limits, and these restraints were deeply frustrating.

The way these frustrations worked themselves out off-stage was often physically, through horse-play and sometimes alcohol. There was also another public way of releasing the safety valve. as I realized talking to a Boston Irish reporter, who like so many idealists was fascinated by Kennedy, and also despaired of him. He told me how on his first visit to California some of the Kennedy aides had been shocked to find the welcoming high school kids, singing doubtless their adaptation of Woodie Guthrie about RFK being 'your man and my man from California to the New York Island', had been paraded on the tarmac. There were several hundred of them, but on the principle that for television purposes this looked unimpressive, they had been herded into a smallish reception lounge, one which

might have held half of them, and the candidate was diverted
through it, and inevitably mobbed, to give the cameramen
something they could dramatize. I too had seen similar non-
events with crowds manufactured on several other occasions. It
was only partly a straightforward TV technique, though as I
have indicated it was peculiarly hard with Kennedy to make
distinctions about what was or was not natural to him when
it came to the media, who were like his third arm. Kennedy
enjoyed creating mob hysteria, and after he had been man-
handled by ecstatic supporters, some of whom were sometimes
actually paid for the job, he always looked happy and fulfilled.
As a speaker he was a long way from the top class but on a
good night, particularly when he was making his underdog
appeals, stressing his favourite word 'care' which had a certain
poignancy when repeated constantly in the nasal Bostonese
that made almost three distinct syllables of it, he could move
impressionable (and usually pre-committed) audiences to tears.
This too made him happy, and perhaps compensated for the
frustrations of hours spent on the telephone. With the help of
skilled assistants, many of them veterans of the campaign
brother Jack won with no policies at all, the candidate had, by
California, been made into an impressive demagogue, though
again perhaps not of the very highest class.

Next to Gene McCarthy, who by this time was finding it
almost impossible to conceal his distaste for campaigning and
also his natural indolence, Bobby seemed positively messianic.
(No one would have dared to touch Gene; Bobby was trying
to touch up the whole state at once.) He ran himself to a stand-
still trying to get people excited, and since Californians excite
easily without any abnormal stimulation, the atmosphere became increasingly highly charged. Kennedy supporters all over
the country had a physical identity, there was something rough
and burly about them, they prided themselves on being practical, and the anti-war element in the campaign did not sit
easily on their husky shoulders. In contrast, the archetypal
McCarthy supporter was a pacific fellow, of higher social class,
of willowy shape and, at the start of the campaign anyway,
flowing hair. By now McCarthy's speeches were as exciting as

five grammes of seconal. Bobby and his men, spurred on by the poor Oregon result, were pulling out all the stops, and they regarded any meeting that did not end in a near riot as something of a failure. Bobby's style was designed to make Californians laugh and cry, shout and scream, and it also of course made one of them shoot.

On polling night I decided to attend the McCarthy party in the Los Angeles Hilton, and not Bobby's counterpart in the fatal Hotel Ambassador, largely because it was nicer to be with McCarthy's crowd in victory or defeat. The only problem was that young America for Gene tended to look so identical in their dissenting reasonable uniform that it was only too easy to say 'Hullo Janie' to Mary-Lou, and 'Hi Peter' to a beaming Jeff. By 11.30 it was clearly a night of defeat, so I went with a friend to eat in the Hilton's downstairs restaurant, which had South Sea pretentions. I was paying the bill when the waiters started going from table to table saying: 'They've shot him.' No one doubted for a moment that the 'him' was Bobby, even though the diners might have been expected to think the unnamed, assassinated candidate was the one three floors up, not his competitor a couple of miles away.

We arrived at the Good Samaritans' Hospital, where Bobby was to die, at the same time as his ambulance. The suffering of his family and aides was horrible to see. Within an hour those cursing, uncommitted men one had got to know from California to the New York Island, were on the spot, setting up their lights and cameras on the lawn in front of the hospital, so that it looked like an old-time façade for a movie set, or the scene of yet another of those Bobby speeches, which ended with a section about brother Jack's American dream (the signal for those with the campaign to get up and start running for the waiting coaches). Soon the police fenced the Good Samaritans off, and typically the only way to get through their barrier to a nearby hamburger joint and telephone was by exhibiting Kennedy press accreditation. After one call to my colleagues who had been on the spot in the Ambassador I used some of my Kennedy cards to get a couple of kids I had met at campaign headquarters in New York back past the cops. Both were weeping copiously, though whether for Ethel and Bobby, for America or simply for themselves was impossible to assess.

Strong men, in fact, were weeping all over the place. One of the strongest, the Olympic decathlon champion Rafer Johnson who could doubtless have thrown Sirrhan fifteen feet with one huge hand, and in fact very nearly did, said to me: 'Man, it's over.' This attracted a hand-held cameraman who moved in to focus on Rafer's tears, and his partner with a microphone who moved in to record this Black epitaph for posterity. I thought Rafer, obviously suffering from the contagious Kennedy hysteria, might easily have started to tear them into pieces but the big man accepted them like a lamb. Suddenly, with immense weariness, I realized that the mourning, like everything else, was going to be turned into a beanfeast for the media. Soon the tears would be glycerine, the blood ketchup and no one would be able to differentiate between the two. It had been the story of the poor bastard's life, and there was no reason to suppose his dying would be conducted on any other level. There was still a long way to go.

It began overnight in a room we had been given thanks to the good offices of a friend of Bobby's, Ed Guthman of *The Los Angeles Times*, from where I was washed up in the stagnant shores of the Ambassador Hotel, where someone was preparing for a wide-screen Bar-Mitzvah. In one of the repellent red-carpeted lobbies I ran into a Kennedy campaigner, a veteran of Jack's successful 1960 effort, who had learnt one trick then, and like an old dog was determined to play it till the end. Just as on Edward Heath's 1964 mini-campaigns there had been a man with no discernible role except to carry the Leader of the Opposition's bottle of malt whisky, so this veteran had quartered the United States solemnly carrying a football, which when photographers appeared he would throw so Bobby could photogenically catch it. Bobby had got tired of this game after a few weeks, but this husky, ageing teller of locker room stories was still there with his faithful ball, presumably in case the Kennedy ghost turned up to order one last punt for the media. His eyes were wet and red, and he offered me a drink in some gimcrack cocktail bar in the Ambassador. It was an occasion for strong men to be stoical and philosophical; our *rapport* was somewhat spoiled by the barman who was complaining bitterly. He said that the commotion of the night before had been used by various unscrupulous clients as an excuse for ducking out without paying for their drinks, and insisted on taking the money from my football friend in advance. 'It's time to leave this fucking disgusting city,' I remarked. It was the first time I had said what I was thinking for about a week.

At around three am the following morning a weeping secretary I had dined with somewhere along the way telephoned my hotel to say she had booked me a place on one of the special planes flying to New York – it was all up. Should she send a car for me or would I like to ride with Mr Gerald Scarfe, the artist? I said he would do, and, too early, Gerry and I, who a few weeks earlier had worked together covering the so-called Poor Peoples' March to Washington from the Deep South, were on our way to the Jetport along the Harbor Freeway, out past the rooftops and finally the topless lunch-counters. We had a bit of trouble because Gerry was carrying a pair of *papier-mâché* figures he had been sculpting for a *Time* magazine cover. 'They're not of Bobby?', I asked in alarm, as he gave me one to lug along the airport's 'People-Mover', a moving platform decorated with mosaics of primary colours. They turned out to be of some dim West Coast comedians, on whose yacht he had acquired an unusual suntan.

The candidate might have been as dead as Lincoln, but the machine refused to lie down, perhaps it simply did not know how to, like the bristle on a corpse's chin. After the 'reception of the casket', as it was called on the mimeographed programme sheet, we ended up in the Commodore Hotel as if the campaign was, as they say, still 'peaking'. There were the same telephones and free drinks, the same efficient aides, the same tickets to be acquired for entry to various places, though now it was no longer the Indiana Real Estate Association but St Patrick's Cathedral and Arlington Cemetery. Frank Mankiewicz, who had officially announced Bobby was dead, was still there, paler and tighter, but as efficient as ever. Others though were flagging.

The Requiem Mass in St Patrick's had been grave, and, in

some ways, important. It had proved, for example, that Edward Kennedy was going to pick up his brother's banner, as long as it was for sale anyhow, and we had heard, presumably for the last time, the Bernard Shaw quotation about dreaming a dream, though by now it had become Bobby's dream of America, and not Jack's. A great deal of pious nonsense was talked about how, had he lived, one of the most highly competitive and instinctively divisive politicians the USA has ever had would have united the country under wings of peace. I found myself seated next to Billy Graham at the ceremony (only later did I learn he had been specifically not invited) and heard him grunt in satisfaction at this piece of hypocrisy, the kind of thing he understood. The Kennedy women were as splendid as ever, combat veterans of mourning.

After staying long enough to satisfy myself that no one had taken a pot-shot at LBJ, who inevitably had got in on the act, I sent London an account of the proceedings, accurate and understated, and as neat as I could make it in thirty minutes or so. My friend Lewis Chester was holding the fort on the train carrying the coffin at eye level along the tracks to Washington. Here, it seemed, the famous Bullshit Machine finally lay down and died; a couple of mourners were killed on the track; the train, the last and latest of all Bobby's expensive – and late – means of transport, got into the Union Station after nine, five hours or so after schedule. Finally, an hour before midnight, the funeral ceremony in Arlington ended by candlelight.

These unfortunate incidents had not inhibited an American agency reporter from filing a so-called 'holding story' some five hours previously. It had described, with a wealth of moving detail, how 'the casket of Robert F. Kennedy had been laid to its final rest in the sunlight. . . .' Widows had been weeping, strong men moved to tears, and even one of the Kennedy dogs, romping or frolicking, I forget which, among the dappled sunbeams, had received its statutory paragraph. The newspaper I then worked for had compared this account with my own, and decided that the agency was 'later' – as the events it described had not actually taken place when this account arrived in London there could obviously be no doubt that indeed it

was. When, the following drab Sunday morning, I weaved my
way between the pimps and junkies in Times Square to pick
up the foreign newspapers, I was irritated to discover this
sunny, canine account of the previous night's events appearing
under my name on page one. It made up my mind to leave
for Paris where, I was assured, they were having a nice, clean
revolution. I have often wondered which version of his burial
Bobby would have preferred. I suspect he would have gone for
the one with the dog in it.

CHAPTER 13

Piers

♣

THE Viennese have a decided weakness for fancy dress but compared with Piers they are a drab lot for all their green cloaks and hats with shaving brushes on them. I first spotted him in a supermarket in the Kärtnerstrasse, where I was arming myself for what looked like an extended stay in Czechoslovakia by buying whisky, typewriter ribbons, transistor batteries and a lot of other items which usually take a week's work to track down in the Soviet satellite countries. Piers was at a neighbouring counter, also stockpiling ammunition, though of a different calibre. He was facing, I learnt later, the identical dreary itinerary, but there was no sign it was getting him down. Instead he was holding court to a bunch of giggling sales assistants from his temporary throne in the precise centre of the women's underwear counter.

With the air of a connoisseur he was working his way through a mounting pile of pants, bras, stockings, suspender belts and frilly garters. His attitude of total absorption and indifference to the stir he was creating argued either superhuman self-possession, or the insensitivity of a robot. His bald, domed head and eagle's beak were striking enough; his outfit was positively mystifying. For his underwear expedition Piers had selected an obviously expensive English suit, perhaps even from Savile Row, tailored for him probably fifteen years earlier when he must have been slimmer. Even so the wide padded shoulders and bell-bottom trousers gve him an anachronistic, bloated look. With this suit he wore white plastic sandals with matching socks, and an open-necked drip-dry shirt. Over this he wore a transparent blue plastic raincoat, and a kind of pixie hood, also of transparent plastic but this time in faded green. Round his shoulders a very long woollen scarf was negligently draped. The colours, yellow and red, were instantly recognizable. They indicated he was a member of the Marylebone Cricket Club, or at least wished to be taken for one.

He was a large man, and the adjective 'elephantine' fitted him perfectly, far better than anything he was wearing. Suddenly flirtatious he held a sack-like bra – size forty-six I later discovered – to his chest, and performed a ponderous, high camp dance step for the sales girls, who shrieked hysterically. I was reminded vividly of an elephant I once saw doing the same trick in a circus near Sochi on the Black Sea. It would not surprise me to learn that Piers had seen the same elephant in the same place and thence drawn his inspiration, but I never dared to ask him. His selection completed he ordered the nearest girl to pile the goods into four square cardboard boxes he had evidently brought for this purpose. He spoke excellent German with the twang peculiar to Berlin, and also with the Berliner's indifferent bellowing rudery. Perhaps he *was* German, and the MCC scarf a coincidence. To my surprise he marched straight up to me, two boxes under each arm. 'English, eh?' said Piers. 'I noticed you before.'

From close range he was even more impressive. His eyes were blue, and apparently mad. His lips were of the kind one sees on Bosch heads personifying lust. His teeth, which he was proud of, were big, white and beautiful. 'Always easy to spot an Englishman, eh?' continued Piers heartily. 'Must be something about their clothes.'

He indicated his own bizarre get-up with satisfaction, as if it were some exclusive formal costume peculiar to the English, and much imitated by envious foreigners. 'My name's Ferdinand, how d'you,' continued Piers, in fruity upper class tones. 'Wouldn't think there was a world crisis up the road, would you? Cold-blooded bastards the Viennese.'

We had a drink in Sacher's, and I saw his point. No hint here of the anguish across the border. Our fellow clients, sleek against the plush *fin-de-siècle* backdrop, addressed each other by honorific titles, and ate cream cakes. I sent a disconsolate cable to London informing them the border was sealed for the night,

and found Piers arguing with the barman – he claimed his milk
was too cold. His anarchic side was appealing so I invited him
to dinner; it would be instructive to see what the head waiter
made of his pixie hat.

The invitation was warmly accepted, but Piers disappoint-
ingly left for the cloakroom 'to wash and brush up'. When he
returned the plastic hat had gone, and his bald dome looked raw
as a frozen fish finger stripped of its protective covering. He was
now wearing a shabby Old Etonian tie, which I discovered he
always carried in his pocket for such emergencies. It went nicely,
I thought, with the white sandals. The overall impression was
of a barmy peer, likely at any moment to start barking, or
delivering a lecture on the nutritive advantages of nut cutlets.
However, Piers turned out to be a hearty and conventional
trencherman. Between gulps of boiled beef he ogled a fat American widow with blue hair and talked, with encyclopaedic examples, of the sad decline of leg spin in modern cricket. I excused
my own lack of animation on the grounds of exhaustion, and the
dim prospects for the morrow. Piers did his crazed laugh, and
with an expansive gesture brushed aside crises, border guards,
visas – those Eumenides so often at my back with their bloody
claws. 'It's all arranged, old boy,' said Piers. 'I'll take you over
in the morning. Least I can do.' He gave a broad lecherous wink,
and made an obscene gesture, jabbing his right index finger
fiercely back and forth through a circle made with his left thumb
and forefinger. The widow looked away, shocked. Piers cackled.

'Get it, old boy? I'm going the same way as you. Tomorrow
I'm dipping my wick in Prague.'

My exhaustion had been unfeigned. I had been woken at
five am in Paris with the news of the Russian invasion. By eight
I had broken the news to a stunned Czech consul, got my visa,
and been turned off a direct Prague flight from Orly, because
the Czechs – or Russians – had closed the airport. So it had to
be Vienna. With Don McCullin I had been refused entry at
various checkpoints, and so had hundreds of other reporters.
Don was suffering from his habitual anxiety neurosis, a nagging
fear that the battle might be over before he had time to station
himself in the crossfire and take photographs of it. The border

was irrevocably closed, and it was only marginally consoling to learn that others trying via East Berlin, Budapest and even Danzig, had done no better. Don, convinced that he had missed the action, drifted off disconsolately in search of another more accessible war.

Piers and I left soon after dawn in his big white Fiat with Vienna plates. The car was oddly equipped. In the back were two sleeping bags; a set of matched Arnold Palmer golf clubs; a cricket bat and stumps; deckchairs, pneumatic mattresses and an expensive picnic hamper containing a spirit stove. The boot held the four large cardboard cartons of assorted women's underwear, style *Vie Parisienne*, all in black. Our cases went on the roof rack.

My typewriter was still at Sacher's because Piers had sternly proscribed it. 'They might think we were journalists, very bad that. Do you carry a gun by the way?'

'Rarely.'

'Jolly good,' said Piers. 'We don't want to create the wrong impression.'

The Viennese police, surly in their green uniforms, were reluctant to let us drive into no-man's-land. Piers bellowed at them with old-style Prussian volume, and finally they not only raised the barrier, but saluted as we drove off. On the Czech side there were pill boxes with heavy calibre machine guns poking out; half a dozen privates in shapeless khaki carrying the machine pistols favoured by the Viet-Cong, and a full lieutenant with shiny red epaulettes. 'This is where the fun starts,' said Piers happily. 'Get out of the car as soon as I stop. If you stay inside it makes the poor sods feel inferior.'

He concentrated on the Lieutenant, while I distributed Rothmans King Size to the soldiery, who like all the Czechs one met at that period, wore an expression of fixed misery as though their bowels were bothering them. Piers saluted the officer with panache, and handed him our passports, a letter bristling with official seals and a cellophane pass with his picture on it.

Piers' linguistic accomplishments did not stretch to very much Czech, it turned out, but he tried what he knew, which were largely obscenities seasoned with the odd practical phrase. '*Ya*

Ctihodny muz' – 'I am an honourable man,' he began, and followed swiftly with the phrases for 'Are you married?'; 'Do you know a quiet place without people?'; and, finally, *'Lozhnite'* – 'bedroom'. The officer smiled uncertainly, the privates snickered and nudged each other. They clearly thought we were insane. The contents of the boot convinced them. While smirking soldiers pawed through the underwear Piers showed his letter to the officers again. Then he selected one of the giant bras, looped it round his barrel chest, and went into the dance routine that had caused such a stir in the Kärtnerstrasse. The lieutenant and his men laughed till they wept, then led us into a wooden lean-to office. 'We're in, old boy,' said Piers. 'How long do you want the visa for?'

My emergency one was valid for three days only. The officer cheerfully extended it to fifteen. Before we left he pointed up the road, said *'Russkis schlechts'*, and did a very effective pantomime of firing sweeps with an automatic weapon. Then he spoke in rapid Czech. 'What was all that about,' I wondered as we drove off. 'I think he was saying the Russians would shoot us,' said Piers. 'History shows the Czechs have always been a nation of pessimists.'

The first Russians were stationed just two hundred yards from the border post round a bend in the road, thus concealed from the sightseers on the Viennese side. They had a light tank, a couple of personnel carriers and had made a cooking fire. The soldiers were only just over five feet, flat-faced gnomes in miniature jackboots that looked as if they had been specially made for children. One told me he was from Tashkent, and his friend was from Alma Atta where I had once been – the famous orchard city whose name means 'Father of the Apples'. These grey-faced little men, who gave off a doggy odour which must have been the result of sleeping too long in tanks, were totally confused and exhausted. Some seemed to think they were in Germany, others neither knew nor cared where they were. They examined the lingerie with the same blank incomprehension as the cricket bat, and waved us on. At the first crossroads all the road signs had been demolished, except one, newly painted, which pointed east and read: 'Moskva, 2,500 kilometres.'

'Don't suppose those chaps have ever seen a pair of lace panties in their lives,' Piers remarked chattily, turning on to the Prague road, which showed signs of tank tracks. 'From my experience most of those Russian pieces, outside the big cities that is, wear bloody great drawers made out of sacking.'

We drove fast through the pine forests and stopped only three times. Twice, involuntarily because of Russian patrols, and once when Piers spotted a middle-aged lady of ample proportions. 'My first forty-four-er of the day,' he said and leaning through the window asked her conversationally if we were on the road to Prague. She was friendly enough, but despite the routine about 'I am an honourable man' and 'Do you know somewhere quiet?' obviously had no intention of accompanying us anywhere. It must have been a decade since any man had made approaches to her, and she obviously found it hard to believe this bald madman was not trying to make her ridiculous for some obscure purpose of his own. It was embarrassing; the lady was old enough to be Piers' great aunt. It was then I discovered that Piers only criterion of female beauty was bust measurement. The face was of no interest, and neither was the rest of the body – he reckoned such considerations were strictly for amateurs. The bras in the back started at forty-two inches, and he would only reluctantly condescend to women of these modest proportions when there was nothing more Amazonian available. In the glove compartment of the Fiat he carried a tape-measure – an English one in feet and inches, which he explained made him feel more at home. The magic figure of forty-four inches had been heavily hatched over with marking ink for easier identification in poor light.

It took us four and a half hour's hard driving before we reached Prague, and apart from two patrols we saw no Russians at all, which made us both happy. The political situation left Piers cold. He talked of his 'piece' in Prague – 'a genuine forty-fiver' – and of innumerable other pieces over the years. He was disappointed that I did not know how many women I had slept with. He himself had recorded every individual sexual act he had been involved in over the previous decade, as well as the woman's name, measurements and individual peculiarities.

Most of his conquests he seemed to dislike heartily. He had once
been in love – with a happily married ear doctor in Bucharest –
but this unaccustomed emotion had led, he believed, to a series
of technical errors on his part, and he had never repeated the
experiment. The lady had not only rejected him, she had called
the police.

'It was in her surgery, old boy,' Piers explained ruefully. 'I
went originally to have my ears cleaned, a bad start that, not
very romantic. Went back every day for a week with flowers and
she got fed up. I said I'd shoot myself if she didn't come for a
ride in the car, and the next thing I knew there were two bloody
great Rumanian cops there, guns and all. Never fall in love, you
only make mistakes.' The underwear was not, it turned out,
intended as an erotic aid. They were just Piers' trade goods, his
equivalent of the beads missionaries formerly equipped themselves with when converting the heathen. That trip taught me a
lot about underwear. For instance, a double pack of black
stockings, Piers assured me, cost sixteen schillings in Vienna,
or about 27p. By some quirk of the capitalist system a single pair
cost only 7½p less, so the thing to do was buy in bulk and split
the purchases into single units afterwards as the need arose.

'Never give a girl two pairs of stockings at the same time, old
boy,' Piers advised. 'They'll think you're soft, made of money.
I sometimes give a pair at each meeting, that's if there *is* more
than one meeting, of course . . .' And on the stories flowed, of
pieces in Sofia and Dresden, Lvov and Budapest, pieces in
woods and on park benches, in trains and, once, in the lavatory
of a plane over-flying Warsaw. The endless and admittedly
rather repetitive saga of a contemporary Don Juan.

But why, I wondered, did he conduct his operations in the
Iron Curtain countries, surely the most depressing and dangerous in Europe? Piers cocked a mad blue eye sideways, and
smirked. 'Did you ever get a girl into bed in London by giving
her a pair of pants that cost five bob?' he asked. 'Or in Paris,
or Rome?' I admitted I had not. Piers looked triumphant.
'Thought as much. To be honest neither have I. This is the only
place it works.'

But surely there were other methods, less standardized ap-

proaches? 'Not for me, old boy. Don't think I haven't tried, lots
of times. But I'm no good at it anywhere except here. Don't
seem to have the knack. Why, I was a virgin until I got stationed
in Vienna.'

The idea of a virginal Piers was as incongruous as a vision of
him wearing a frou-frou, or writing an ode to Spring. He must
have thought so as well, because he snorted with laughter.
'Except for professionals, of course. But you can't really count
them, can you?'

He looked a bit guilty as if he had been caught out. 'Don't
think I count professionals when I'm adding up My Score. I *note*
them sometimes, if they're special, but I wouldn't count them
in the Grand Total. That wouldn't do at all.' I said I had never
suspected him capable of such deception, and he looked pleased.
It was a waste of energy making ironical comments to Piers:
he never even noticed.

'I never got a commission, too intelligent I suppose, so I was
only a poor bloody driver in the Ordnance. Bloke I knew was
a poacher by trade, a border Scot, and we heard there was
bloody good hunting up round Brno. We wangled a forty-eight
together, borrowed an old jalopy, and drove up to take a
butcher's. It was NBG, guards all over the shop, so we buggered
off to have a few beers. Jock, that's what we called him, started
chatting up a couple of pieces. I didn't say much, I was a bit
shy in those days.' Again he was struck by the incongruity of the
youthful, naive Piers, and he cackled.

'To break the ice I offered one of the pieces a cigarette, I had
a packet of Player's. She practically went spare, held it up to
the light to examine the workmanship, showed it to her mate,
eyes went all gooey. Might have been the Koh-i-Noor diamond.
So I gave her the rest of the packet, wouldn't do *that* nowadays,
I can tell you. She was tickled pink, and beckoned me into some
kind of garden place they had at the back. I didn't think anything much of it, and then all of a sudden she started undoing
my fly. Wouldn't believe it, would you? I nearly went mad. She
wasn't on the game or anything, just bowled over with gratitude
by the fags.' Piers looked very solemn, and turned full face on
as he recalled his conversion on the Road to Damascus.

'I tell you, old boy, I never looked back from that day on. I'd Seen the Light.'

This same Light, which Piers had been doggedly following across the length and breadth of Eastern Europe for over ten years, finally led us to Prague in the later afternoon. My mind was already worrying about telephone lines and telex circuits while I tried to take in what was going on: the crowds smothering the Wenceslas statue with flowers; the bullet holes in the façade of the National Museum, which the Russians had mistaken for the Central Radio Station; the shell of a burnt out tank covered in graffiti with 'Russkis Go Home' (in English) among the slogans. The Russian tank crews, exhausted and angry, were usually being harangued by groups of young Czechs, and they didn't seem to be enjoying it. There were occasional crackles of small arms fire; no one seemed to take any notice. 'Quite a scene,' I said to Piers. 'Marvellous,' replied my companion enthusiastically, his eyes flickering up and down the crowded pavements. 'Just look at those mini-skirts.'

I wanted to get to the Alcron Hotel as soon as possible because I knew that such of my colleagues who had managed to sneak in would be gathered in the deplorable tea-lounge that serves as a substitute for a bar. Piers at first ignored this suggestion and then without warning suddenly changed gear, accelerated fiercely across the tramlines, and seemed to be turning up Stepanska Street, a hundred yards from the revolving glass doors which lead into the Alcron's murky and crumbling foyer. But on the corner, with an unnecessary screech, he stopped the Fiat altogether.

Piers wound down his window and leant out, beaming at around 170 pounds of early middle-aged lady with synthetic, angry-looking red hair, plastic glasses with wings, and – I should have known at once – a heavy, sloppy bust under a tight dress. Piers spoke to her, in German, very slowly. 'Can you tell me the way to the Alcron Hotel, please? I am lost.' He then got out of the car and so, sadly, did I. It was obvious that Piers was going to be occupied for some time. As I left he asked her name, again slowly, and she replied with a frightening smirk: 'Ich bin Drahamira.'

It's quite a common Bohemian name. I left before he had time to ask whether she knew a quiet place without people; or to assure her he was an honourable man.

The next ten days saw the so-called Dubcek Spring give way ineluctably to a long, masochistic Autumn, from which the country has never emerged. It was an acutely depressing period. Each day the Czechs lost a little more heart, grew less impertinent to their invaders, prepared themselves for the long haul of just getting by. There were fifty thousand militia men with weapons in their homes trained to carry out guerilla resistance in precisely this kind of emergency – except it had always been assumed that the invader would be the forces of West German capitalism, rather than their fellow socialists from the east. If ever a time was ripe for Viet-Cong resistance this was it, with the Russians confused and hopelessly inadequate, and the whole country providing the ideal water for the revolutionary fish to swim in. But, unlike their Polish comrades, the Czechs are imbued with common sense, and to hell with national pride.

History has made them a nation of masochists and they were soon sullenly accommodating to the Russians, just as their parents had to the Germans. Those who were not prepared to knuckle under left while they could, and daily one's contacts vanished, shortly to reappear in Switzerland or Paris or British provincial universities. Communications were vile and Piers was a luxury one had no time to enjoy. Not that I didn't see him around; he was, as ever, conspicuous, and seldom far from the Alcron tea lounge, where he spent long hours leering at the twenty or so whores the secret police kept there, or parading through Wenceslas Square in his plastic outfit, endlessly asking strange women with big breasts the way to the Alcron or some other prominent monument in the direction they were already walking. On the night of our arrival I had seen him briefly again, signing Drahamira into the Hotel Alcron, while tracer bullets blasted blue and red along Stepanska Street – the Russians' typically delicate way of underlining the eight pm curfew. Piers was obviously well known to the management, and was greeted with smirks and dirty jokes. 'Wie geht's?' I heard him say to the night manager.

'Everything OK, everything under police control,' replied this unshaven, putty-faced functionary. Anywhere but Prague it would have been meant as a joke.

Piers, hustling Drahamira towards the antique lift, was indifferent to the tracers outside and the near-hysteria within. He leered at me happily over her shoulder and raised two fingers she could not see – not, I believe in any obscene spirit, but simply to indicate his Grand Total had advanced in the course of the afternoon. Perhaps he had found an unoccupied tank.

When things quietened down my colleagues in the Alcron found time to ponder the mystery of Piers, and decided to a man he must be a secret agent. He had played chess with them all, and beaten them, so I assumed they had decided he was too intelligent to be a journalist, and there seemed no other conceivable justification for being in that hotel at that period. I tried to explain about forty-four-ers and the rest but everyone thought I was naive. In the course of one afternoon a man from the BBC, who was always trying, heroically, to make his pleasant west of England brogue sound like middle fifties Chelsea, assured me that Piers was working for the West Germans ('because of his accent, old boy') only to be followed by a Central European freelance, whom I had decided several years previously actually was working for them, with a tale about Piers' important role in East German intelligence.

'Watch that bald guy, David,' he said. 'He's a Berlin spook, I know it. What did he say to you just then?'

'Asked me if I knew the Test score. We're forty-six for three if you're interested.' The Middle European looked at me with deep suspicion, and has probably been going round ever since boring people with stories about my role in the Czech secret police. Piers was unworried by this suspicious undercurrent; he was, after all, used to it, it was inevitable, given his chosen beat, and as he said: 'You've got to make *some* sacrifices old man. You can't just go around expecting to get it for nothing.'

Later Piers appeared in Paris for Christmas and made a spirited attempt to seduce my washerwoman. He left reasonably content though, as ever outside that Iron Curtain, with no additions to either the Score, or the Grand Total. Later yet, Jan

Palach committed suicide, the kind of occasion the Czechs really get their teeth into. Before being expelled I discovered that Palach had in fact been number three on a list of student candidates for self-immolation, and had performed the act under heavy sedation after the first two, who had drawn even lower cards than him, had suddenly recalled pressing engagements elsewhere. The usual crowd were in the Alcron, including Piers, who came pounding over the carpet to greet me like a cheerful St Bernard.

By this time *The Observer*, a newspaper always interested in espionage – after all, they had employed Philby, the best practitioner of modern times – had discovered about Piers. They were about a year late, but found this in no way inhibiting. An exuberant piece appeared saying that Piers was known to the press corps as 'The Naked Tape', a late-night joke which referred to his baldness, and the known fact that all bedrooms in the Alcron are bugged via a pleasant man who sits with his recording devices in an office on the left of the hotel's underground garage as you go in. Piers, it seemed, had been seen talking to this man (about his sister, as I later learned, 'a forty-fiver if ever I saw one') and *The Observer* had jumped in.

This piece of journalistic enterprise revived the old topic of Piers' credentials, a matter that interested him little as he was engaged in the pursuit of what he called 'a very decent little nurse, looks very clean too'. My Paris colleague Alex Macmillan had heard all about Piers from me previously, and was fascinated to see the fabled ungainly figure revelling in the chase. As Alex was beyond doubt a real pukka Etonian, possibly the only one between the Alcron and the Bosphorus, I suggested he bought my friend a coffee, and tried to pump him about his background. Alex, as always a good reporter, wasted no time.

He returned an hour later with the look of a man who had been attempting to chat about Pop and M'Tutor in a casual kind of way, and been sorely frustrated. I asked him for his verdict. 'Weird bloke, isn't he?' said Alex cautiously.

'Certainly,' I said, 'but is he a weird *Etonian*? You didn't look as if you were warbling the Boating Song together.'

'No, we didn't, scarcely mentioned the place as a matter of fact, not that I didn't try.'

'What did you talk about then?'

Alex smiled disarmingly, and shook his head a couple of times. 'That's what I meant by weird. The chap didn't seem to have any conversation at all, except, er . . .'

'Except, er, what?'

'I know it sounds insane but actually he refused categorically to discuss anything except, er, tits.'

CHAPTER 14

Jay

♣

IF AN analyst checking on my word associations said the name
'Paris', my home and great love, I might riposte with something
banal but apparently quite sane like *Eiffel* or '*Service non Compris*'.
On the other hand it might quite easily come to me to say 'Jay',
or even 'JayBee', a common variant on the same name, though
now largely fallen out of use.

Jay Berman Finkler liked to be called by his first two initials
during his high commercial period around 1964. He obviously
believed that this dated company executive affectation reinforced what he would doubtless have then called his 'business
image', though in fact it always made me think of some sinister
mutant, half bird and half insect. This was highly misleading
because the man is far from sinister. Jay is simply an American
in Paris, a professional American in Paris that is, the purest em-
bodiment of a traditional species, whose relationship to the
French capital is that of fly to sticky paper. Round every Paris
corner some tiny experience lies in wait – a gratuitous insult, a
traffic accident, perhaps just somebody shouting about something. If the corner happens to be in the Fifth Arrondissement
there is a reasonable chance that Jay will be there too, on duty
as it were, blending confidently in against the Gallic backdrop.

On my earliest, schoolboy visits to Paris I did not cross his
path, though I am sure he was there, reading the *New York
Times* by the old League of Nations building and sending snapshots of Napoleon's Tomb home to uncomprehending relatives
in the middle west. As a hitchhiker my main concern was to
dodge past the centre of town as fast as possible in order to find
a good pitch on the N7 around the Porte d'Italie, and one
therefore skirted Jay's natural habitat. I ran into him, on the

other hand, within days of my first period of real residence in the
city, and ever since he has been as reliable an adjunct of the
capital of Europe as clear white dawns along the Quai des
Grands Augustins.

An English girl who was working in George's *librairie* on
Place St Julien-le-Pauvre took me to see Jay one winter's afternoon in the studio he then had somewhere off the Boulevard de
Montparnasse (I have never been able to locate this little street
since, and suspect it has been sacrificed in the interests of the
monstrous new Montparnasse station). There was no purpose to
the visit, like so many at this time, except that people like us
who were sharing an eight franc room in the Hotel de Notre-
Dame tended to cultivate people who had apartments of their
own, mainly to get out of the cold. Our favourite shelter by far
was on the Quai aux Fleurs where some other Paris Americans,
Jim and Gloria Jones, were endlessly hospitable – they had
known hard times themselves before *From Here to Eternity* had
made him the best war novelist of his generation. In sneakers
and T-shirt he still looked like a marine on leave. But Gloria
was pregnant with Haley, and we were careful not to bother
them too often. They said she had been Marilyn Monroe's
stand-in: judging by the way she looked six months gone it
should have been the other way round. Anyway that day we
went to Jay's. With his unvarying politeness he made tea, and
showed us his latest paintings, accomplished and totally un-
forthcoming abstracts which betrayed an obsession for the
palest of washed-out blues. But the conversation was mainly
political.

And so it largely passed over my head. There were lots of
names which then meant nothing to me – Moch, Pinay and
Mendès-France, Pleven and Thorez – cabinet ministers of the
moment I assumed, because this was during de Gaulle's long
exile when new French governments were as common as
quarter days. Jay knew what was going on from the inside,
or almost from the inside: I remember he was the first person
I ever heard refer to the Communist Party, familiarly as
it were, as 'The Party'. In the same kind of way he kept talking
about 'Albert', and it was some time before I realized he meant

Camus. Had Sartre figured in the conversation, or rather mono-logue, he would certainly have been 'Jean-Paul', but as far as I remember the great philosopher of French sixth formers was only present by proxy, represented by Jay's black cloak which hung on the door ready for sorties into the Boulevard St Germain, and also by his fringe beard.

At that period Jay also favoured hair *en brosse*, GI boots, and Boyard cigarettes, a brand that has always exercised an irresistible appeal for a certain kind of French intellectual, for whom they symbolize old fashioned provincial academicism: anti-clerical discussion in cafés like Les Deux Garcons in Aix, a nostalgia for a lost way of life which is stimulated by reading *Le Grand Meaulnes* or *Le Diable au Corps* and St Exupéry at an impressionable age. God alone knows what they symbolized for Jay, whose grasp of the French language was then still tenuous, but it was absolutely certain they symbolized something. Perhaps he had seen 'Albert' smoking them, or even 'Jean-Paul'.

When we left Jay asked my beautiful girl friend if she wanted to borrow any money. She said she didn't, and Jay looked relieved, though surprised.

'Most people do,' he said. And then: 'Come again, I mean any time you're passing.'

It was hard not to feel a certain sympathy, and even admiration, for a man who was so much a prey to bohemian sharks, and yet remained so polite. When we were back on the icy boulevard my friend remarked that Jay was sad because his wife had left him. I replied, half ironically, that he seemed very good at controlling his feelings. Privately, I doubted that anyone with eyes that shade of blue – like his canvases, they were preternaturally pale – was likely to be much troubled by deep passion.

The next meeting with Jay was distinctly more dramatic. He appeared suddenly from the street, black cloak aswirl, and transfixed the company with an expression laden with doom. 'I've just heard,' he said, as if citing his private line to the Archangel Gabriel, 'Albert Camus has committed suicide.' I remember wondering why he hadn't simply called the writer 'Albert'.

We were crouched round in the bookshop then officially called the *Mistral*, and now transmogrified into *Shakespear & Co.*, in honour of Sylvia Beach. The gesture is entirely appropriate because George, the proprietor, numbers among his more amiable eccentricities the belief that he is inhabiting the American Paris of the 1920s so minutely documented by anyone who ever spent a long weekend there, and learnt how to spell '*Contrescarpe*', or fall off a bar stool in the Crillon. Miss Beach's shop and George's have little in common except the name, and the fact that they both served as a magnet for expatriate Americans. While the original shop was patronized by Joyce, Hemingway, Henry Miller and so on, its successor tends to attract people either writing about these luminaries in order to acquire postgraduate degrees, or just plain bums. On the day of Jay's announcement his audience consisted of perhaps six from each category, uneasily drawn together by a common need to find somewhere out of the cold that didn't cost anything.

Jay's announcement went down pretty flat. George, who looks like a starved goat and likes to be gnomic, made the peculiar throaty clucking noise which is his trademark and at once retired to his squalid quarters upstairs, either to ponder the cosmic significance of the great man's suicide, or more likely to take a snort of rum and coke from his private supply without having to offer a drink to anyone else. Jay began to harangue his captive and largely apathetic audience.

'He could no longer live with that blindingly, searingly honest vision of man's predicament . . .' he began, and after about ten minutes of this both graduates and bums began to be stirred. It was the first hint I had that Jay was a talented salesman. A quaker from Ohio who was said to be 'researching into' Sherwood Anderson remarked that we had witnessed the passing of a great man, which seemed a mild exaggeration. He also thought that suicide was setting a bad example. One of the bums remarked you got fifteen hundred francs from the Prefecture for pulling a suicide's body out of the Seine, and that maybe if one studied the tides there was real money in it. He was rebuked for his insensitivity by a young divorcée who had published a totally impenetrable short story in a review called *Two Cities*, and she and Jay raised the spiritual tone with an earnest discussion of the sun and sea imagery in *l'Etranger*. When I finally slipped out for a drink in the rue St Severin, deftly forestalling an attempt by one of the bums to accompany me, the bookshop was taking on the aura of an Irish wake, passionate, solemn and also rather sexy. Jay had finally succeeded in communicating his own excitement to the others, and they were all extracting the maximum possible gratification out of the suicide. A genuine customer, one of those rare birds who evidently had come to buy a book, was actually turned away as if he were intruding into private grief.

Jay's news affected me less than it might have done because I had long been filled with priggish disapproval over the writer's apparently colonialist and unprogressive views on the liberation and independence of his native Algeria. (Since then first hand experience of liberated Algeria which Boumédienne has managed to turn from a fertile and potentially enormously prosperous society into a ruined and sinister slum has given me more sympathy with his views.) In my bar I picked up *France-Soir*, and to my surprise discovered the truth.

Far from committing suicide Camus had in fact died in a vulgar road accident. He had been killed instantaneously when a Facel-Vega driven by Michel Gallimard, his publisher's son, had left the road at high speed in a rain storm and finished up wrapped round a tree. So much for Jay's 'searing vision'. He had obviously been misled by the headline read over someone's shoulder: '*Camus Se Tue.*' Instead of going back to break the news I had another drink; there was no point in shattering so many solemnities about the human condition. When I did finally return the *émigrés* were engrossed in a discussion about the duty free concessions the French authorities allowed visitors who purchased scent with dollar cheques. Camus was studiously not mentioned, and Jay had departed. That was the last day of his existentialist period, and I never saw him wearing that black cloak again.

Instead Jay became a beat. This became clear at a party the cultural counsellor at the American Embassy unwisely gave in the Boulevard St Germain for the heroes of the Beat Generation, most of whom were then supposed to be in Paris. Allen Ginsberg, it turned out, was meditating on a beach in southern Spain and Kerouac, as was his wont, had disappeared no one knew where. But still there were a few lions, scruffy, destroyed-looking lions though they were. William Burroughs, skeletal in a grey suit, trembled in a corner like some dusty ghost, attended by a beautiful English girl who was allowed into his room in the Hotel Gît le Coeur to sweep up, and an equally beautiful boy who had similar privileges, though his duties differed. Burroughs contributed little but it didn't matter because Gregory Corso, very drunk or high or both, was reciting a free-verse poem to an audience of American Embassy staff who looked a bit uneasy. Sure, they seemed to be thinking, he's a poet, we all know about Dylan Thomas and all that. But wasn't that f**k he just said?

The Embassy people were unwontedly animated. Generally their major preoccupation, attending as they did occasions of this kind seven times a week, was remaining moderately sober, and avoiding seducing the wives of senior colleagues. But this party – for 'poets and bohemians' – was different; they could let their hair down a shade, it was even expected. Accordingly, a crew-cut second secretary tried, unavailingly, to engage Burroughs in conversation about Kafka. Burroughs twitched at him. And various cocktail-dressed wives surrounded Gregory feeding him whisky and things on bits of toast. With his small stature and curly hair he looked like Eros in a Titian. Someone put dixieland records on the Hi-Fi, and among the Embassy personnel there was decorous jiving. Burroughs began to talk, or rather croak, under the influence of Scotch, and Corso, his eyes glowing and bloodshot, was making a speech, mainly about the cats who inhabit the Colosseum in Rome.

Jay, dressed in an army surplus combat jacket and smoking marihuana, was prominent in the group of listeners: he was in fact the only member of the small audience who looked uncritically enthusiastic. Corso switched topics – he was now talking about the beauty of women, the way their souls breathed through their eyes. The wives looked pleased, and particularly our hostess, a stout honey blonde in her middle forties whose placid features wore a slightly dopey expression of generalized goodwill. She was probably the secretary of the Embassy wives' committee devoted to charitable works among Paris slum children and doubtless she had bridge afternoons twice a week. Poets, or anyway the kind who smoked dope and said fuck, probably did not figure largely among her acquaintance. She found Gregory exciting, and he was not a man to miss a chance. 'You must have a very interesting life, Mr Corso,' she began tentatively. Gregory beamed at her in a way that suggested he wasn't focusing too well.

'Dig,' he said.

'I beg your pardon?'

'Dig,' said Gregory encouragingly, as if talking to a backward child. 'You know, like I dig you. You know, I think you're great, dig?'

The lady looked confused but fell back on the training so painfully acquired over the years bringing American culture to the Thais, the South Koreans, the Chileans and other incomprehensible foreigners (whom her husband heaped indiscriminately together into one category – they were all 'Gooks' to him).

'Very interesting,' she said sincerely. Gregory obviously found her an unsatisfactory interlocutor; he did not feel obliged to prop up dull conversations. 'You know something,' he said. 'I think you're pretty, dig? Yeah, whooee, yeah you're beautiful, like a picture.'

This was the kind of thing she understood, though one imagined compliments came her way fairly rarely. She simpered, as she might have done at thirteen, and her cheeks, already flushed from highballs, glowed crimson. 'You're a flirt, Mr Corso,' she said roguishly.

'Right,' said Gregory. 'Pretty as a picture. One of those crazy Breughels up there in Amsterdam. You know the thing I mean . . .' he paused to ensure the whole group was drawn in for the punch line. One or two of them, including, I noticed, Jay, nodded to establish their familiarity both with Breughel and Amsterdam. 'You know those crazy peasants in the fields? You know those great fat women with red cheeks? That's you, baby. Just like a great beautiful sack of potatoes tied round the middle.'

Considering the man's intake of drink and dope that night his poetic reflexes were functioning remarkably well. She looked precisely as he said. A couple of the group laughed a bit nervously, Gregory beamed hazily, happy with his *bon mot*, the lady burst into hysterical sobs, and had to be led from the room by her husband, who looked as if he were worrying about whether the incident was going to affect his next promotion.

Later the same night I bumped into Jay and Gregory in a bar off the rue de Seine. Gregory was suffering, and kept disappearing to the lavatory. Jay was in a state of euphoria. 'Isn't he great?' he wanted to know. 'Jesus, there's a guy who's really spontaneous.'

I said mildly that perhaps he should reserve his spontaneity for those better equipped to deal with it than the lady who looked like the potato sack. Jay, with a pitying expression I was to know well over the years, shook his head.

'It's that English education. If you don't mind me saying so it leaves all you guys kinda, kinda emasculated.'

Gregory reappeared and said he had to 'split'. 'Lay some bread on me, can you,' he said to me.

'No.'

Gregory smiled beatifically. 'Dig man,' he said, and turned to Jay with the same request. Jay gave him fifty dollars which was generous, because in those days he was a poor man.

Gregory's spontaneity did not inhibit him from establishing the correct rate of exchange and noting it on a beer mat. Then he left, a weaving, determined little man who seemed to have trouble supporting the weight of all that curly hair. Jay was still enthusiastic. 'You know he's going to stay with Peggy Guggenheim in Venice? She said he could have her chauffeur to drive him down. You know what he said? He said "Screw chauffeurs". He says he's going to hitchhike like he used to do with Kerouac and Neal Cassady. He says that's the way to see the poetry in the country.'

'What do you think the chances are of seeing that fifty again?'

Jay looked pained. 'Man,' he said, (he had recently started referring to everyone, male or female, in this way) 'Man, wouldn't it be great to hitch right down there to Venice?

Wouldn't it be great to bum rides right across the States, from New York to California? Route 66, you dig?' To extract some enthusiasm he ordered two more red wines.

'You know that English poet Thom Gunn, the cat who wrote "A Sense of Movement"?' I said I did.

'He digs, that cat. I tell you, the next time I see you I'll probably have been right across the States, just bumming rides and digging the scene.'

'Okay, Jay.' I wished him luck, and didn't see him again for nearly three years.

It was 1965, the year of the presidential election, the year all the anti-Gaullists had, albeit reluctantly, agreed to support whichever opposition candidate did best on the first vote in the hope of unseating the old man.

In Rouen I had seen the mayor, Jean Lecanuet, who was engaged in launching what he thought of as a 'Kennedy-style' campaign, which largely involved the distribution of wide angle photographs of himself looking purposive and youthful. In Marseille I had talked to Mayor Gaston Defferre, who as 'Monsieur X' had been preparing to run for the office of president for over a year. In the Aveyron in south-west France I had spent a hallucinatory day with Pierre Poujade, the former leader of the small businessmen's party.

Finally, I went back to Paris and specifically to the Crillon Bar, where it seemed worth checking my impressions against those of Sam White, *doyen* of the Paris press corps, and probably the best client the Crillon has had in its long history. He was of course there perched on his throne-like stool, but before I had a chance to speak to him I was intercepted by Jay, a Jay whose plumage had taken on such brilliant courtship hues that he was virtually unrecognizable. Gone was the rough beard, the long hair, the down-at-heel ex-army outfit he had worn so long. Instead he was resplendent in a suit of black silk, which made him look remarkably like a Mafia button man, and gave his carroty hair a curiously livid look. His tie was of heavy silk cut squarely, evidently in Dior's workrooms judging by the label that seemed to be on the outside. Jay's Italian shoes had silver buckles on them, and he had acquired a toothbrush moustache, a rather gingery one.

'Hullo there, I'm waiting for my date.' Jay's fruity welcoming tones, so unlike the old cool manner, reminded me very much of Billy Graham, with whom I had recently spent several tedious hours. Simultaneously, Jay placed his manicured right hand on my left upper arm and delicately squeezed it three times as if he were a cannibal connoisseur checking on the fatty content.

'I'm drinking whisky sours,' Jay suggested, calling 'Gilles' familiarly to the barman. When the bill came I noticed he initialled it – 'J.B.'. This was the finest flower of the 'JayBee' epoch. Not only had Jay's speaking voice ripened into a timbre of continuous *bonhomie* his subject matter had also been refurbished. No more abstract painting; no existentialism, no beat ravings. Instead he talked like an article in *The Wall Street Journal*. It passed above my head; one phrase only stuck in my mind: 'Communications satellites, they'll be high flyers.' I laughed, and Jay for the first time switched off his permanent smile. 'Dave,' he said looking pained, 'don't you see I'm talking about *growth*.'

Jay, it emerged, was selling stock in an offshore mutual fund based in Geneva. He seemed to be peddling this paper to some effect as he now owned a house on the lake, and a speedboat to go with it. As if to keep his hand in he tried to sell me an insurance scheme: I was being treated as 'Mr Prospect,' as the suckers were called in the salesmen's instruction pamphlets. He jotted capital growth percentages down for me in a crocodile skin notebook with 'J.B.' monogrammed in gold when there was a transatlantic phone call for him. Gilles, whom I had known in his earlier days at the *Closerie des Lilas* on the Boulevard de Montparnasse, passed the phone to Jay with a good deal more respect than he had ever shown me. It was obscurely irritating. Behind Jay's back Gilles allowed himself the undue familiarity of rubbing his thumb and index finger together in the gesture which in France means *'fric'* – cash.

Even Sam, a man not over-impressionable by any standards, evinced mild interest.

'Who's your rich cobber?' he wanted to know. 'I've seen the

bugger's face a hundred times. . . .' 'You should have done. He's
The American in Paris, the original archetypal one. He's the
contemporary Wandering Jew, the . . .'

My whisky sour eloquence was cut short as Sam raised his
memorably bushy grey eyebrows. 'He seems to have been wandering in the right direction. . . .'

Jay's 'date' had arrived, a Negress of perhaps six feet two,
who had acquired a certain local fame as the star model of
Cardin's most recent show. On the way out Jay introduced her
and explained they were driving to Geneva that afternoon – he
reckoned in his new Maserati they would do it in under five
hours. The car enthused him, and he discussed its particular
merits for some minutes. 'Why don't you hitchhike?' I asked
unkindly. Jay looked blank.

'Remember Thom Gunn, the sense of movement, swinging
free down "66", remember Gregory? Did you ever see those
fifty bucks?'

Jay brushed the questions aside airily. He indicated that in
the mutual fund world, Gregory Corso, like the Pope, had no
divisions behind him, and as for sums like fifty dollars – that
was the kind of money you used for lighting your Havanas.

From then on for a couple of years whenever I went anywhere conventionally smart Jay, like Kilroy, was there. When
dining with my publisher in New York at The Four Seasons Jay
appeared gesticulating across the fountain. On the one occasion
when against my better judgment I went to the London Hilton
to play poker with a visiting actor I found Jay sitting in the
repulsive lobby watching a mannequin parade of mink stoles.
When King Constantine lost his throne so clumsily I booked
into the Hotel de la Ville in via Sistina instead of my usual
Roman journalistic fleapit because the ex-King's dim and hos-
tile advisers were lodged there. In the Edwardian lift I met Jay,
with a starlet from Cine-Città. He still squeezed my shoulder
but in a more perfunctory fashion, I noticed. There was a
growing uneasiness about the eyes; he talked less Wall Street
and more Hollywood. It seemed he had attended film festivals
at both Cannes and Venice. Geneva, I noticed, no longer
loomed in his conversation as a kind of mutual fund Mecca.

The King's *coup* took place, or rather failed to take place, in December 1967, and I stayed on for Christmas to see President Johnson's slightly ignominious arrival for a Papal audience: the demonstrators ensured, or so a Roman colleague assured me, that LBJ was unable to set foot on Italian soil, except when changing helicopters. After that I was travelling incessantly to a whole series of totally unJaylike places, and lost track of him for eighteen months – to be precise until June 9, 1968. The reunion, as might have been guessed, took place in his favourite Latin Quarter of Paris. I was coming in from Orly after an exhausting transatlantic flight looking for signs of a revolution in which I found it hard to believe. If it *had* taken place at all then the key must have been distinctly minor, despite the pictures. People in shirt sleeves were strolling in the Luxembourg Gardens, and the sun on the Boulevard St Michel made this normally slum-like thoroughfare look almost lyrical. There were the shells of three burnt-out cars, but none was burning now. I noticed a CRS riot cop laughing with a pretty girl, and also Jay.

He was installed by the St Michel Fountain, a new Jay, or rather a reincarnation of a past, once rejected, *persona*. He wore his combat jacket, which must have hung neglected for a decade in some dusty cupboard. The beard, though still at no more than the advanced stubble stage, indicated that his decision to grow it – as one might have guessed – had coincided with the beginning of the troubles in Paris, less than three weeks earlier. Round his neck he wore a black handkerchief which though dirty appeared to be of silk, a relic presumably of the executive period. Its purpose, I learnt eventually, was to protect the wearer from tear-gas attacks, though by then there was little gas going. Jay was effusive, but shocked to learn I had only just flown in from New York.

'If you leave Paris too long you miss all the action,' he reproved me. 'Listen, I think we can still win,' and he launched his fist forward from the shoulder as if he were singing the *Internationale*. He was already explaining the revolution.

I was too exhausted even to laugh. But, as always, it was impossible to be unmoved by Jay's blithe assumption that this pocket of northern Europe was the warm centre of the universe and that the rest of the world was as fascinated as Jay himself by what was happening there. Revolution, or a new trend in action painting, it was all the same to Jay. I remember wishing weakly he would stop using superlatives all the time. He was saying how spontaneous and beautiful it had been when Cohn-Bendit had spurned Waldeck-Rochet. Such was Jay's eloquence that for a moment one had a vision of this grubby opportunist, not as an undergraduate on the make (one's usual image of the lad), but beatified, and swirling a white cloak. Even for a moment it was possible to believe there was a real revolution going on, not simply an adolescent charade which one could already see was likely to have as its most important consequence a France even more rigid and oppressive than before.

Grinning inanely, behind the stubble he wore like a medal ribbon, Jay seemed to be expecting a word of praise, as if the whole thing were his creation. Or rather perhaps, thinking of his commercial past, as if it were a fast-growing company in which he had acquired a controlling interest on the cheap. Jay mentioned that a tiny and enormously solemn political group called 'the Situationists' were meeting that night at his apart-ment. I enquired who the hell they were. Jay, shocked, shook his head in disbelief that anyone could be so ignorant. 'This is June 1968, remember?' He rebuked me. 'Oh man, where have you been?'

In good years Paris enjoys a majestic, orange season of autumn until the third week of October when winter suddenly descends on one virtually overnight. November always seems the month when Paris gets nearest to being ugly and drab, in the way London is; the French could do, one always feels around that time of year, with a Guy Fawkes' Day. In the rue Gay-Lussac there were no more fireworks that November, only an ex-hibition of photographs taken during what were euphemistically called 'les événements du mai'. These images of six months ago were, I reflected, looking at the pig-snouted cops gassing and beating up students, already as remote as the Brady sepia studies of the American Civil War. Jay, who showed up after a while as has always been his wont in the Latin Quarter, felt the same too.

'Like since then man the whole place has turned into plastic,' he said, after a perfunctory '*Salut*'. 'A kind of happiness has gone out of Paris.'

'They went about it the wrong way,' I said, slightly worried to find myself in agreement with Jay on any matter. 'Right on,' Jay replied. 'They had all these political hang-ups – analysis, dialectic, all that Marxist shit. They weren't into love, did you notice that?' I grunted noncommittally, recalling how one minor student leader had described the five girls he claimed to have had during a twenty-four-hour Sorbonne sit-in. Would Jay have considered him 'into love', I wondered. More to the point, what did this odd remark signify in Jay's Parisian evolution?

'A fuck,' said Jay very loudly, as one declaiming some Old Testament text in a Baptist Church, 'can be a great revolutionary weapon.' What precisely he meant by this was puzzling; evidently he had embarked on yet another mysterious Paris voyage heading God knew where. 'Tell me, Jay,' I said. 'What exactly are you, er, into?'

Instead of replying he invited me to visit his apartment as if I would find the answer there. Perhaps he had realized the fascination that place had always held for me. Jay's eclectic headquarters, the fruit of fifteen years of 'getting into' this and that, made me feel like an archaeologist starting a dig on some new Cnossos. By charting the 'levels' of his finds, the archaeologist would bit by bit establish a chronology for the rise and fall of Minoan civilization and in the same kind of way Jay's apartment bristled with historical clues to his development, passing as it did through several very distinct phases. The apartment had grown with him. His old *atelier* had been the nucleus, out of which had grown the kind of private theatre he had acquired during the big money period by purchasing adjoining apartments, knocking down walls, and generally subsidizing half the phoney interior decorators in Paris. They had created a huge central space with rooms opening off and, among other refinements, a minstrels' gallery of the kind one might have expected to find in San Simeon, or one of the other great American follies. Significantly the *atelier*, like the mediaeval core of a house developed during the renaissance, had now fallen into disrespect. He used it as an attic only.

It contained the earliest traces of Jay's European period, a pile of canvases in abstract impressionist style recalling Jay in besmeared painter's smock living frugally off the GI Bill. Along one wall he had stored a row of dusty and long unopened filing cabinets in chic aluminium, a relic of the Captain of Industry period which, as it had been a time of buying, was liberally represented throughout the whole house. There were the obvious executive accoutrements: the battered Eames chairs; the intercom system (now broken) between master bedroom and hall; the electric typewriter, the revolving steel bookcase devoted almost entirely to grim though gaily jacketed studies of abstruse commercial matters published by the Harvard Business School. Jay had talked about Harvard so possessively at this time that a lot of people, possibly including Jay himself, believed he was an *alumnus*. The books traced Jay's development chronologically; cheap art books giving way to book club editions on politics and current events, and these sober labels leading to the more eye-catching editions of the City Lights Bookstore – Ferlinghetti, Ginsberg and Gregory Corso. Then the highly materialistic Harvard series, soon to be followed by piles of coffee table volumes devoted to the cinema in all its multifariously dull aspects. There were also rows of challenging looking paperbacks, often it seemed in German, devoted to the careers of film directors I had never heard of. That film period had been one of Jay's stubbornest, and the apartment contained a projection and sound unit, as I knew to my cost. How many films had I been forced to watch on Castro, how many on Che? How many times had I heard Jay solemnly elucidating some particularly meaningless piece of filmic self-indulgence, and nodding gravely to himself the while as if in the presence of genius. There had been the film that consisted of one shot of an empty room which lasted for forty minutes against a background of electronic music. There had been another about a homosexual who achieved satisfaction through having his nipple slowly transfixed by a needle. This had lasted a very long time; Jay had said it was the most beautiful film of the century.

All this, plus the repellent ten foot high head in *papier-mâché* which had been used in some horror movie, had been Jay

'getting into films'. But, as I realized within seconds of entering
the place after a two-year absence, all these familiar symbols
representing various things Jay had 'got into' in the past,
were as nothing compared with what he was getting into
now.

Though it was mid-afternoon the place was sunk in crepuscu-
lar gloom; green shades had been drawn across the sloping
studio windows thirty feet up. Out of this gloom came a smell
which seemed very clearly to be a compound of three lesser
smells – incense, cannabis and dirt. At first I thought we were
alone, except for the white head, and then I saw a group of five
or six long-haired kids sprawled in an undulating heap on what
I later learned was the water-bed, a Greenwich Village fad Jay
had imported. They were not making love, as Jay had probably
been hoping. Instead they formed an amorphous hairy pile
blurring distinctions of sex, and indeed of individuality in any
form, as the mattress filled with oily water made its wave-like
effect. Periodically this bloated plastic bag, which had all the
aesthetic appeal of a giant contraceptive, emitted a squelching,
farty noise. It was the only sound in the place as someone had
broken the stereo system. No one uttered or even looked up as
we came in. The silence was complete, and it did not have the
texture of a pause in conversation resulting from our intrusion;
this was a solid, well-established silence of some standing. They
must have been lying there for hours mutely slopping around
on top of the warm water.

This struck me as funny, and I chuckled. Jay shepherded me
promptly into another room looking aggrieved as if I had burst
out laughing during a funeral. 'I suppose they're into love,' I
began.

Jay, with no hint of a smile, cut me off.

'They're just some kids trying to get their karma together.'
It was irresistible; I sniggered again.

Jay looked pained. 'Dave,' he said, and it was the old mutual
fund voice, the one Bernie Cornfield had taught him, the voice
that had made him a millionaire who met his beautiful mistresses in the Crillon bar.

'Dave, don't you see I'm talking about *love*?'

It took several visits to realize that Jay in kaftan and bells was more than another run-of-the-mill middle-aged hippie. When he did something he did it seriously, and his energy and organizing capacity, qualities rare indeed among his new 'underground' acquaintance, had given him an elevated rank in the hierarchy of what he called 'The Movement'. Jay had turned the apartment, now known as 'a crash pad', into an oasis on one of the more popular hippie trade routes, the one that goes from New York to North Africa with refuelling stops in Paris and Avignon. His fame had also spread much wider afield as I discovered when I briefly looked after the place while he was in America. Dead stumbling voices would come out of the telephone, often an hour or so before dawn, instructing me to hurry down and open the outside door as they needed 'to crash'. When one demurred the voices would take on some slight animation and demand that Jay be brought to the phone immediately in the manner of a disgruntled customer summoning the manager. Nobody ever believed Jay was really absent, and at the same time virtually none of the hopeful crashers who presented themselves at inconvenient times as Jay's nearest and dearest had ever met him. This I learned to establish through interrogation. 'Like I got the number from this chick in Goa (or Haight-Asbury, or Marrakesh, or Khatmandu)', the disembodied voice would say down the phone.

'*She* said it would be cool to crash. She's called like Jeanie or Joanie or somethin', with this freakie long hair. You know, way out. You never even heard of Joanie? Hey, who is this on the line anyway?'

And so on. One caller announced ingenuously that he had found the magic phone number written on the wall of a jail in Ankara. I kept him out too.

Occasionally Jay would get pettish – when the stereo system was fooled around with, or when one of his more spectacularly feckless lodgers on some hallucinating trip left the huge skylights open during a snowstorm, turning the apartment briefly into a stage set for the retreat from Moscow. But generally Jay, who was always a kind man, would let anyone in. He seemed to adore his picturesque guests, and after a while they acquired a certain morbid fascination for me too. I took to dropping in from time to time, watching the rich panorama of Jay's life unfold. My motives were not sexual though they might well have been. A few of the girls were beautiful, though it struck me that hippie standards in these matters (of which they made something of a speciality) were noticably lower than those of, say, the 'straight' foreign correspondents I knew. Without exception these creatures with frizzed hair and flowing robes were promiscuous as alley cats – though a good deal less animated – and at times the apartment seemed to be floating on the groans of love. But there was a snag. A lot of them had the clap, or hepatitis, or both. A girl called Samantha made a joke about a boy friend who had caught 'psychological clap' from her – he had developed all the symptoms after a night they spent together, *even though she was clean*. Everyone thought this an amusing example of how 'straight' and 'square' the boy had been, but they all failed to see what this story implied about the girl. I felt a vivid flash of sympathy for him; after a night with Samantha I too would doubtless have acquired psychosomatic symptoms. Another girl, Janet, carried in her Moroccan shoulder bag a certificate from the Hôpital de la Salpêtrière, which I found very original. It announced, 'To Whom It May Concern' as it were, that she 'was no longer suffering from syphilis. It was a shabby and ageing document which, like Janet herself, was suffering from the effects of extended and indiscriminate handling. It did not inspire me with confidence.

But the girls were much more interesting than the boys all the same. They did, for example, talk – about 'getting it together', about the Age of Aquarius and its effects on their horoscopes, about 'vibrations', both good and bad, usually the latter. I spent many happy hours being told how 'groovy' Woman's Lib was, and earned a reputation for incredible sagacity by drawing a map of the South American continent which showed the whereabouts of Brazil. This encouraged a girl, who had apparently been trying unsuccessfully for some weeks to find out where this exotic country was, to join the Living Theatre in Rio and eventually go to jail with them in Belo Horizonte. I felt guilty about this, but treasured a letter she wrote describing, insofar as she was capable, how the 'Living' were liberating the Brazilian consciousness.

'These Brazilians,' she confided, 'aren't into THE REVOLUTION, they even aren't into acid! All the Living have been going round the streets, improvizing a bit, and then rapping quietly to the people about The Movement. I think they dig even though we don't know Spanish, of course.'

That 'of course' stopped me short, and I thought of it again when the news came that the whole lot of them had been arrested, as had always seemed inevitable. What kind of society was it that *assumed* ignorance of geography and languages as a norm? It was probably connected in some way with the strong aversion all the boys felt for what they described as 'the verbal number', or speech as it used to be called. Going one evening from Jay's where no one was saying anything, to a run-of-the-mill second rank diplomatic cocktail party, I suddenly realized why casual conversation was regarded by Jay's lodgers with such vivid suspicion. In the course of an hour I had talked to people about their families and jobs, their views on living in Paris, their ambitions to travel or to be allowed to stay where they were. All these minor exchanges were subtly imbued, it seemed to me fresh from Jay's neutral limbo, with the protestant ethic. The conversations were all erected on a series of axioms involving, for instance, a sense of reason, an awareness of the relationship between present and future, an interest in *doing* various things. These, in the Jay world, were all highly dangerous concepts to be avoided at all costs. If you had asked a hippie whether he preferred Rome to Rabat he would at best have replied that they were both cool, or possibly uncool. Similarly, polite enquiries about where someone lived (answer: 'like around, you know') or what they were doing in Paris as opposed to Kansas City (answer: 'getting myself together') suggested in their very core all kinds of positives which the hippies found challenging, and in some cases actually frightening. There was also the problem of identity. Since all their hair was long, their clothes were identical, they seldom spoke and the apartment was in a permanent artificial twilight, identifying Julie from Janie, or Dick from Dan, posed insuperable problems. Jay found so too.

'Hi Joanie, everything cool?' he said cheerfully one evening to a blonde waif who wandered abstractedly through the room we were in. 'Cool,' she replied, in the obligatory manner, and floated off ectoplasmically.

'Joan's a new one isn't she?' I asked.

'Her name's Joan, is it?' he replied, infuriatingly.

'That's what you called her, for God's sake.'

'Yeah, but I call them *all* Joan. You'd be surprised how many of them *are* Joans. Why did Jewish moms twenty years ago call their daughters Joan?'

I gave up, as so often with Jay. This was a period during which the girls, with staggering lack of skill, were preparing macrobiotic dishes so vile they would have been angrily rejected by a bush Mashona or a Hottentot. The apartment had acquired a new smell – the flat, bland odour of brown rice over-cooked to burning point. Jay had naturally thrown himself into hippie dietetics with imprudent zeal, and was now almost visibly shrinking day by day. Understandably, these meals, known as 'feasts' with characteristic hippie inaccuracy, were also affecting his powers of concentration.

* * * *

No one who was in Paris during that autumn of 1971 will ever forget it, particularly if, like Jay and myself, they were living close to the chestnuts in the Luxembourg gardens, or were so placed that they could see above that grey wall in the rue de l'Abbé de l'Epée, and into the secret garden of the Deaf and Dumb school, where the pupils gesticulated wildly in sign language as if drawing each other's attention to the cornucopian country profusion concealed there in the middle of the city. One morning I watched a small boy stand nearly an hour next to a clump of ivy which glowed like antique, hand-beaten copper. Had he been given, I wondered, a special keenness of vision to make up for the lack of other faculties? Was he drunk on that joyous copper? Or had he, perhaps, simply been dismissed from the classroom as a punishment for bad behaviour?

A chance meeting with Jay, the last in a long line, provoked similar thoughts about him. It was in the very centre of the

gardens in that odd little children's enclave, secure from Japs
with cameras and roving Senegalese rolling mad eyes at passing schoolgirls. It was late – the last week of October – and a
thousand chestnuts were shimmering in golds and yellows and
the most delicate greens, each tree different, and each contri-
buting to a spectrum of amazing subtlety. The fallen leaves
were brown and yellow, swishing under one's feet, or swept into
little rectangular wire cages provided by the tidy-minded Hôtel
de Ville. Their function, I suppose, was to moulder there into
manageable and useful compost; meanwhile, their perfume
was so heavy one imagined somewhere in those symmetrical
heaps exotic fruit were buried. And, as I say, there was Jay, as
impassive and apparently transfixed as the dumb boy beside
the ivy.

I had been making my morning proprietorial stroll, noting
that the man in the beret who runs the Rucher School of Bee-
Keeping ('*Apiculture*') was busy with some obscure bee oriented
activities, and that the chestnut glow on the Baudelaire statue
was making the old boy look unusually philanthropic. There
were three out of season little girls conscientiously riding miniature bears on the little nineteenth-century merry-go-round, and
there was Jay, childless and wifeless. What, I wondered, could
he be doing? His presence implied a certain seriousness I had
not suspected – a depth of feeling for Paris of which I would
have believed him incapable. For a man without children he
must have done a lot of solitary walking to stumble on this spot.
It is the kind of thing you only discover about a city after conducting a love affair with it or, at the very least, after a mutually
respectful friendship of many years' standing. Jay was staring
at the beloved marionette theatre.

They were showing *La Belle au Bois Dormant* as they have for
twenty years – though only on what they call 'Gala Days',
Thursday and Sunday afternoons. Now the stage door at the
back was open, and as I came up behind Jay I noticed he was
staring in. The tingling sunlight revealed some monstrous coils
of Victorian electricity cables and, on a shelf, the time-honoured
props – there was a puppet-sized crown of silver paper; a sword
(of painted wood); an old cardboard box in which the puppeteer

kept his treasure of paste diamonds; papered gold bricks; pearl necklaces as lush as hothouse grapes, and a brace of silver stars.

Jay seemed as rapt before these wonders as my daughter Judy when she sees them on stage (Judy, it will shortly be announced in the Guinness Book, is engaged in establishing a world record for attendance at *La Belle au Bois Dormant*). The sunlight striking the tinsel through the door gave the old props a deceptive authenticity; perhaps because of this trick of weather Jay was seeing the glow which for Judy is there all the time. It seemed wrong to disturb him.

His namesake Gatsby, of course, was a great man for staring at lights. There had been Daisy's lights, twinkling at him from her new French villa across the Long Island Sound. And then there had been his apotheosis, the vision of that famous green light, the orgiastic future receding year by year, which could never be caught no matter how fast he ran. That light had been used as a symbol for the American experience and the romantic quest of the pioneers heading westwards. Gatsby's quest had involved turning round and travelling eastwards; his romantic roots were bearing him 'back ceaselessly into the past'.

Jay had gone even further back, from Chicago to Europe, pursuing his future through rediscovering his roots. Certainly, Jay's had been a longer, braver journey than any I had dared to undertake so far. Perhaps there was something serious about him after all, and it was silly of me to mock his ever-shifting earnestness. Later I confided something of this to someone who knew Jay well, and he laughed 'He was probably hoping to pick up an *au pair* girl,' this friend said. And when I was sceptical – for Jay was notoriously uninvolved in the voracious *coucheries* of his *protégés* – he was more specific.

'Suppose you had met Jay in the Boulevard Raspail under the Balzac statue. Would you have assumed he was there because of Balzac? Or Rodin? Of course not. You would know perfectly well he was on his way to the Boulevard de Montparnasse to have a drink at the Coupole with a con man from San Francisco who wanted him to put up the money for a teenage masturbation contest, or a psychedelic light show using laser beams and a background of Ginsberg doing the Om chant, or to sign up that girl in Denmark who makes it with pigs to turn her into the latest Superstar. You're getting old and sentimental.'

He was, I suppose, right, and in any case one will never know the true answer. Still, I intend to preserve my picture of Jay shriven by the paste jewels of the marionettes, and assuming by osmosis the autumnal brightness of his adopted city where the lights are always on and someone, somewhere – even at the saddest hour just before dawn – is optimistically launching yet another impromptu party.